OECD Territorial Reviews

Istanbul, Turkey

OECD

ORGANISATION FOR ECONOMIC CO-OPERATION AND DEVELOPMENT

The OECD is a unique forum where the governments of 30 democracies work together to address the economic, social and environmental challenges of globalisation. The OECD is also at the forefront of efforts to understand and to help governments respond to new developments and concerns, such as corporate governance, the information economy and the challenges of an ageing population. The Organisation provides a setting where governments can compare policy experiences, seek answers to common problems, identify good practice and work to co-ordinate domestic and international policies.

The OECD member countries are: Australia, Austria, Belgium, Canada, the Czech Republic, Denmark, Finland, France, Germany, Greece, Hungary, Iceland, Ireland, Italy, Japan, Korea, Luxembourg, Mexico, the Netherlands, New Zealand, Norway, Poland, Portugal, the Slovak Republic, Spain, Sweden, Switzerland, Turkey, the United Kingdom and the United States. The Commission of the European Communities takes part in the work of the OECD.

OECD Publishing disseminates widely the results of the Organisation's statistics gathering and research on economic, social and environmental issues, as well as the conventions, guidelines and standards agreed by its members.

This work is published on the responsibility of the Secretary-General of the OECD. The opinions expressed and arguments employed herein do not necessarily reflect the official views of the Organisation or of the governments of its member countries.

Corrigenda to OECD publications may be found on line at: *www.oecd.org/publishing/corrigenda.*

Foreword

Across the OECD, globalisation increasingly tests the ability of regional economies to adapt and exploit their competitive edge, as it also offers new opportunities for regional development. This is leading public authorities to rethink their strategies. Moreover, as a result of decentralisation, central governments are no longer the sole provider of development policies. Effective and efficient relations between different levels of government are required in order to improve public service delivery.

The objective of pursuing regional competitiveness and governance is particularly relevant in metropolitan regions. Despite producing the bulk of national wealth, metropolitan areas are often characterised by unexploited opportunities for growth, as well as unemployment and distressed areas. Effective policies to enhance their competitiveness need to address their functional region as a whole and thus call for metropolitan governance.

Responding to a need to study and spread innovative territorial development strategies and governance in a more systematic way, in 1999 the OECD created the Territorial Development Policy Committee (TDPC) and its Working Party on Urban Areas (WPUA) as a unique forum for international exchange and debate. The TDPC has developed a number of activities, among which are a series of specific case studies on metropolitan regions. These studies follow a standard methodology and a common conceptual framework, allowing countries to share their experiences. This series is intended to produce a synthesis that will formulate and diffuse horizontal policy recommendations.

Acknowledgements

This Review was produced by the OECD Regional Competitiveness and Governance Division in co-operation with the Istanbul Metropolitan Municipality (IMM) and the State Planning Organization (SPO) of the Republic of Turkey.

Special thanks are given to Mr. Lütfi Elvan (Deputy State Secretary, SPO), Mr. Mesut Pektas (Secretary General, IMM), Ahmet Yaman (General Director, SPO), Mr. Taner Kavasoğlu (Regional Development and Strategic Planning Expert, SPO), Mr. Lütfi Altun (Director, Urban Transformation Directorate, IMM), Mrs. Rabia Filiz Atay (Project Manager, IMM), Mr. Ali Sabuncu (Expert, SPO), and Mrs. Ayse Gokbayrak (Deputy Director, IMM). Socio-economic information, analysis and statistics on Istanbul were provided through a background report prepared by a team of local experts co-ordinated by the Istanbul Metropolitan Municipality.

The OECD Secretariat also wishes to thank the business association TUSIAD, especially Mr. Haluk Tükel (Secretary General), for the in-kind support provided to the project.

A team of peer reviewers participated to the process:

- *Canada*: Mr. Adam Ostry, Head of Unit, Policy and Strategic Initiatives, Cities and Communities Branch, Infrastructure Canada, Chairman of the OECD Working Party on Territorial Policy in Urban Areas;
- *France*: Mr. Vincent Fouchier, Deputy Director, Institute for Spatial Planning and Urban Development for the region Ile-de-France (IAURIF), Vice-Chair of the OECD Working Party on Territorial Policy in Urban Areas;
- *Italy*: Mrs. Flavia Terribile, Public Investment Evaluation Unit, Department for Development Policies, Ministry of Economic Development, Italian Delegate of the OECD Territorial Development Policy Committee;

- *Japan*: Mr. Satoru Nishikawa, Director for Disaster Preparedness, Public Relations and International Cooperation, Japanese Cabinet Office;
- *Mexico*: Mr. Roberto Villarreal, former Undersecretary for Urban and Regional Development.

A team of international experts participated to the review process: Mr. Jeroen Klink (Director of Community Relations of the Federal University of the Greater ABC Region – Metropolitan São Paulo) and Mr. Andrew Thornley, (Chair in Urban Planning and Director of Planning Studies Programme, London School of Economics and Political Science). Several experts from Turkey also contributed to the report: Mrs. Nese Kumral (Department of Economics, Ege University, Izmir), Mr. Çağaçan Deger (Department of Economics, Middle East Technical University, Ankara), Mr. Hamdi Gargin (Head of the Urban Observatory of Istanbul) and Mr. Jean-François Perouse (Assistant Professor in Galatasaray University, Istanbul).

This Review was directed by Mr. Mario Pezzini, Head of Regional Competitiveness and Governance Division, and co-ordinated and drafted by Mrs. Lamia Kamal-Chaoui. Members of the OECD Secretariat that participated to the review included: Mrs. Dorothée Allain-Dupre (governance), Mr. Olaf Merk (local finance), Mr. Javier Sanchez-Reaza (socio-economic analysis) and Mrs. Ritsuko Yamazaki-Honda (transport, housing and disaster prevention). Mrs Eda Alidedeoglu, (internal consultant) provided support to the organisation process and data collection. Statistical data were produced by Ms. Brunella Boselli and Mr. Javier Sanchez-Reaza. Mrs. Erin Byrne prepared the Review for publication.

Table of contents

Assessment and Recommendations **13**

***Chapter 1.* Istanbul: The Bicontinental Mega-city** **29**

Introduction 29
1.1. What is the Istanbul metropolitan region? 30
1.2. Main socio-economic trends 35
The demographic and economic motor of Turkey 35
A dynamic and vulnerable economy… 46
The impact of the macroeconomic context 50
Major structural changes in this industrial mix 52
1.3. Istanbul on the international market place 69
International competitiveness, exports and FDI 69
An emerging regional hub? 73
1.4. Towards a competitive and sustainable mega-city: the challenges ahead 87
Obstacles to a competitive business environment 88
Impact of over-migration 100

***Chapter 2.* Fostering Istanbul's International Competitiveness** **113**

Introduction 113
2.1. Promoting Istanbul's international competitiveness 115
Upgrading Istanbul's economy 115
Building a regional hub 138
2.2. Coping with congestion and risks 160
Managing congestion and transport 161
Land use, urban regeneration projects and housing development 167
Environmental issues and earthquake risks 175
2.3. Istanbul in Turkey: the challenge of regional development policies...... 186
Conclusion: Towards the implementation of a coherent and comprehensive strategy 189

Chapter 3. **Governance for a Sustainable Mega-city....................................201**

Introduction..201
3.1. The institutional and fiscal challenges..203
The institutional framework in Turkey and Istanbul...................................203
The allocation of responsibilities within Istanbul......................................206
The organisation of local government finance...207
The decentralisation process in Turkey and its impact on Istanbul............214
3.2. Ensuring a better management for urban development..........................218
Streamlining institutional governance and inter-governmental relationships 219
Establishing a consistent strategic planning framework.............................223
3.3. Promoting a regional growth strategy..236
Conclusion: Istanbul governance is a local and a national challenge 241

Annex. **Regional Disparities in Turkey: A Slow Convergence Process......247**

Bibliography...248

Tables

Table 1.1. Basic indicators of Istanbul Functional Area 34
Table 1.2 Evolution of population shares for Istanbul and the Marmara region 36
Table 1.3. Fertility rates in Istanbul (%) 39
Table 1.4. Regional share of national GDP by sector 41
Table 1.5. Labour force by economic activity (2000)....................................53
Table 1.6. Contribution of services to total gross value added in OECD countries (2004) 54
Table 1.7. Specialisations of the manufacturing industry in Istanbul (2000)..56
Table 1.8. Sectoral share of employment in the Polycentric Greater Istanbul (2000)..63
Table 1.9. Wage evolution in Istanbul and Turkey 98
Table 1.10. Emissions caused by road traffic in Istanbul............................101
Table A.1. Summary of β-convergence regressions 247
Table A.2. σ- Convergence 247
Table A.3. Conditional convergence regressions for 1987-2000.................249

Figures

Figure 1.1. Istanbul in the Marmara Region Context.....................................31
Figure 1.2. Institutional framework in Turkey...31
Figure 1.3 Population trends in Istanbul and Turkey (1927-2000) 35

Figure 1.4. Urbanisation growth in OECD countries....................................36
Figure 1.5. Average annual population growth rates among a selection of OECD metro-regions (1995-2002) 37
Figure 1.6. Population density among a selection of large cities 38
Figure 1.7. Share of Istanbul population born in another province (2000) 39
Figure 1.8. Immigration to Istanbul and the Marmara Region.......................40
Figure 1.9. Net migrants in Istanbul...40
Figure 1.10. Differences in per capita GDP of metro-regions and their national level (2002) 42
Figure 1.11. Productivity differences between the metro-regions and their national level (2002) 43
Figure 1.12. Regional disparities in Turkey...44
Figure 1.13. Comparison of regional disparities in OECD countries.............45
Figure 1.14. Economic growth in a selection of OECD metro-regions 46
Figure 1.15. Real GDP growth in Istanbul and Turkey (1989–2004).............47
Figure 1.16. Evolution of GDP per capita in Istanbul and the Marmara Region (1987–2001)...48
Figure 1.17. Difference in productivity, unemployment and activity rate among provinces of the metro-region 50
Figure 1.18. Sectoral composition of GDP (2000)...53
Figure 1.19. Change in specialisation in Istanbul 61
Figure 1.20. Concentration of services sector in the Marmara Region...........63
Figure 1.21. Change in specialisation in Kocaeli...65
Figure 1.22. Change in specialisation in Yalova..65
Figure 1.23. Change in specialisation in Bursa..66
Figure 1.24. Change in specialisation in Tekirdağ...67
Figure 1.25. Change in specialisation in Sakarya 68
Figure 1.26. FDI stocks in a selection of OECD and non-OECD member countries..71
Figure 1.27. Net FDI flows as % GDP among Turkey's main competitors 72
Figure 1.28. Total value of stock trading in emerging markets 75
Figure 1.29. Total value of bond trading...76
Figure 1.30. Stock market significance in the national economy 77
Figure 1.31. Outstanding securities in the Istanbul Stock Exchange (2000-2005)..78
Figure 1.32. Foreign equity investments in the Istanbul Stock Exchange (1989-2006)...78
Figure 1.33. Size of the capital in the Istanbul Stock Exchange (1999-2006) 79
Figure 1.34. "Mediterranean gateway ports" throughout 2000-2004..............82
Figure 1.35. Second-tier world top travel destinations and expenditures 83
Figure 1.36. Arrivals of non-resident tourists staying in hotels and similar establishments 84
Figure 1.37. Tourism arrivals in Turkey and Istanbul (1999-2004)................86

Figure 1.38. Conferences and exhibitions tourism........87
Figure 1.39. Informality by sector........89
Figure 1.40. Informality by level of education........91
Figure 1.41. Gross domestic expenditure on R&D........92
Figure 1.42. Number of triadic patent families........93
Figure 1.43. Composition of large firms in Istanbul........93
Figure 1.44. Major obstacles to FDI in Turkey........98
Figure 1.45. Road fatalities........102
Figure 2.1. Governance complexity for transport in Istanbul........164
Figure 3.1. Institutional framework in Istanbul Metropolitan Area........205
Figure 3.2. Local government revenues as percentage of GDP (1980-2000)208
Figure 3.3. Composition of municipal revenues (2002)........209
Figure 3.4. Revenues on the budget of Istanbul Metropolitan Municipality (2004)........210
Figure 3.5. Sub-national tax revenues as a share of total tax revenues (2005) 210
Figure 3.6. Sub-national expenditures as share of total government expenditures (2004)........215
Figure 3.7. Different types of plans in the Istanbul Metropolitan Area........224
Figure A.1. Average growth rate *versus* initial level of GDP per capita by province........248
Figure A.2. Migration and regional income........250
Figure A.3. Migration and regional growth........250
Figure A.4. Public investment and regional growth........251
Figure A.5. Incentives to lagging regions and convergence........251

Boxes

Box 1.1. How large is Istanbul's functional metropolitan area?........33
Box 1.2. Forms and causes of informality........90
Box 1.3. Strengths and handicaps of Turkish firms according to their size....94
Box 2.1. The microeconomics of research partnerships: the case of Brazil's Law on Innovation and the Madrid Institutes for Advanced Studies........119
Box 2.2. North East Productivity Alliance: United Kingdom........122
Box 2.3. The role of business improvement districts in Michigan, United States........135
Box 2.4. National Linkages Programme: Ireland........139
Box 2.5. Linking cities and their ports: the example of the "Kop van Zuid" project in the city of Rotterdam, Netherlands........144
Box 2.6. Banking sector reform in Turkey........147
Box 2.7. Restructuring in Dynamic Dubai........150
Box 2.8. Tourism Vision for Istanbul........151

Box 2.9. Sustainable development after heavy industry?: the role of IBA in reinventing and "re-branding" the Ruhr 159
Box 2.10. Fighting informal settlements: the case of Mexico 170
Box 2.11. A successful approach to integration between squatter settlements and the urban fabric: the Integrated Slum Upgrading Program "Favela Bairro" in Rio de Janeiro, Brazil 172
Box 2.12. Water management in Istanbul 176
Box 2.13. Lessons from urban earthquake disasters in other countries 181
Box 2.14. NUTS 2 regions in Turkey 188
Box. 3.1. Improving skills and capacity in local government: the example of the Improvement and Development Agency (IDeA), England and Wales 218
Box. 3.2. Examples of strategic planning approaches: Johannesburg and London 226
Box 3.3. Encouraging citizen participation in controlling corruption: the example of the Seoul Metropolitan Government 232
Box 3.4. Neighbourhood level participation: the examples of Busan and Porto Alegre 235

Assessment and Recommendations

A big population magnet and an emerging metropolitan economy...

Istanbul, the demographic and economic heart of Turkey, has gone through enormous changes over the past century. The mega-city of about 13 to 16 million inhabitants (depending on the unit of analysis), 20% of Turkey's total population has registered a dramatic population increase since 1950 (more than tenfold). Although the pace of population growth has slowed since 1990, it remains the highest both nationally and among the largest OECD metro-regions. Istanbul has benefited from a favourable national economic environment, triggered by broad and continuous reform process, strengthening its position within Turkey and on the international marketplace. In Turkey, Istanbul concentrates 27% of national GDP, 38% of total industrial output and more than 50% of services, and generates 40% of tax revenues. Its GDP per capita exceeds the national average by more than 70% (*i.e.*, the highest level among OECD metro-regions) and its productivity level by almost 50%. Though Istanbul ranks low compared to other OECD metro-regions on GDP per capita, the bi-continental megalopolis is one of the fastest growing cities for this indicator. Istanbul has half of total Turkish exports, impressive within a country with one of the highest trade-to-GDP ratios among OECD countries. Istanbul also gets the lion's share of total FDI in Turkey, which although relatively low by OECD standards, registered a historical record in 2006 of a total amount of USD 20.2 billion. Thanks to a combination of factors – including its unique geographical location, historical and architectural assets, major infrastructure investments, increasing economic linkages with the European, Asian and Balkan regions, a large and cheap labour force – Istanbul has established itself as the industrial, financial and logistics centre of the country.

...challenged by other emerging economies

Increasing international competition from low-cost and labour-intensive emerging economies in China, India and other Asian countries is now challenging Istanbul's economy. Typical to large metropolitan areas, Istanbul tends to have a more diversified economic basis, with a higher share of services in its sectoral mix (about two-thirds), with an expansion of advanced services in the central city. But contrary to many OECD metro-regions, Istanbul maintains a sizeable manufacturing sector, specialised in relatively labour-intensive, low-technology activities, *i.e.*, mainly textiles and supply chain. This sector represents 37% of the total labour force and 26% of GDP and around 80% of total exports. A productive restructuring has been ongoing in the textile cluster with an increase of employment in apparel and a reduction in knitting, while the design and fashion-intensive sectors appear as promising niches. Specialisation is also apparent in some high-value-added activities such as pharmaceuticals and to a lesser extent in electronics. Yet, this overall process is taking place slowly, as traditional and labour-intensive sectors have been shifting only gradually to other complementary segments.

An ambitious strategic role within the country and within the Euro-Asia area...

Policy makers at all levels of the government share an ambitious vision for Istanbul: making it a major economic centre and the central node for international trade flows. To achieve this, many advocate for two related objectives:

1. *Istanbul as the innovation and knowledge-based centre of Turkey:* creating a more dynamic learning economy to compete more effectively with other metropolitan areas in the international arena while generating positive spillovers for the rest of Turkey.

2. *Istanbul as a regional hub in the Euro-Asia region:* as a global gateway city between Europe, Asia, the Middle East and the former East European countries, and as a regional provider of financial services, a logistic hub and a tourism and cultural centre.

...which requires accelerating economic restructuring

(1) The first pillar of the strategy, ***Istanbul as the innovation and knowledge-based centre of Turkey,*** will require accelerating the positive trends in restructuring towards complementary segments. This includes Istanbul's activities to progressively upgrade towards higher technology content activities (*e.g.*, chemical, pharmaceuticals and medical devices, and electrical equipment and devices) and continued restructuring in the textile industry, expanding employment in apparel linked to global markets and contracting in knit fabrics. However a lack of microeconomic adjustments and institutional bottlenecks are slowing the pace of industrial transformation. Many of the actions to be taken are related to national macroeconomic policies, products and labour market regulations, tax and national sectoral policies (*e.g.*, education, labour markets, etc.). Specific territorial-based policies should also target the upgrading of Istanbul's industrial mix. The combination of a series of policy actions at the national and the regional levels could help to strengthen the networks between firms, encourage links up and down supply chains, and facilitate the insertion of small firms into the wider processes of technological and managerial change.

Public policies are needed to accompany the adjustment process...

Current policies to foster innovation, productivity and business and technology development could be further strengthened. Significant efforts have yielded positive results for segments such as pharmaceuticals, logistics and textile. In the textile industry for instance, the Istanbul Textile and Clothing Export Union (ITKIB), a semi-public organisation located in the Under-Secretariat of the Prime Ministry for Foreign Trade, has managed to improve mechanisms for information sharing, and co-operation among small and medium-sized enterprises and facilitate penetration into export markets. The implementation of Technoparks and the increased priority on National Science and Technology Development Policy initiatives have been positive moves towards fostering Istanbul's learning and innovation system. The government has also taken the initial steps toward establishing a national level industrial and technological development policy, with positive spin-off for sectors such as logistics and textile. The national agency KOSGEB has set up an enabling framework to help small and medium-sized enterprises implement strategies aimed at their managerial and technological modernisation. All these promising initiatives, still at a limited scale, could be further strengthened. For instance, they could be complemented by specific policies to tap all the potential of FDI in technology transfer (*e.g.*, through supplier-buyer relations, quality certification programmes sponsored by foreign firms, technical assistance, etc.). In the logistics sector, this would mean incorporating foreign know-how related to multi-modal and logistics chain management. Moreover, the techno parks initiative currently limited to three sites (one in Istanbul and two in the neighbouring province) could be extended and complemented with programmes within universities focusing on increasing research and development in partnership with the private sector. Finally, in their efforts to foster innovation, national and local authorities could pay more attention as well to the potential of regional and local clustering, and to the role of collaborative stakeholders' networks of component suppliers, universities and business associations, that have so far been largely driven by private initiatives.

...and foster the potential of specific niches

A cluster policy would be relevant to exploit specific niches and move towards complementary segments. The textile and clothing sector is an example of how large industrial sectors offer both potential and challenges that could be dealt with through specific public policies. The challenges of niches in design and fashion are that they currently operate according to informal work practices, and generally with outdated managerial and technological production processes. In practice, dealing with the multi-faceted structure of the textile sector will require a policy framework that is able to simultaneously create a Textile Cluster Agency or a Fashion Institute, and create incentives for informal businesses to transform into economic units that offer sustainable jobs. Pharmaceutical manufacturing, medical and surgical equipment, and soap and detergents also have the potential to trigger positive technological externalities on other sectors like biotechnology. Already contributing 18% of value added of the Istanbul economy, these sectors might be considered a strategic niche in science and research-driven industrial development. Other promising sectors include the chemical and medical sectors, which have shown recent growth patterns and the prospect of health tourism.

The extent of the informal sector requires a broad-based strategy

A main priority for fostering productivity and innovation, and upgrading Istanbul's economy is to address the informal sector. This sector represents about the 30% of the city's working labour force. The large number of small firms that make up the informal sector has helped to relieve urban employment tensions during the economic downturns (unemployment rates stand at 11.4% against 10.3% for Turkey). However, the large informal sector also explains the low activity rate due to less employee access to adult education, on-the-job training, and other means of human capital development; all necessary for upgrading skills and increasing the innovation capacity and productivity of firms. Moreover, taxation leakages and unfair competition make these firms less productive than those in the formal economy. Yet the informal sector offers a great entrepreneurial potential impeded by product market regulations, tax system and labour market legislation. Overall, the transition will require a long-term strategy that includes broad-based and integrated reforms, with a particular focus on creating a legal framework for micro-firms. While there is a role for central government, local government could promote formalisation through incentives like reducing local red tape, simplifying export rules and regulations potentially creating a free trade zone or a tax cut, or more efficient and speedier tax rebates. Also, connecting small firms and the sector of internationally competitive, export-oriented firms would contribute to bridging the technology gap due to lack of information about production methods and processes. This combined with lack of access to modern equipment are clear problems for micro-firms that undermine the productivity of individual firms and whole sectors. The policy challenge is to reach these firms through a cost-effective enterprise development strategy that provides access to financing and creating venture capital systems with complementary programmes to increase the number of formal self-employed micro-businesses (capacity building, micro-credit (currently underdeveloped in Turkey) and support to co-operatives and home-based activities of women). Further diagnosis will be required to design a comprehensive and a long-term policy, and appropriate actions for the sector.

A "smart" logistics hub strategy for an environmentally-friendly city

(2) The *logistics* sector has been one of three main targets of the second strategic pillar, *i.e.*, ***Istanbul as a regional hub in the Euro-Asia region***. Istanbul's assets are its relative proximity to new formed market economies in former Soviet bloc countries and its experience as the node of Turkey's international transportation corridors, processing 60% of the country's total trade volume. Turkish policy makers have intensified relations with existing and potential trading partners and developed transnational transport infrastructure through a number of international co-operation projects. Moreover, a number of actions have been taken to promote an efficient combination of different transportation modes. An explicit effort is made both by the central and the municipal governments to expand and shift the modal transport split away from trucks (currently managing 90%) to other transportation modes (railways, maritime and seaports). Also, like the most competitive ports in the world, the focus here is on creating "intelligent" port systems, *i.e.*, capable of planning and managing a chain of activities for their clients (just in time management, insurance, economies of scope, distribution, finance, etc.). This is particularly relevant given Istanbul's environmental concerns, especially related to over-use of the Strait of Istanbul. Improvements will benefit from increased private sector participation in investment, operations and port maintenance, and the dissemination of information technology. Local stakeholders in port management (freight forwarders, businesses) should also be actively involved in creating new market and product combinations in order to position ports in the global economy. More generally, Istanbul's port strategy has to fit into a broader strategy for urban development. In other words, it is important to avoid a fast track implementation of specific projects, without consideration of their impact on the overall urban development pattern.

A wise and pro-active policy to foster Istanbul's tourism and cultural centre potential

Istanbul has strong assets to be further exploited in order to position itself as a *tourism and culture* centre, the second strategic sector of the regional hub strategy. The city's historical heritage gives it significant cultural and natural assets, making it an attractive tourism destination. Comprehensive strategic plans related to the city's tourism policy have recently included concrete projects in areas of the city with explicit land use and zoning guidelines. Istanbul's recent nomination as the "2010 European Capital of Culture" has given new impetus to the strategy for preserving and protecting the city's cultural heritage. A series of renovation, restoration and demolition projects, complemented with financial incentives are underway with several projects in co-operation with civil organisations and the central government, to increase the capacities of hotel, museums and other cultural amenities. The implementation of the vision, however, suffers from significant physical challenges (limited capacity, infrastructure deficiencies and inner city congestion) as well as policy challenges (overlapping responsibilities, cumbersome administrative procedures, limited access to financial resources). The metropolitan government has recently initiated more pro-active marketing and communication strategy with support from private initiatives. Further efforts could be made to develop some market tourism niches, such as conferences and exhibitions. This relates to a strong commitment towards building Istanbul's international brand image. A significant surge in tourism revenues could be obtained if the city were to focus on variables such as the duration of stay and tourist spending patterns, through innovative means to attract repeat visitors and cultural events, or promote competitive creative industries linked with traditional industries.

More regulatory reforms for a competitive financial centre

Important reforms are needed in the *financial* sector – the third sector identified in regional hub strategy – for Istanbul to stand as a regional centre, especially in light of fierce international competition in this field. The Istanbul Stock Exchange (ISE) has witnessed a dramatic increase, largely outstripping other countries' financial centres in the Eurasia region. However, the lack of financial instruments and big international institutional investors along with a low level of saving prevent it from reaching a higher capitalisation rate. Weaknesses include the capital markets being dominated by public securities over stock and other financial instruments. The banking sector, more experienced than other places in the Eurasia region, needs further restructuring to make the limited number of large banking groups more competitive. Increasing financial competitiveness will require regulatory policy to reduce high transaction and intermediary costs, and the financial intermediary institutions' high dependency on the stock exchange. These reforms are even more pressing as Istanbul faces tough competition, particularly from cities like Dubai. In this respect, Istanbul needs to develop a more aggressive and pro-active differential branding strategy.

Environmental and social risks are obstacles to competitiveness

Going beyond a mere pro-growth strategy, Istanbul has to deal with important negative externalities that infringe upon (or could infringe upon) its attractiveness and competitiveness. Rapid urbanisation growth and a large influx of domestic and foreign migrants to Istanbul in a relatively short period of time have raised issues threatening Istanbul's sustainability and social cohesion. They include:

1. *Transport congestion*: Istanbul has to face huge traffic congestion costs in the city centre and along the two bridges crossing the Strait of Istanbul (the Bosphorus), both running above capacity. The newly developed public transport systems (tramways, light rail and metro) are too limited and lack sufficient capacity to alleviate metropolitan wide congestion.

2. *Uncontrolled land use development*: Informal settlements, housing around 50% of the population, have proliferated, sprawling towards water reserves and preserved forest areas, raising concerns for service provision. This issue is further worsened by the city's geological structure.

3. *Environmental risks*: Informal settlement, rapid motorisation and industrial waste have caused serious environmental concerns (air, water and soil pollution). The Strait of Istanbul is considered one of the most crowded, and potentially dangerous waterways in the world. The 1999 earthquake, one of the most damaging earthquakes in the world, and the threat of another major earthquake in the next 30 years makes addressing these issues even more pressing.

4. *Social cohesion*: Increasing competition from low-labour-cost countries has impacted the real income of workers in labour intensive activities, a large number of which operate in the informal sector. Rapid economic growth has been insufficient in creating jobs for newcomers to the labour market. Income disparities have increased with the new, highly educated and high-wage group working in more advanced and services oriented activities. This process is common in economies experiencing a major shift in industrial mix, but the effects in Istanbul have been magnified, with the large influx of low-skilled migrants over a relatively short period.

A better decision-making process to address transport congestion…

(1) *Dealing with transport congestion* requires bold political measures. Several new projects are ongoing, including the Marmaray project, an undersea rail tunnel across the Strait of Istanbul, and the relocation of workshops off of the peninsula. Moreover, since early 2006 the city has undertaken promising initiatives to introduce efficient integrated tariff management, giving incentives for mass transportation over car use as well as a number of other measures aimed at a cleaner transport system. These efforts remain however limited compared to that needed to address the scale of the issue. A main obstacle to improvement is the highly fragmented decision-making process characterised by a large number of actors, operating both formally and informally, many of which are large private companies. The former Transportation Master Plans (last one enacted in 1996) have not been implemented, and the proposed shift in the modal split, away from cars towards the railway system, has not yet materialised. In this context, it is crucial to streamline and clarify the governance system for transport issues, better integrate land use and transportation planning, further prioritise railway over road networks, and integrate and improve public transport modes to maximise the use of public transportation, by enhancing its efficiency and facilitating the modal exchange.

…and deal with informal land use

(2) Stopping *uncontrolled land use development* is probably one of the most challenging spatial issues in Istanbul. Since the 1960s the "*Gecekondu*", or squatter settlements have proliferated and become the most typical and well-known forms of illegal occupation and construction. They are mainly the homes of the new low-income populations that migrate to Istanbul, although there are also illegally owned lands that hold skyscrapers and luxury villas along the shores of the Strait of Istanbul. Such illegal settlement proliferation often onto scarce and protected forest areas and water reserves has exacerbated environmental risks, representing substantial threats in terms of health, environmental and earthquake risks. These trends are also partly the result of Istanbul's planning difficulties by which the system accommodates projects already in progress, leading to an unsustainable pattern of urban growth. Within the current urban regeneration policies, a number of negotiations, mechanisms for financial compensation and initiatives aimed at urban regeneration have been introduced to deal with the issue, though the low-income dwellers have not been involved in

the process. More generally, urban planning in Istanbul addresses the over-concentration of population in a limited way. It provides a vision for a polycentric metropolitan supported by a transportation system, major housing and infrastructure development projects and targets a more even pattern of urban development. However, there is no attention devoted to a broader perspective on the growth management in Istanbul.

A stronger emphasis on environment for a metropolis at risk

(3) *Promoting a more environmental approach* is even more pressing in such a congested and at-risk region as Istanbul. Remarkable achievements have been made in water management and adopting a wider concept of the environment, one which includes air pollution caused by transport, the use of coal (or brown coal) for heating and, to a lesser extent, from unregulated industrialisation. Initiatives aimed at reducing traffic congestion and by the same token pollution, include the regulation of heavy goods vehicles in transit, measures to direct automobile traffic to the second bridge (though still crowded), preferential pricing policies and incentives in "public" collective transport (*e.g.*, a single pricing system to encourage the use of boats, as a more environment-friendly transport mode), the banning of private collective transport within the historical peninsula and the introduction of green buses that run on gas. These initiatives however remain limited. A more cross-cutting environmental policy is needed to co-ordinate these and additional efforts. A consortium of academics and representatives from the Istanbul Metropolitan Municipality has produced the Istanbul Earthquake Master Plan, a valuable document that provides a checklist of critical actions for comprehensive earthquake prevention policy with an important focus on the need for seismic resistant buildings. Although the political will and the expertise are present, a critical link with implementation is missing. A draft bill on addressing urban area needs for transformation, development, and investment, currently pending in the Turkish parliament, is expected to address and clarify these issues. Positively, there are however individual elements of the Master Plan that are being adopted and implemented, such as a public awareness campaign, major projects for seismic reinforcements, the establishment of an emergency operations centre and intensification of law enforcement on illegal occupation.

Deepening the social dimensions as intrinsic elements of a pro-growth strategy

(4) *Further incorporating social development concerns* in current economic and urban policies is essential not only to deal with – and cushion against – eventual macroeconomic shocks but also to provide the social capital necessary for a long-term competitiveness strategy. Whilst the social dimensions of the policy reforms in Turkey are a national matter, local authorities have also a key role to play. For instance, it is essential that current urban regeneration policies, in particular the relocation policies for families and small-scale industries, be implemented without disrupting socio-economic ties and community relations, and with sufficient infrastructure to support the newly planned neighbourhoods. In this respect, mass production of low-income housing and specific mortgage programmes, like those implemented recently in other parts of Turkey, will be necessary but insufficient responses. Instead, upgrading and regulating squatter settlements would create a more solid base for local economic development strategies and social capital in these areas. When addressing the informal sector, an integrated approach aimed at the microeconomic inclusion of the so-called "moderately poor" (a target group located in between the extremely poor and the non-poor population, which has been growing over the last few years) could be realised through programmes aimed at adult education, school certification, labour training and the provision of child-care facilities.

Governance of a mega-city like Istanbul requires constant improvement…

The implementation of a competitiveness strategy, along with the necessity to deal with issues related to migration, congestion, social polarisation and environmental concerns make governance of the mega-city region especially challenging. The system of governance in Istanbul has undergone a major transformation, improving management and planning in the region, particularly in urban planning. Istanbul has benefited from the decentralisation process in Turkey and new actors have emerged at the local and metropolitan levels. The recent expansion of the metropolitan boundary to coincide with the province presents an opportunity to formulate a good strategic framework that covers a reasonably large area and improves the possibility for co-ordination between the municipality and the provincial special administration. Moreover, the planning responsibilities previously under the central government's responsibility have been transferred to the

Istanbul metropolitan municipality since 2004. The scale of planning reflects the functional evolution of the metropolitan area (*i.e.*, beyond the geographical area covered by the Metropolitan Municipality), and new concepts are being introduced in the planning exercise such as urban regeneration ideology, earthquake and tourism, environmental and transport issues. Also, a wider range of actors are being involved in planning, and flexibility and time phasing have been introduced. Yet, further efforts are needed to establish a robust governance system that will ensure better urban management and long-term strategies.

...such as streamlining inter-governmental relationships and the institutional framework...

Typical to large metropolitan areas, inter-governmental relationships and institutional governance needs to be further streamlined. Istanbul's governance system is complex, and fragmented which can lead to duplication and conflicts, retarding rather than stimulating urban development. In areas like transport, there are a large number of bodies involved from all levels of government and from the private sector. Conflicts also often arise because of a strong control of the central government and the provincial authorities over local matters as well as overlapping responsibilities. Several ministries intervene in some local policy areas such as infrastructure and land-use development, sometimes in contradiction with municipal interests and urban plans. Co-ordination between the metropolitan municipality and central government is often made more difficult by differences of opinion between ministries. Finally, some inefficiency may arise for the second tier local authorities (sub-province and first level municipalities for which most of them have at least 200 000 inhabitants) who have limited responsibilities and who are funded from the metropolitan municipality. In this context, there is an opportunity to clarify individual competencies among the different institutional actors, implement the principle of subsidiarity and simplify the municipal pattern.

...establishing a consistent, long-term strategic plan...

Istanbul would benefit from a less iterative planning process and a clearer implementation programme. Despite significant improvements, the planning process in Istanbul faces several implementation issues. First, there is a multitude of plans that involve a large number of actors with ill-defined competences leading to a diluted global vision and focus on the principal priorities. This is particularly apparent in transport and land-use planning. Second, in terms of physical planning, the strategy functions are divided between the metropolitan municipality and the lower level municipalities – the former focussing on the broader master plan with the lower level producing implementation plans in conformance with the master plan. This highlights the urgent need to ensure a clear hierarchy among all these plans; too many plans kill the planning. Third, the common local authorities' practice to depart from the plan renders the plans inefficient or obsolete. The multiplication of special laws and regulations also tends to reduce the value of these plans. Finally, planning suffers from a lack of clearly phased implementation projects and a large number of unplanned projects, which cause tensions and doubts about the effective role and legitimacy of the urban planning process. More generally, the planning process should go beyond purely land-use oriented decisions, to inspire better conformity between the plans and more systematic integration of spatial planning, earthquake and environment, transport infrastructure, and socio-economic development.

...and improving local public management.

Endowed with a large administration, Istanbul could well consider improving its local management through a modernisation reform. Istanbul now covers a large territory, providing significant advantages for co-ordinating policy. Yet, like other large organisations, it faces internal tensions for co-ordination and resource allocation between municipal departments. Some local governments throughout the OECD like those in Seoul or Madrid have undergone beneficial large scale local public management reforms. Generally, these reforms are aimed at introducing greater transparency in urban decision making and further accountability, a rationalisation of the local administrative framework, measures to enhance the local workforce capacity, new rules in human resources management, nomination procedures based on competition and transparency, and control and audit procedures on the allocations of resources to various extra-municipal actors including for the attribution of public works contracts. Meanwhile, enhancing the role of civil society in the local decision-making process, through better access to information, and more involvement in municipal decision-making structures, would contribute to creating a more consensus-oriented approach. While efforts in this area have been significant in recent years, civil society in Istanbul still remains a source of ideas, though providing a less real input into decision making.

Decentralisation in Turkey must mean preparing local capacity

The implementation of the subsidiary principle in Turkey will have a determinant impact on many of these governance challenges. Since the early 2000s, decentralisation of public administrations has been a key government priority. Laws have been enacted or are under discussion, but changes are taking time to implement and some are concerned whether laws can be put into effective practice. One priority area in this process will be to ensure that lower level authorities have the local capacity to carry out their new duties. An interesting step in the decentralisation process – that will provide an additional institutional tool for governance in Istanbul – is the establishment of Development Agencies (DA) on a country-basis in 26 NUTS 2 regions. The DAs have a number of broad objectives as they combine the functions of an investment promotion agency with that of a regional development agency. They will be set up as corporate bodies subject to private law and will take a participatory approach to encourage public-private dialogue. Whilst the DAs appear as a promising and necessary addition to the Istanbul region's institutional structure, it is still unclear to how the DAs will fit into the existing structure and networks. In particular, it will be important to establish clear relationships between the decision-making process of the forthcoming DA and those of the provincial and the municipal authority in Istanbul. Finally, the administrative capacity for the evaluation, implementation and monitoring of programmes and projects at the municipal level would need to be ensured. In this respect, Turkey could establish technical units like Italy, both at central and regional levels, for the evaluation and monitoring of public investments – coupled with sanction and reward mechanisms in the regional allocation of funds.

Istanbul: a national challenge

Looking forward, the challenges facing the Istanbul metropolitan region cannot be tackled without considering the national context of huge regional disparities. The central government understands the importance of fostering the economic development of its major metropolitan area and dealing with the major urban issues: Istanbul is a national pole of growth that needs to be sustained. However, the increasing challenges faced by the mega-city will constantly be threatened so long as the rest of the country is lagging behind. Turkey has the largest disparities among OECD countries. While a slow convergence process has been detected, it could take decades to bridge the income per capita gap between regions. Meanwhile, Istanbul has registered dramatic demographic growth, much of which comes from other regions of

Turkey. The resulting over-concentration in Istanbul has reached its sustainable limit, necessitating a national strategy for managing future growth. A new approach to regional policy is emerging and a number of concrete actions have been taken in this direction. For instance, the 2004 and the 2006 National Development Plan as well as the 9th National Development Plan for 2007-2011 included plans to overcome inter-regional migration problems, including the development of regional cities to strengthen the competitiveness of other regions and counterbalance the weight of Istanbul. The DA projects intend to provide the institutional tools for the co-ordination and the implementation of the regional development policies, though it has been a slow process. It is urgent for this process to be expedited not only for the development of the country, but also for the success and the sustainability of Istanbul under the continuous threat of increasing pressures from inward migration.

Chapter 1

Istanbul: The Bicontinental Mega-city

Introduction

Istanbul has gone through enormous changes over the past century. Its population has grown tenfold. Today, Istanbul is home to between 13 and 16 million inhabitants. It is one of the largest metropolitan areas both in the OECD and throughout the world. It has a unique geographical location spanning two continents, and it has a wealth and diversity of historical, cultural and architectural assets. The city has experienced success on many fronts: economic growth, productivity, trade and tourism, to name a few. Yet, competition among metropolitan areas is fierce around the world and emerging cities in China, Eastern Europe and other Asian countries are threatening Istanbul's economic base. Istanbul is also a victim of its own success: economic growth has resulted in it attracting dramatic waves of migrants from other parts of Turkey as well as from neighbouring countries at one of the fastest paces in the world. Such inflow of migrants has put the city's physical infrastructure under considerable strain and led to sizeable congestion costs and pollution issues. Migration has also spurred the informal sector of the economy as the, albeit rapid, economic growth has been insufficient in providing jobs for a large number of newcomers into the labour market.

But Istanbul is ambitious. It would like to take advantage of its location to become a regional hub in finance, logistics and tourism. It would like also to become an "Innovative City" and aims at earning the recognition of a "Global City". This chapter presents key socio-economic trends and assesses comparative advantages, untapped potential and major challenges in light of these objectives. It will start by discussing the definition of the metropolitan area from a functional perspective and explore the drivers behind Istanbul's influence within Turkey as the economic motor of the country and the largest concentration of value-added production. It also explores Istanbul's influence on the wider region. Consideration of the macroeconomic impact of ongoing socio-economic and political restructuring provides a picture of the changes the city has undergone and an indication of the changes still to come. The chapter then addresses the structural and spatial specialisation trends in the metro-region's economic base, within the international context of competition among cities, with particular focus given to the region's hub strategy. Finally, the chapter concludes with a survey of some of the challenges the city must overcome if it is to realise its ambitions. These challenges range from those affecting its business environment to those affecting the city's long-term sustainability.

1.1. What is the Istanbul metropolitan region?

Metropolitan areas frequently have a larger influence beyond their administrative boundaries and Istanbul is not the exception. Istanbul is located on the western end of Turkey in the Marmara Region, stretching over both sides of the Strait of Istanbul (Bosphorus) which connects the Black Sea and the Sea of Marmara, and separates Asia and Europe (Figure 1.1). Over time the city has grown, sprawling into neighbouring regions leading not only to the emergence of a self-contained labour market, but also deepening socio-economic interdependencies among the different parts of the metropolitan area. Suburbanisation and urban sprawl have been especially prominent along the southern coast of the metropolitan area, not only on the European side, but also on the Asian side stretching along the coast of the Marmara Sea and into the Izmit Bay. With a population of 13 to 16 million, depending on the unit of analysis, Istanbul has grown from a mono-centric metro-region towards a polycentric mega-city characterised by a dominant core and multiple urban nuclei.

As with most polycentric mega-cities, defining the functional area of the metropolitan area of Istanbul is not an easy task. Accurately defining the functional area facilitates a more precise analysis of the spatial and socio-economic trends (linkages within production chains, mobility and commuting patterns, etc.) that determine future growth trends; however, the definition also contributes to potential challenges in policy design, especially in terms of planning. Istanbul usually refers to the City of Istanbul, represented by an administrative local government, the Istanbul Metropolitan Municipality, whose boundaries also coincide with the province (Figure 1.2). Contrary to many OECD metropolitan regions, but much like metro-regions in Korea and Japan, the Istanbul Metropolitan Municipality covers quite a large area, almost tripling in size when its administrative boundaries were extended from 1 864 km^2 to 5 343 km^2 in a 2004 legislative law. Yet, the Istanbul Metropolitan Municipality does not cover the entire functional area. The size of this polycentric functional metro-region is subject to some debate as there is critical lack of data, including on commuting flows (Box 1.1).

Figure 1.1. **Istanbul in the Marmara Region Context**

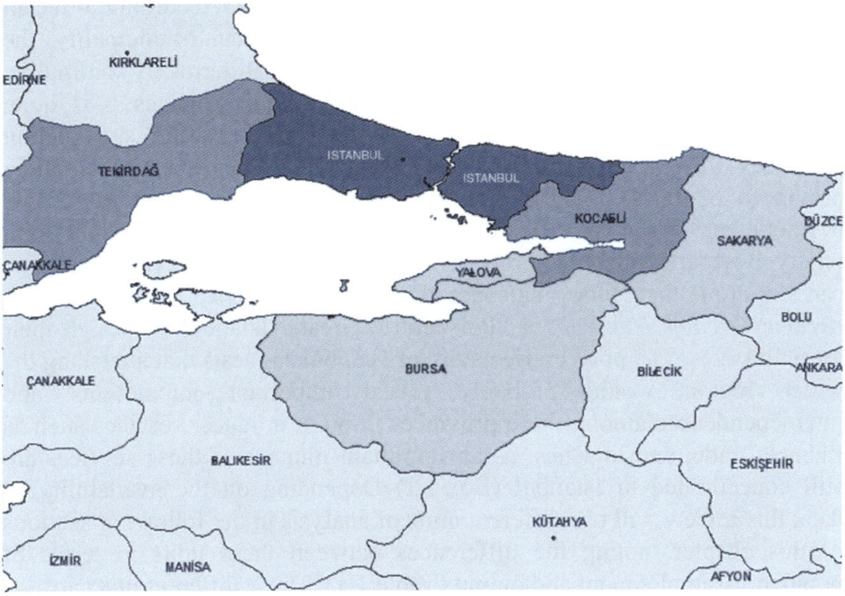

Source: Istanbul Metropolitan Municipality.

Figure 1.2. **Institutional framework in Turkey**

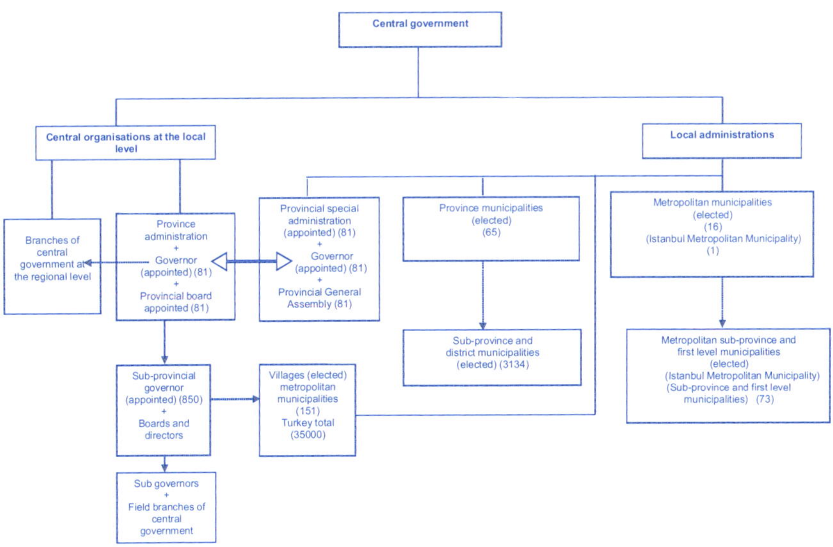

For the purpose of the analysis, this review will opt for a pragmatic approach to define the Istanbul functional metro-region. According to recent field research undertaken by the Istanbul Metropolitan Municipality, the Istanbul province is a relatively self-contained area in terms of commuting flows, but in terms of production and consumption linkages it is quite integrated within a functional area that also includes the surrounding provinces of Kocaeli and Tekirdağ. Meanwhile, the other surrounding provinces of Bursa, Yalova and Sakarya, have experienced their own development. More specifically, cities like Bursa have developed into relatively separate manufacturing centres outside Istanbul. Nevertheless, one can still argue that Bursa, Yalova and Sakarya remain part of a *Polycentric Area of Greater Istanbul* (or "Polycentric Greater Istanbul") through their loose linkages. The polycentric nature of Istanbul suggests that analysing the wider region would probably reveal important interactions and interdependences among these provinces through producer services such as finance, trade, and logistics, as an important number of these services are still concentrated in Istanbul (Box 1.1) Depending on the availability of data, this review will use different units of analysis in the following sections of this chapter, noting the differences between these units in terms of population, employment and output (Table 1.1). These different units are:

- ***Istanbul***, represented by the Istanbul Metropolitan Municipality; in the institutional framework of Turkey, the boundaries of the Municipality also coincide with those of the province;[1]

- ***Istanbul Metro-Region***, that includes Kocaeli and Tekirdağ provinces in addition to Istanbul; this unit can be considered a close proxy to the functional area;

- ***Polycentric Greater Istanbul***, which includes in addition to the Istanbul Metro-Region, Bursa, Sakarya and Yalova provinces;

- ***The Marmara region***, in which Istanbul is located, is one of the seven geographical statistical regions in Turkey. Since the introduction of the NUTS classification in Turkey, these statistical units have lost their relevance; we will however use this unit as a proxy for the larger functional area when other data is not available.

Box 1.1. **How large is Istanbul's functional metropolitan area?**

The OECD has developed a methodology to define metro-regions based on three main criteria: population size, density and functional labour markets. While Istanbul satisfies the first two conditions as it is a large and densely populated area, the third one is not as clear, due to a lack of data on commuting flows that would facilitate the definition of a single self-contained labour market based on the movement of workers.

Although there are no official data to help analytically define the functional area, several planning and academic studies undertaken in the past have underlined that Çorlu and Çerkezköy (sub-provinces of Tekirdağ) in the West, and Kocaeli province in the East, are part of the Istanbul *functional area*. There are dense economic relational networks, and intense flows of goods, people and services between the areas that justify this definition. Kocaeli has developed as an industrial extension of Istanbul following political decisions to push industrial activities out of the city centre in the 1963 "Eastern Marmara Plan".

A more recent study conducted by the Istanbul Metropolitan Municipality, based on a sample size of 3 098 industrial establishments, confirms that the Istanbul province is self-contained in terms of commuting patterns of industrial workers (IMM, 2007). However, when exploring the nature of production linkages (spatial profile of raw material purchases and final sales), the same study concludes that the Istanbul functional area includes the provinces of Kocaeli and Tekirdağ. For example, 83% of the firms confirm that they buy their raw materials from within Istanbul (particularly the European side), while only 27% buy from outside the province. It also points out that Yalova, a part of Istanbul until 1995, and Bursa are excluded from the functional area. Moreover, the proportion of establishments buying from the Marmara region is substantially lower (*e.g.*, 10% for Bursa). In fact, both in terms of producer and commuting patters, Bursa is becoming relatively self-contained in light of the substantial growth that has taken place in the car manufacturing and textile industries. Consequently, the city has developed a sizeable qualified and pooled labour force and a strong consumer market, which is reflected in much looser linkages between Bursa and Istanbul. Along the same lines, the initial analysis of the commuting patterns confirms that there is no strong relationship between Istanbul and Yalova. The notable exception to this rule is Gebze, where 38% of the labour force comes from Istanbul, thus confirming strong commuting patterns and labour market interdependencies.

Yet, it is important to consider the existence of a larger region, which could be called the *Polycentric Greater Istanbul*, that is not functionally integrated but has important economic interdependencies that cover the five provinces (Istanbul, Tekirdağ, Kocaeli, Yalova, Bursa and Sakarya). This larger area is consistent with historical developments in the region. First, the Regional Development Programme for the Eastern Marmara Region in the 1960s used investment incentives to promote the de-concentration of manufacturing activities in Istanbul

Box 1.1. How large is Istanbul's functional metropolitan area? (*cont.*)

and spurred companies to transfer production to sites in Kocaeli, Sakarya and Bursa along Trans-European Motorway (TEM) axis. As a result, manufacturing progressively migrated to the western provinces of Kocaeli and Sakarya. Second, more recently, land and rent prices in Istanbul have induced manufacturing relocation to the European province of Tekirdağ, just to the west of Istanbul. The axis now extends from Tekirdağ to Sakarya passing through Istanbul and Kocaeli. Third, to the south of Istanbul is Bursa, the second largest populated agglomeration in the Marmara region and an important urban trading area dating back to the Ottoman Empire that has recently been favoured by trade liberalisation in Turkey, and is becoming an important FDI manufacturing hub. Changes in employment and specialisation among the different provinces within the larger functional area suggest an increasingly dense pattern of relational and socio-economic networks between the city of Istanbul and the outskirts of its larger functional metropolitan area.

Table 1.1. **Basic indicators of Istanbul Functional Area**

	Population (2005*)	Employment(1) (2000)	Labour Force(1) (2000)	GDP pc (PPP USD) (2001) (2)
Istanbul Metro-region	*13 387 624*	*4 047 150*	*4 605 112*	*9 566*
Istanbul City/province	11 331 963	3 471 400	3 977 241	8 752
Kocaeli	1 362 869	502 950	548 622	17 612
Tekirdağ	692 792	301 628	321 892	7 137
GREATER ISTANBUL	*16 703 287*	*5 679 424*	*6 378 368*	*9 327*
(Istanbul Metro-Region) plus				
Bursa	2 361 933	825 531	910 349	7 163
Sakarya	771 433	505 115	541 015	6 023
Yalova	182 297	72 800	79 249	9 893
TURKEY	*72 065 000*	*22 081 000*	*23 578 000*	*6 132*

Notes: *mid-year population projection by provinces.

1. Employment and labour force statistics by provinces (NUTS 3) for the more recent years have not been produced by TURKSTAT. Employment and labour force statistics for 2004 and 2005 are available only at NUTS 2, NUTS 1 and national (NUTS 0) levels.

2. GDP per capita (USD PPP) have not been produced at the regional level (NUTS 1, 2 and 3) since 2001.

Source: TURKSTAT, *www.turkstat.gov.tr*

1.2. Main socio-economic trends

The demographic and economic motor of Turkey

A big population magnet…

Istanbul has been one of the fastest growing metro-regions both in Turkey and amongst other OECD member countries. Over a half century, the Istanbul metro-region has become a mega-city both by UN and OECD standards, ranking eight out of 78 OECD metro-regions in terms of population.[2] In the first 25 years of the Turkish Republic, population both in Turkey and Istanbul seemed to grow steadily, then after 1965 the population growth went faster in Istanbul than in Turkey (Figure 1.3). By international comparison, this increase in urbanisation has been quite impressive, with Turkey ranking first among OECD countries for its urbanisation growth during the period 1980-2004 (Figure 1.4). In fact, Istanbul registered a dramatic population increase from 1.16 million to more than 10 million from 1950-2000 (during the same period, the Marmara region population grew from 3.1 to 17.4 million). As a result, Istanbul's share of Turkey's total population grew from 5.6% to 14.8% during the period 1950-2000 (and from 14.8% to 25.6% for the Marmara region) (Table 1.2). Since 1990, the pace of population growth has slowed (from 4.5% in 1990 to 3.3% in 2000). However, this rate remains higher than the national level and the highest among OECD metro-regions for the period 1995-2002 (Figure 1.5).

Figure 1.3. **Population trends in Istanbul and Turkey (1927-2000)**

Population (in millions)

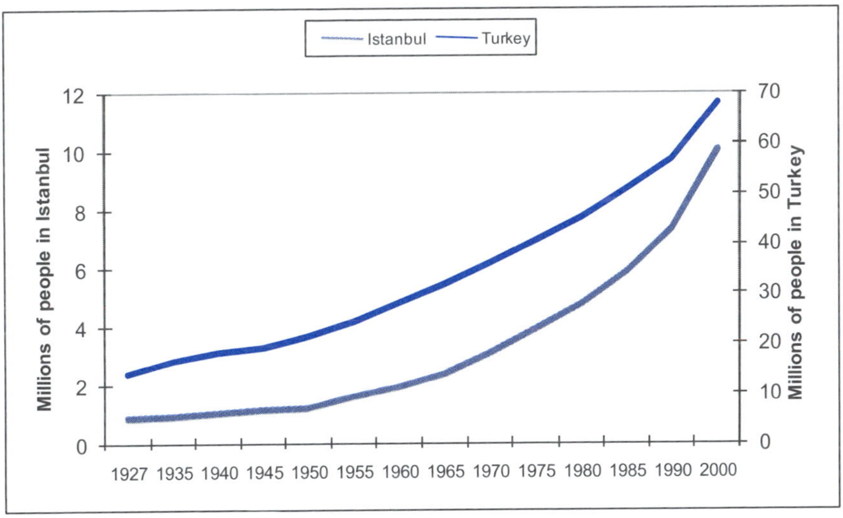

Source: Turkish Statistical Institute (TURKSTAT), 2000 Census of Population (*www.turkstat.gov.tr*).

Figure 1.4. **Urbanisation growth in OECD countries**

Average annual growth in population in predominantly urban areas (1980-2004)

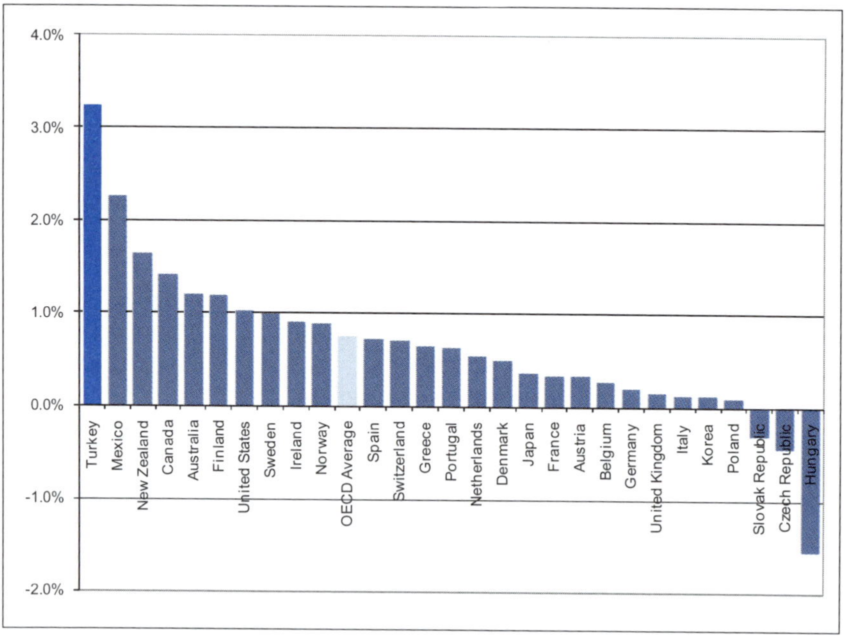

Table 1.2 **Evolution of population shares for Istanbul and the Marmara region**

	1950	1960	1970	1980	1990	2000
ISTANBUL	1 166 477	1 882 092	3 019 032	4 741 890	7 309 190	10 018 735
Share % (of the total population in Turkey)	*5.6*	*6.8*	*8.5*	*10.6*	*12.7*	*14.8*
MARMARA REGION	3 097 683	5 181 850	6 837 167	9 435 210	13 295 878	17 365 027
Share % (of the total population in Turkey)	*14.8*	*18.7*	*19.2*	*21.1*	*23.5*	*25.6*
TURKEY	20 947 188	27 754 820	35 605 176	44 736 957	56 473 035	67 803 927

Source: Turkish Statistical Institute (TURKSTAT), 2000 Census of Population (*www.turkstat.gov.tr*).

Figure 1.5. **Average annual population growth rates among a selection of OECD metro-regions (1995-2002)**

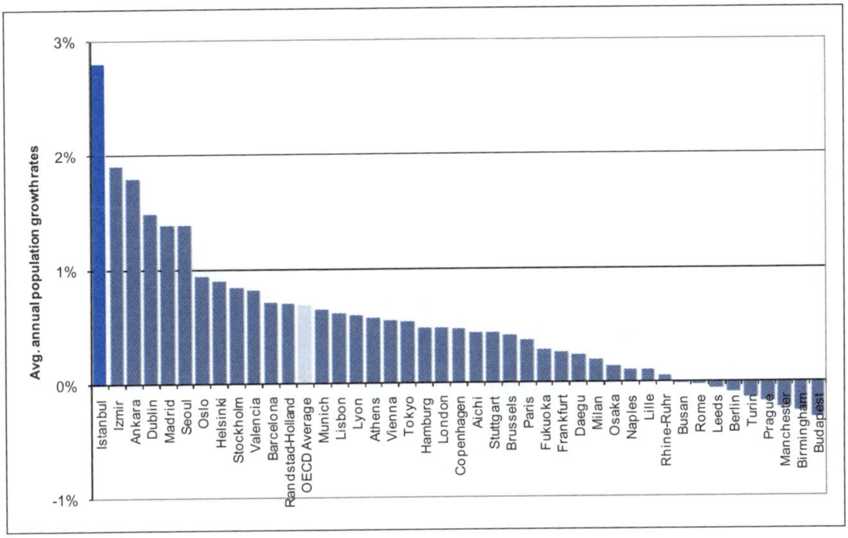

Note: OECD average refers to the average of OECD metro-regions.

Urbanisation has been accompanied by increased population density. The spatial concentration of the population within the Istanbul Metro-Region is particularly high, partly due to the constraints of Istanbul's geographical morphology. Half of Istanbul's northern coast, particularly on the Asian side, is covered by forest and water nature reserves where settlements are forbidden. While many OECD metro-regions have tended to grow through outward expansion at progressively lower densities, Istanbul's fast urban growth has gone hand in hand with increased density, particularly in the peninsula. In fact, Istanbul has a higher density than most OECD metro-regions and as large as that of many metro-regions from non-member countries (Figure 1.6).

Population growth has been largely fuelled by domestic and international migration. Though Istanbul, as other regions in Turkey, has greatly benefited from a decline in mortality rates and pro-active governmental policies to promote fertility rates implemented from 1927 to 1960, the more recent population growth in Istanbul has mainly been due to migration waves. Actually, fertility rates in Istanbul have been consistently lower than the national average since 1980 (2% against 2.5% in 2000) (Table 1.3). The demographic transition process is about to be achieved whilst population growth is now largely supported by important migration flows. Between 1970 and 2000, Istanbul alone – excluding other provinces – received almost 4 million migrants. Depending on the unit of analysis (Istanbul, the Metro-Region or Polycentric Greater Istanbul), the proportion of residents in Istanbul that were born in a different province represent about one-third to one-half of that born locally[3] (Figure 1.7).

Figure 1.6. **Population density among a selection of large cities**

People per km^2

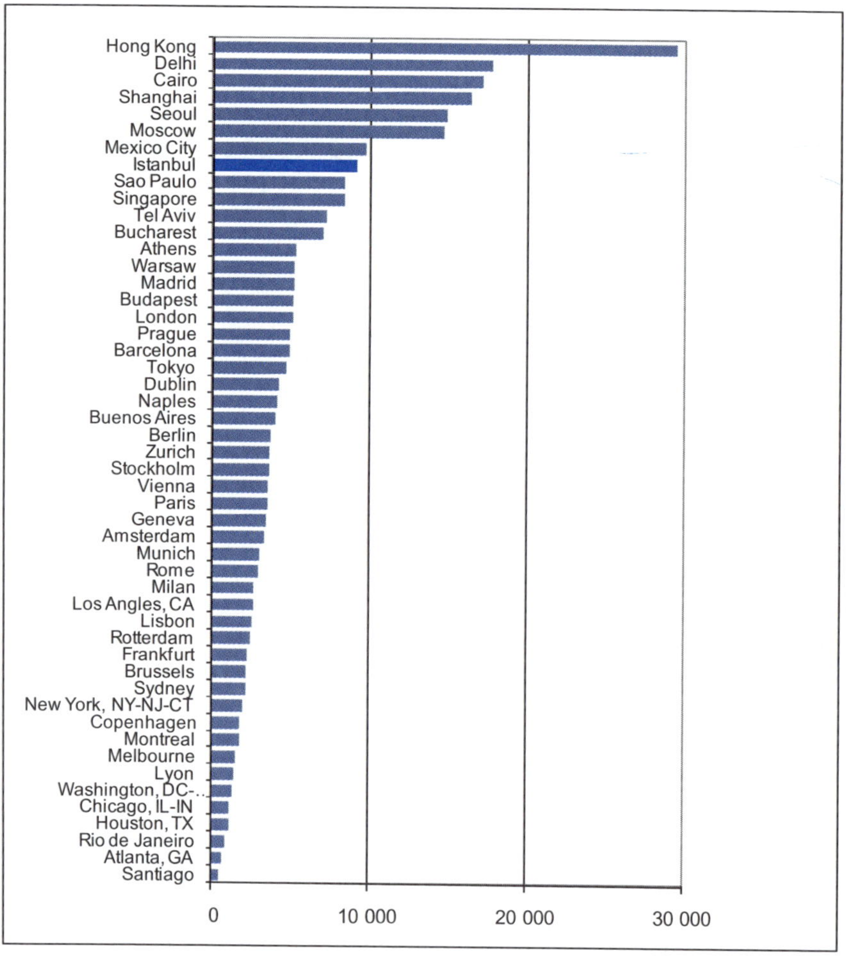

Note: Most of the data come from *www.demographia.com*; Moscow, Warsaw, Prague, Budapest: Millennium cities database 1995; London: Census 2001; Paris: Insee 1999, American cities: US Census 2000.

Source: Istanbul Metropolitan Planning and Urban Design Centre (IMP).

Table 1.3. **Fertility rates in Istanbul (%)**

	1980	1985	1990	2000
Istanbul	2.7	2.0	2.1	2.0
Turkey	3.4	2.6	2.7	2.5

Source: Turkish Statistical Institute (TURKSTAT), 2000 Census of Population (*www.turkstat.gov.tr*).

Figure 1.7. **Share of Istanbul population born in another province (2000)**

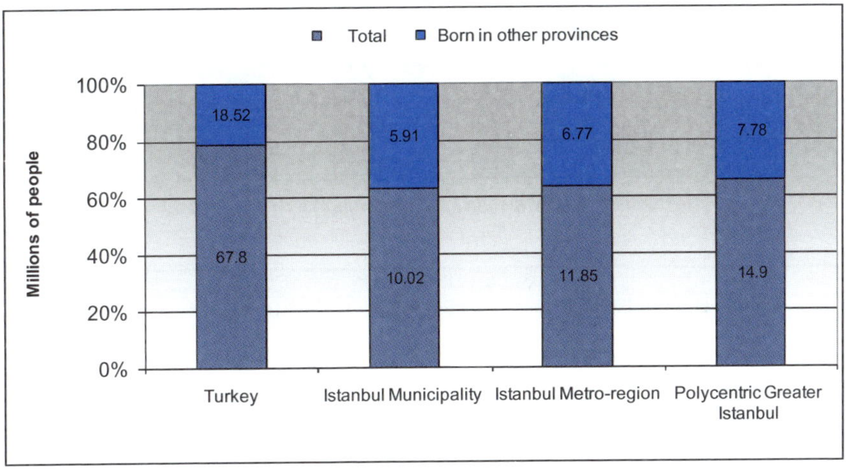

Source: Based on data from the Turkish Statistical Institute (TURKSTAT), 2000 Census of Population (*www.turkstat.gov.tr*).

The pattern of migration trends has changed over the time. The mechanisation of agriculture along with highway network improvements financed by foreign aid in the 1950s kicked off the first wave of migration from Anatolia, mainly to the three largest metropolitan areas – Istanbul, Ankara and Izmir. During the second wave of migration after 1965, Istanbul received more of the migration than the other two large metro-regions. Migration accelerated during the 1980s with the development of new opportunities in western provinces given the opening up of the economy, as well as by foreign migration mainly from countries of the former Soviet bloc. While the first wave of migration in the 1950s was primarily of single men, the post-1965 trend initiated by the second phase of industrialisation involved the migration of entire families. Moreover, in addition to inflows of migrants from remote rural areas, Istanbul increasingly attracted people from other parts of the Marmara region, reinforcing the polarisation effect (Figures 1.8 and 1.9). Finally, in the last decade Istanbul has also been attracting migrants from other surrounding countries.

Figure 1.8. **Immigration to Istanbul and the Marmara Region**

Cumulative, thousands of people

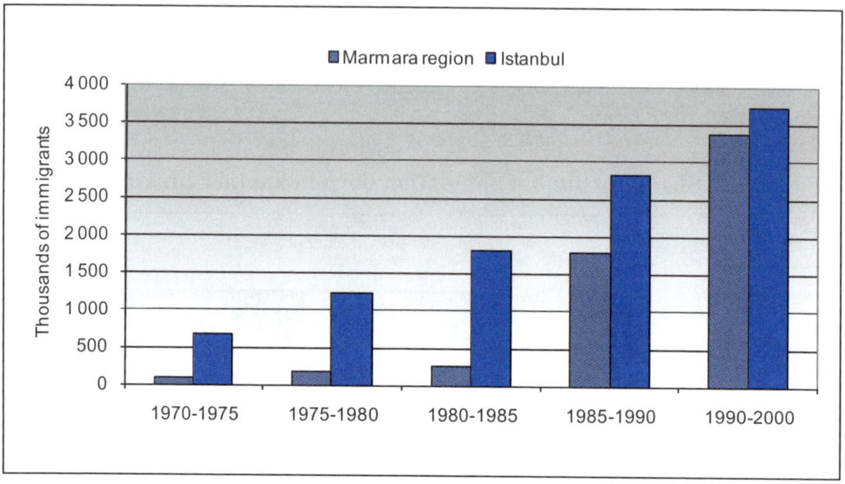

Note: Immigration to Istanbul includes migrants from the Marmara Region.

Source: State Planning Organization (SPO), Regional Statistics, *www.dpt.gov.tr.*

Figure 1.9. **Net migrants in Istanbul**

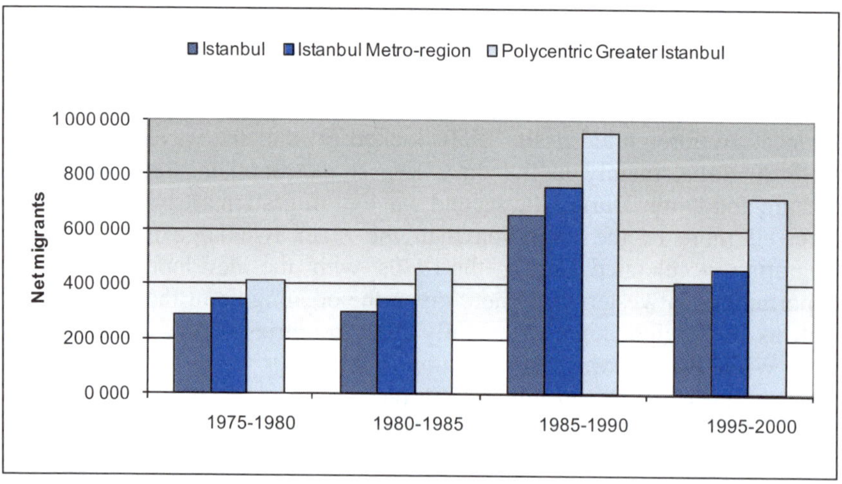

Source: Turkish Statistical Institute (TURKSTAT), 2000 Census of Population (*www.turkstat.gov.tr*).

...that concentrates the bulk of the national economy

Istanbul is undoubtedly the leading economy in Turkey, with the largest concentration of high-value-added productive activities in the country. In 2001, Istanbul generated almost one-quarter of the country's GDP (27.1% for the metro-region), while the Marmara Region accounted for 38% of Turkey's GDP. In 2000, Istanbul Metro-Region's GDP per capita exceeded the national average by more than 70%, making the leading metropolitan area of Turkey rank third among the 78 largest OECD metro-regions for this indicator just after Warsaw, Poland and Monterrey, Mexico (Figure 1.10). Istanbul also has a relatively large labour force as it concentrates 15.6% of Turkey's total labour force, *i.e.*, slightly higher than its 14.7% share of the population. More importantly, Istanbul concentrates high shares of national production in every sector except for agriculture, including those that generate the highest value-added activities. For instance, Istanbul accounts for almost one-third of Turkey's manufacturing and this figure rises to 52.1% for the Marmara Region as many of these activities have relocated to other provinces in Polycentric Greater Istanbul like Kocaeli or Bursa (Table 1.4). The services sector represents more than two-thirds of Istanbul's economy, accounting for more than half of Turkey's financial services and almost 40% of business and personal services. With a stronger specialisation in higher-value-added activities, Istanbul's productivity level exceeds the national average by almost 50%.[4] This differential is comparable to productivity gaps between Paris and France, New York and the United States, and Mexico City and Mexico – with the Istanbul Metro-Region ranking tenth among the 78 OECD metro-regions for this indicator (Figure 1.11).

Table 1.4. **Regional share of national GDP by sector**

	Istanbul		Marmara Region	
	1987	2000	1987	2000
Agriculture	1.4	0.7	15.6	15.0
Manufacturing	26.8	29.2	47.9	52.1
Construction	17.8	18.8	29.2	32.0
Trade	29.3	27.5	38.8	37.4
Transportation, communication	21.7	21.7	33.4	35.0
Financial services	43.0	55.2	53.9	64.1
Business and personal services	38.8	39.5	46.8	48.9
Total sectors	21.0	22.6	35.2	38.1
Public services	12.7	13.6	24.5	26.5
Private non-profit institutions	8.5	6.4	11.6	10.8
Import duties	26.7	21.7	54.9	46.7
GDP	20.7	22.1	35.3	38.0

Source: Turkish Statistical Institute (TURKSTAT), 2000 Census of Population (*www.turkstat.gov.tr*).

Figure 1.10. **Differences in per capita GDP of metro-regions and their national level (2002)**

Sample of 78 metro-regions in the OECD

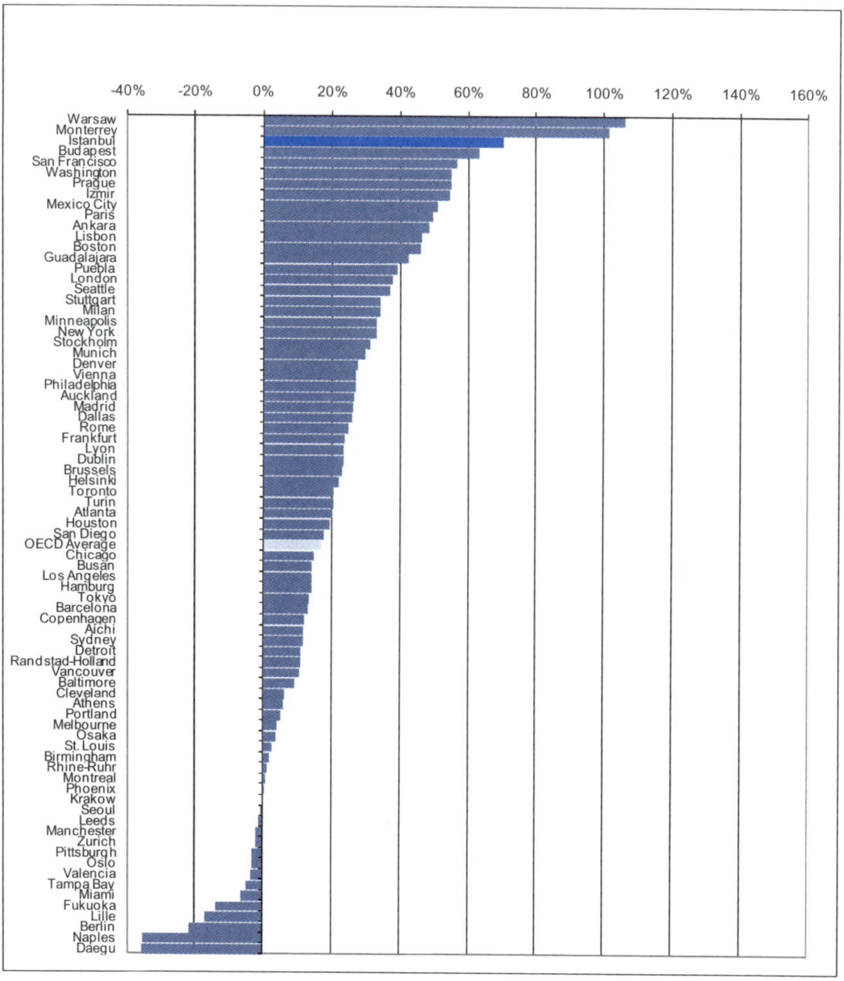

Note: OECD average refers to the average of OECD metro-regions.

Figure 1.11. **Productivity differences between the metro-regions and their national level (2002)**

Sample of 78 metro-regions in the OECD

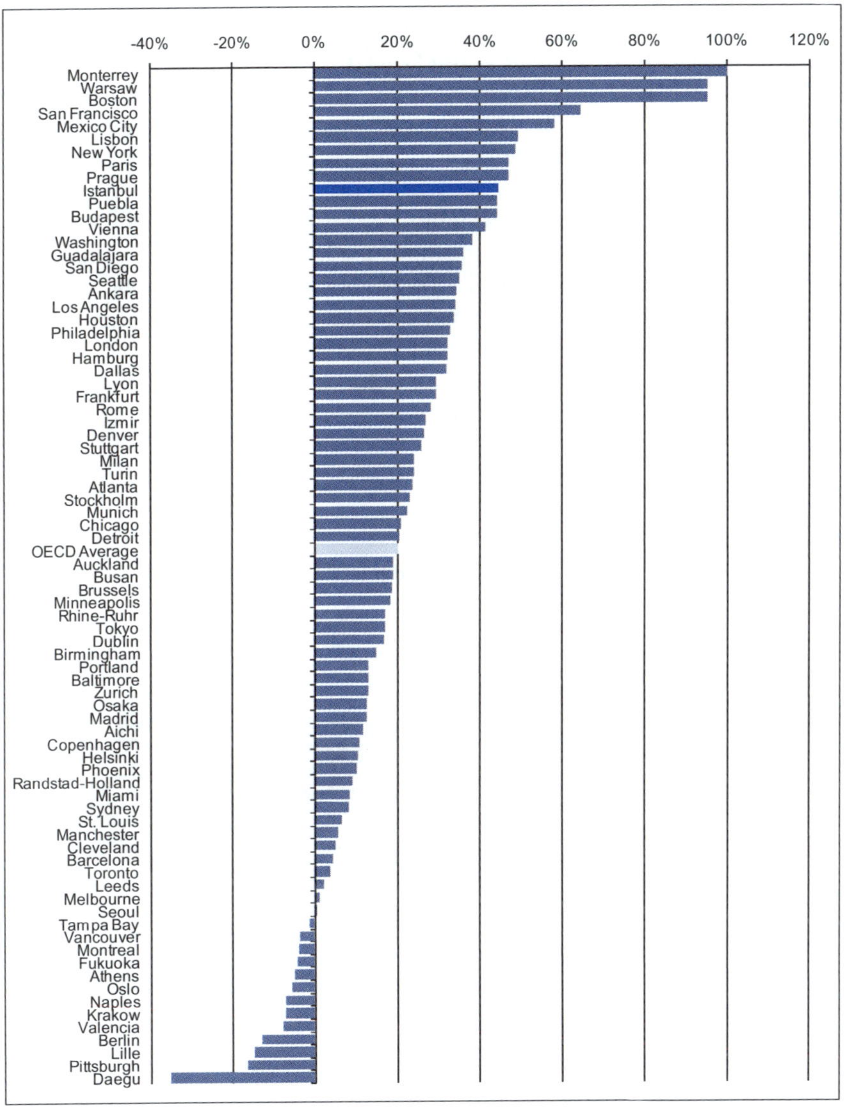

Note: OECD average refers to the average of OECD metro-regions.

The concentration of output in Istanbul contributes to the large regional disparities in the country. Turkey is characterised by a historical "East-West divide" that has been growing since the 18th century with increasing trade relations with western European countries. With the more recent opening to the international economy, fragmented land, difficult climate conditions, and large distances from regional markets have contributed to lower relative agricultural efficiency in the eastern rural areas, accelerating their decline and migration flows to the western provinces. In 2003, Istanbul and its surrounding provinces (Kocaeli and Bursa), along with Ankara and Izmir, ranked the highest among the 81 provinces for the SEDI index that compiles 58 socio-economic variables (Figure 1.12). By international standards Turkey is the OECD country that features the largest levels of regional GDP per capita disparities (Figure 1.13). Although a process of regional convergence can be detected, it remains rather slow given the current extent of regional disparities (see Annex). This issue has been widely recognised as a major challenge in Turkey not only for lagging regions but also for Istanbul and other large metropolitan areas that have to accommodate a large influx of migrants.

Figure 1.12. **Regional disparities in Turkey**

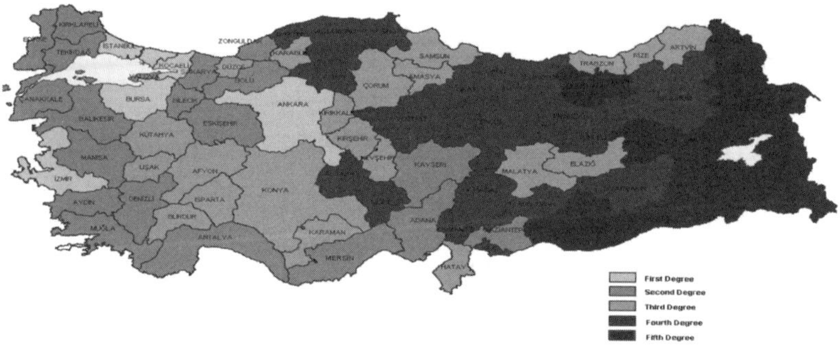

Note: The SEDI index developed by the State Planning Organization compiles 58 variables from social (demographic, employment, education, health, infrastructure, other welfare) and economic (manufacturing, construction, agriculture, financial) fields. Thus, five separate groups have been identified according to their level of development (The Socio-Economic Development Index, SPO (2003), "Survey of Provinces and Regions").

Source: The State Planning Organization.

Figure 1.13. **Comparison of regional disparities in OECD countries**

Gini index for GDP per capita

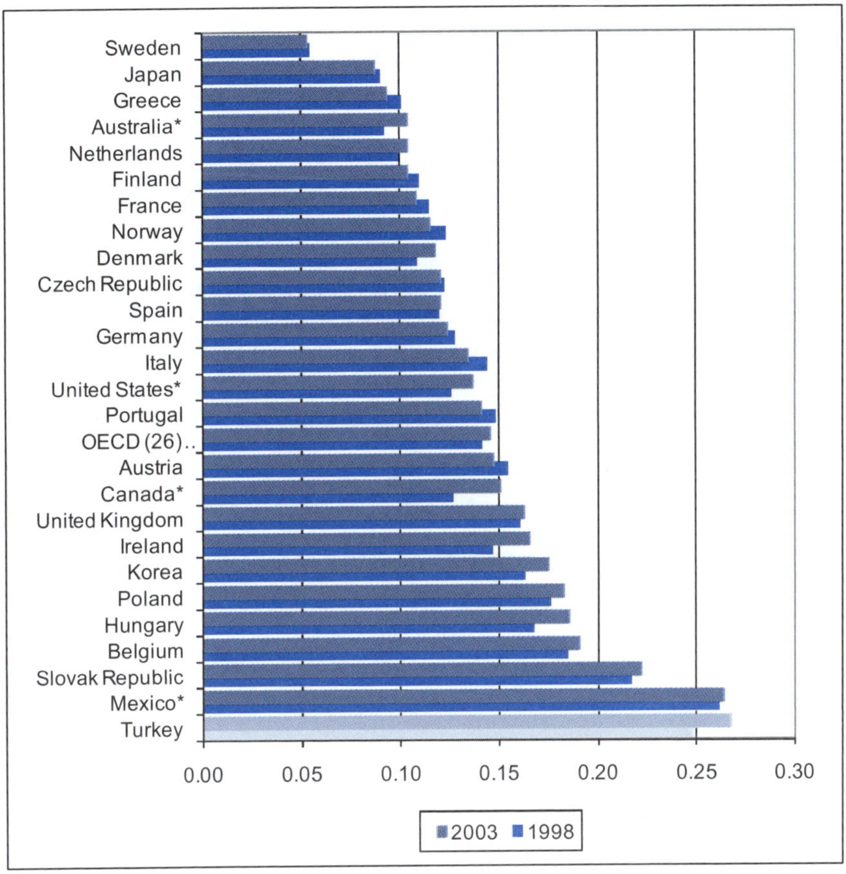

Note: The Gini index looks not only at the regions with the highest and the lowest values but also at the differences among all regions. It ranges between 0 and 1 with the higher the value, the larger regional disparities. The Gini index for GDP per capita is obtained from the *OECD Regions at a Glance 2005*. The regional population figures are collected from Statistics Sweden.

Source: OECD (2007), *OECD Regions at a Glance 2007*, OECD Publications, Paris.

A dynamic and vulnerable economy…

As one of the largest metropolitan areas from a relatively fast developing country, Istanbul has registered high levels of output and productivity growth. Between 1987 and 2004, Istanbul registered an average annual growth of 3.7%, as compared to 3.2% for Turkey during the same period. By international standards, Istanbul ranks 12th among a selection of 45 OECD metro-regions for its growth rate from 1995-2002 (Figure 1.14). High growth rates have been generated by increased labour productivity, *i.e.*, around 1.8% average annual growth over the period 1995-2000. This is less than the national average (2.9%) for the same period; however, labour productivity growth is likely to be higher if more precise measures of labour productivity were available at the local level (GDP per man-hour worked instead of the current one based on GDP per employee). Higher employment growth over the same period in Istanbul as compared to Turkey has created this statistical confusion. Actually, from an international perspective, Istanbul ranks 12th out of 38 metro-regions for productivity growth over the period 1995-2002.

Figure 1.14. **Economic growth in a selection of OECD metro-regions**

Average annual growth rates (1995-2002) using GDP per capita in PPPs – Sample of 45 metro-regions

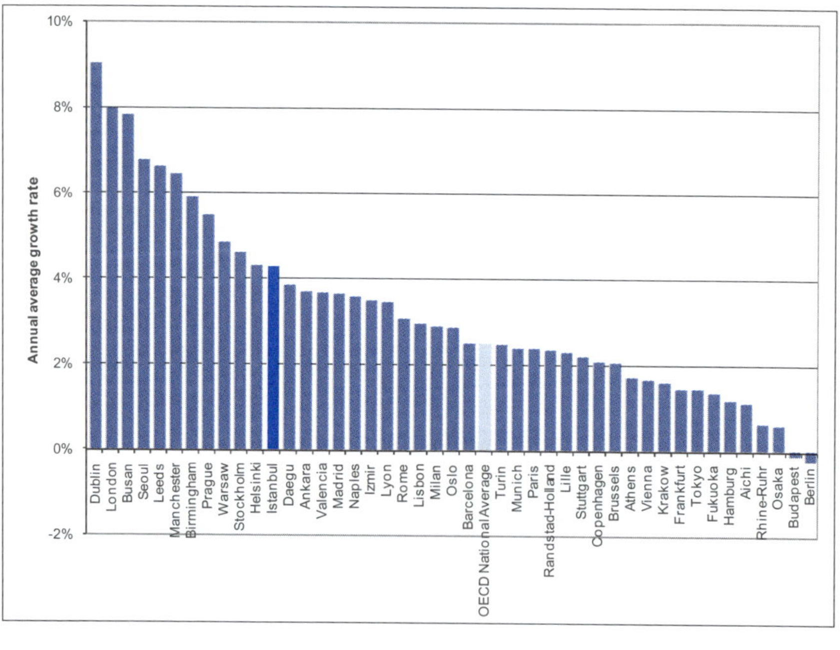

Yet, Istanbul's economy remains particularly vulnerable to economic cycles. Economic growth in both Istanbul and Turkey, but more so in Istanbul, has been tainted by slowdowns and negative growth rates throughout Turkey's recent economic history, but at the same time characterised by outstanding growth rates above 5% and in some years even above 10% (Figure 1.15). Such a trend resembles a boom-and-bust cycle with crises in 1994 and 2001, and a deep recession in 1999. In the aftermath of every financial crisis, the economy would enjoy a rapid recovery with rates of around 8%. As financial services constitute a significant part of Istanbul's economy (around 10%), during the 1994 and 2001 financial crises Istanbul's economy shrank almost 5 percentage points more than the national economy. Although Istanbul's fast recovery after crises was based on short-term capital inflows, after 2002 it has been recovering at a slower pace than the national economy.

Figure 1.15. **Real GDP growth in Istanbul and Turkey (1989–2004)**

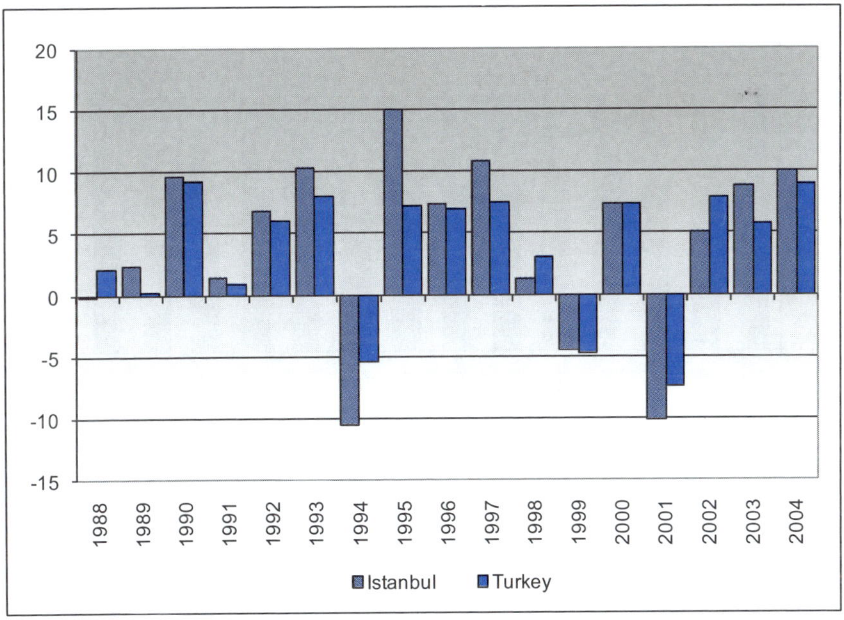

Source: Turkish Statistical Institute (TURKSTAT), 2000 Census of Population (*www.turkstat.gov.tr*).

The vulnerability of Istanbul's economy is putting pressure on its level of wealth per capita, especially within the city. First, whilst Istanbul's GDP per capita[5] exceeds the national average by 70%, GDP per capita growth has slowed down over the 1990s (0.9% over 1990-2000 against 1.7% for Turkey) (Figure 1.16). If Istanbul is excluded from the Marmara Region, the gap between the two in terms of GDP per capita widens. In 2001 this gap reached a record level of 30 percentage points difference due to a sharper decline in services compared to manufacturing, whose activities are located outside the city. Similarly, the average growth rate for the Marmara region, excluding Istanbul for the period 1990-2000, stands largely above that of Istanbul (1.8% *versus* 0.9%).

Figure 1.16. **Evolution of GDP per capita in Istanbul and the Marmara Region (1987–2001)**

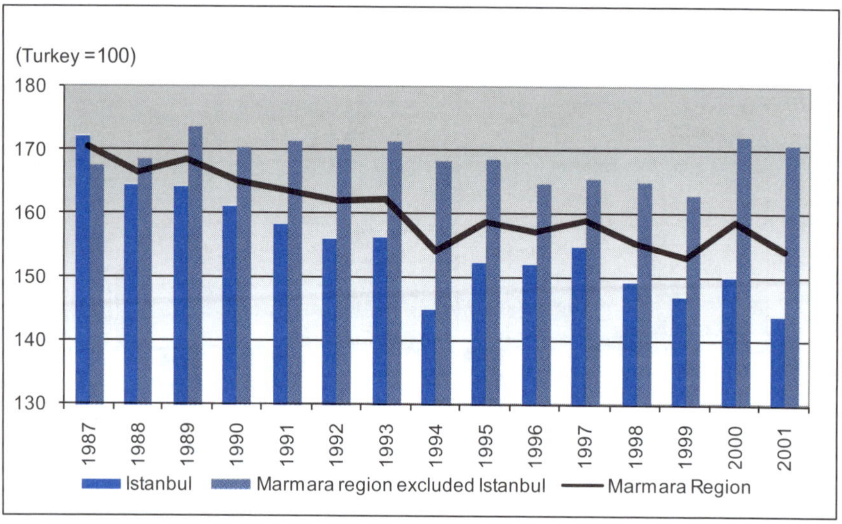

Source: Istanbul Metropolitan Planning and Urban Design Centre (IMP).

Istanbul's labour market is facing increasing strain as well. The employment rate in Istanbul declined by 4.3% between 2001 and 2004 due to the 2001 financial crisis. The economic crisis took its toll on employment especially in fields such as the financial, construction, and commerce sectors. Despite a positive employment growth trend after 2001, Istanbul was not able to restart employment generation as rapidly as prior to 2001. Since then, the employment rate for Istanbul grew slightly, reaching 88.6% in 2005, but remains lower than the average for Turkey (90.7%) which is to a certain degree driven by a lower activity rate in Istanbul. In the same vein, unemployment reached 12.1% (in 2001), *i.e.*, considerably higher than the national average (9%). Unemployment came down to 11.4% in 2005 but still stood above that of Turkey (10.3%). Meanwhile, Istanbul features a lower activity rate than that of Turkey due to its large informal sector. These trends clearly highlight structural problems in Istanbul's labour market.

Istanbul is typically confronted with an "Urban Paradox" that has been reinforced by migration flows. Although it concentrates the bulk of national output and labour force, and generates productivity levels higher than the national average, it also features lower employment and activity rates, and higher unemployment than its country average. Similar trends affect a number of OECD metro-regions (*e.g.*, one-third of the 78 OECD metro-regions have above national average unemployment rates and urban regions as a whole feature lower activity rates than other types of regions).[6] Despite the high concentrations of wealth and agglomeration associated with its leading sectors and being the focal points of their national economies, metro-regions also suffer from a high number of unemployed residents; in other words, wealth is not adequately translated into job creation. It seems, however, that Istanbul, like Mexico City, contains a disproportionate number of people who are inactive. The main reason is a large informal sector whose employment level has recently increased to the detriment of formal employment (see below). The other reason for the low activity rate is low female participation in the labour market. Although Istanbul's female participation rate grew very rapidly from 14.3% in 1980 to 36% in 1991, it then fell to 25.9% in 2000, below the national level of 36%. Increased productivity and output in Istanbul has not created sufficient jobs, especially for low-skilled workers particularly given the extent of new migrants that continuously join the local labour market. Meanwhile, the lower activity rate and higher unemployment levels in Istanbul as compared to the two other provinces in the metro-region might suggest that the impact on the labour market of migration to Istanbul and extent of the informal economy might be greater here than in other parts of the region (Figure 1.17).

Figure 1.17. **Difference in productivity, unemployment and activity rate among provinces of the metro-region**

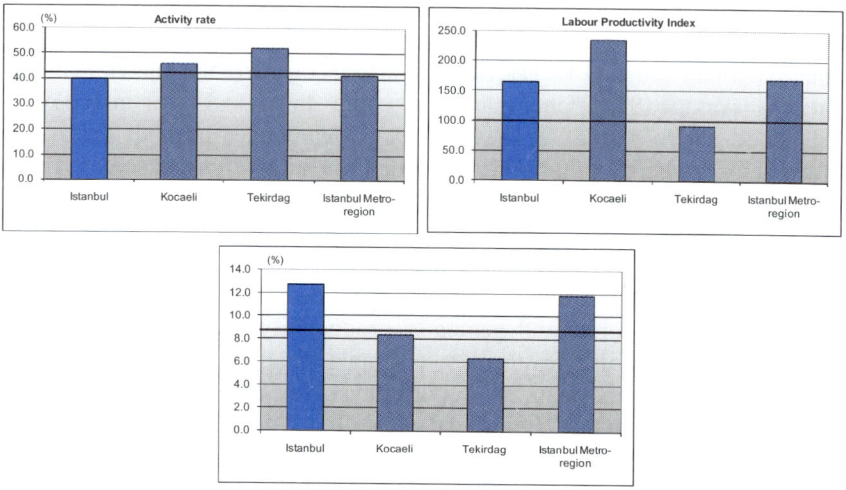

Note: Black line represents the national average.

The impact of the macroeconomic context

Turkey is going through a phase of rapid transition, characterised by significant changes in its policies and an intense process of socio-economic and political restructuring. First, and as part of a process that was triggered in the 1980s, the country has shifted from an import substitution system to a more open and export-oriented macroeconomic framework, which implied a liberalisation of its principle restrictions on factor and product markets. Such a structural adjustment focused on price flexibility, removing price controls and quotas, reducing the state's involvement in economic activities and avoiding fiscal deficits. Since the 1990s, and also following two severe 2000-2001 financial crises, the country negotiated a new stand-by agreement with the IMF and the World Bank, and also deepened its commitments towards liberalisation and structural reform. In addition, Turkey started discussions to enter the European Union, which has implied a series of chapter negotiations related to its socio-economic, political, institutional and legal framework.

Istanbul is likely to benefit from the ongoing policy reforms that are being implemented in Turkey. The city concentrates the majority of national economy's employment and value-added activities, and reflects many of the challenges and potentialities the economy and society of Turkey will be facing over the coming years. Therefore, it can be expected that many of the net economic benefits of overall broadening and deepening of the reform process set in motion by policy makers is likely to be concentrated in the economic heartland of Istanbul. Considering its good geographical location, its historical connections within the European, Asian and Balkan regions, and the increasing tendency towards the liberalisation of factor and product markets with Europe, the city is likely to reap substantial benefits from its increasing institutional and socio-economic linkages with the European Union. Thus, under the likely assumption that these reforms will be continued and deepened, there will be a tendency for Istanbul to strengthen its socio-economic and geo-political role in the international arena.

Istanbul also concentrates the bulk of net costs related to macroeconomic adjustment processes undertaken at the national level and delays in the reform's implementation process. The process of reform started by replacing an autarky with an open-market economy, and by reducing the role of the State as a producer, which resulted in increased price flexibility. By the same token, the strategy included reducing high tariffs and eliminating quotas that limit international trade. With soaring exports, the economy of Turkey enjoyed high-growth rates between 1980 and 1990. However, in the aftermath of the 1990s financial liberalisation, a lack of fiscal austerity resulted in consumption-driven economic growth financed via short-term capital inflows. This brought considerable volatility in macroeconomic aggregates, triggered high and persistent inflation and hid the financial sector inefficiency (which is mainly concentrated in Istanbul). Furthermore, the mounting public debt that reached 101% of GDP in 2001 prevented the financial sector from growing in line with economic activity. The real sector suffered the consequences of the higher deficit, which was financed by the issuance of bonds in the form of crowded-out investment in plant and equipment which led to reduced output growth. This cycle, caused by domestic debt, reached its peak in 2000 and culminated in severe twin crises in 2001 (fiscal deficit and current account deficit reached 15.4% and 4.1% respectively of GDP). The inflation and exchange rates also increased by 20 and 50 points respectively, more than their previous year averages.

A rigorous macroeconomic policy framework has led to improved economic performance but the mid-2006 financial turmoil highlighted the need for further structural reforms. The ambitious 2001 reform agenda established in agreement with the IMF has provided an economic transformation based on a new institutional framework for monetary and fiscal policies as well as for product, labour and financial markets. Over the period 2002-2005, output increased by a third, representing the strongest pace of growth among OECD countries. Turkey also succeeded in fighting against high and chronic inflation, bringing it down from more than 70% at the beginning of 2002 to less than 10% within a time span of about two years (OECD, 2006b). Turkey's positive macroeconomic performance between 2002 and 2005 was the result of a strong governmental commitment to pursue structural reforms, and was also supported by a favourable international environment, characterised by strong world trade and – despite higher oil prices – relatively low inflation and low interest rates, and a strong global appetite for emerging market assets. But towards mid-2006 interest rate hikes in major industrial countries prompted a change in the risk appetite of the international financial markets, which affected Turkey the most severely among the emerging economies. Turkey experienced the strongest deterioration in its risk premium in international markets[7] and the largest exchange rate depreciation (28.3% between April and June 2006). A main consequence has been a surge in the inflation rate that exceeded 2 points in May, June and July with an annual inflation of 3.3 for 2006. This short-run turmoil in the international financial markets again highlighted Turkey's economic vulnerability to external shocks, and the need to strengthen fiscal discipline and budgetary transparency, and to further pursue structural reforms (OECD, 2006b).

Major structural changes in this industrial mix

Beyond recent macroeconomic trends, structural change in the industrial mix has had an impact on Istanbul's economy. These changes are linked with both external factors (increasing integration – and competition – with the world trade system) and internal factors (population movements in Turkey, large regional disparities and urban sprawl). They include: (1) an ongoing shift towards a higher-value-added and more service-oriented economy; and (2) a spatial redistribution of economic activities throughout the larger functional area.

Towards a higher-value-added economy?

Istanbul has increased its service sector's share in its industrial mix. This trend is typical of large metropolitan areas which tend to have a more diversified economic basis. Both in terms of output and labour force, Istanbul's tertiary sector represents about two-thirds of its economy, *i.e.*, largely exceeding the national average (Figure 1.18 and Table 1.5). Comparative data on the contribution of services to the total gross value added at the national level shows that Turkey's economy is much more specialised in services, like wholesale, retail trade, restaurants, transport, storage and communication, than other OECD countries; whose service specialisations focus more in finance and insurance and to a lesser extent in real estate, renting and business services (Table 1.6) As Istanbul concentrates the bulk of advanced services in Turkey, reflected by its recent development of financial, business and personal services (see below), one can conclude that Istanbul remains the wholesale trade centre of Turkey whilst developing new specialisations in more advanced services.

Figure 1.18. **Sectoral composition of GDP (2000)**

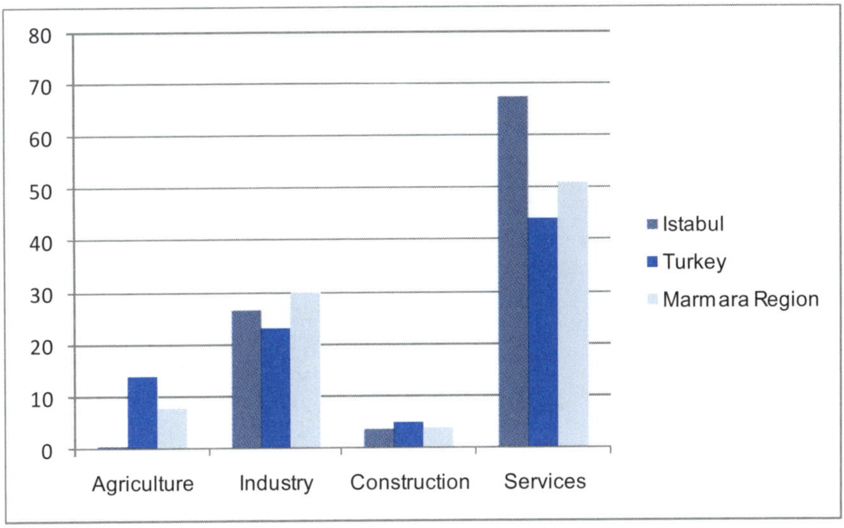

Source: Turkish Statistical Institute (TURKSTAT) (*www.turkstat.gov.tr*).

Table 1.5. **Labour force by economic activity (2000)**

	Total	Agriculture	Industry	Construction	Services
Turkey	*21 791*	7 400	3 988	1 029	9 374
(%, share)		34.0	18.3	4.7	43.0
Istanbul	*3 318*	26	1 236	176	1 880
(%, share)	*(15.2)*	0.8 (0.4)	37.3 (31.0)	5.3 (17.3)	56.7 (20.1)

Source: Turkish Statistical Institute (TURKSTAT) (*www.turkstat.gov.tr*).

Table 1.6. **Contribution of services to total gross value added in OECD countries (2004)**

%

	Wholesale and retail trade, restaurants and hotels	Transport, storage and communi-cation	Finance and insurance	Real estate, renting and business services	Public administra-tion and defence	Education, health, social work and other services
Australia	14.1	7.9	7.5	21.3	4.2	14.6
Austria	17.6	7.2	5.5	17.0	5.8	14.4
Belgium	14.7	8.2	5.9	21.9	7.3	15.9
Canada	13.8	7.1	6.1	19.8	5.7	14.3
Czech Republic	14.5	10.9	3.1	13.2	6.0	11.1
Denmark	13.4	8.8	5.4	18.6	6.3	21.3
Finland	12.2	10.8	2.6	18.3	5.1	17.4
France	13.1	6.3	4.9	26.5	7.6	17.3
Germany	12.4	5.6	4.6	24.5	6.0	16.4
Greece	21.1	9.4	5.6	14.7	7.4	14.1
Hungary	12.6	8.1	3.4	17.3	9.4	14.5
Iceland	12.7	7.1	7.3	16.2	5.8	19.2
Ireland	12.6	5.4	10.1	13.3	4.4	14.1
Italy	15.5	7.7	4.7	21.9	6.4	13.1
Japan	12.7	6.8	6.5	11.7	5.5	17.4
Korea	9.8	7.3	8.2	12.4	6.1	11.5
Luxembourg	12.2	9.7	21.6	21.4	5.8	11.4
Mexico	20.6	10.3	3.4	9.5	4.3	22.2
Netherlands	15.0	7.5	7.4	19.4	7.3	16.9
New Zealand	15.4	7.1	5.8	21.1	4.3	13.0
Norway	10.3	8.8	3.8	15.6	5.0	17.5
Poland	20.7	7.7	2.3	14.1	7.1	13.1
Portugal	17.5	7.0	6.6	14.2	9.1	16.0
Slovak Republic	15.1	10.7	6.8	14.5	7.1	9.8
Spain	18.6	7.4	4.6	16.2	6.0	13.6
Sweden	12.1	8.2	3.7	20.7	5.5	21.0
Turkey	***20.2***	***15.2***	***5.1***	***7.6***	..	***11.3***
United Kingdom	15.4	7.4	5.1	23.8	4.9	17.4
United States	15.4	6.1	7.9	24.5	7.5	15.8
Average	*15.1*	*8.4*	*4.8*	*17.6*	*6.4*	*14.1*

Source: OECD (2006), *OECD in Figures 2006*, OECD Publications, Paris.

Contrary to many OECD metro-regions, Istanbul maintains a sizeable manufacturing sector, specialised in relatively labour-intensive, low-technology activities, *i.e.*, mainly the textile cluster and its supply chains. In 2004, this sector represented 37% of Istanbul's total labour force (*i.e.*, higher than for any other province or region in Turkey) and 26% of its total GDP. If we classify activities according to the intensity with which technology is used, the low-technology group (such as apparel and other textiles) accounts for more than 25% of Istanbul's value-added and the group of medium-low technology (such as plastic products or cutlery) makes up about 5.5% of the value-added in Istanbul (Table 1.7). In 2000, these two segments represented 57% and 17% respectively of the total number of formally registered firms in Istanbul, and 75% and 4.7% of the total exports. At the same time, as can be seen by the percentage of imports that is financed by exports (52% and 65% respectively), these two segments are relatively self-sufficient, and characterised by a large presence of small and medium-sized enterprises.

Table 1.7. **Specialisations of the manufacturing industry in Istanbul (2000)**

	Four digit code of ISIC classification		Share in Istanbul value added (%)	Number of firms (2000)	Share in Istanbul exports (%)	Ratio of imports covered by exports	Sector/cluster
High-tech sectors	2423	Manufacture of pharmaceuticals, medicinal chemicals and botanical products	13.13	46	0.78	7.33	Chemical and medical
	3210	Manufacture of electronic valves and tubes other electronic components	0.23	10	0.06	1.54	Electronics
	3220	Manufacture of television and radio transmitters and apparatus for line telephony and line telegraphy	2.99	5	0.51	2.79	Electronics
	3230	Manufacture of television and radio receivers, sound or video recording or reproducing apparatus, and associated goods	1.23	17	1.93	73.57	Electronics
	3311	Manufacture of medical and surgical equipment and orthopaedic appliances	0.28	7	0.10	4.16	Chemical and medical
	3312	Manufacture of instruments and appliances for measuring, checking, testing, navigating and other purposes, except industrial process control equipment	0.40	15	0.11	5.09	Electronics
	TOTAL		**18.25**	**100**	**3.48**	**8.75**	
Medium-high tech sectors	2424	Manufacture of soap and detergents, cleaning and polishing preparations, perfumes and toilet preparations	4.39	32	1.67	107.06	Chemical and medical
	2912	Manufacture of pumps, compressors, taps and valves	0.79	54	0.61	23.68	Machine building and metal equipment
	2915	Manufacture of lifting and handling equipment	0.44	33	0.16	17.07	Machine building and metal equipment

Table 1.7. **Specialisations of the manufacturing industry in Istanbul (2000)** *(cont.)*

	Four digit code of ISIC classification		Share in Istanbul value added (%)	Number of firms (2000)	Share in Istanbul exports (%)	Ratio of imports covered by exports	Sector/cluster
	2919	Manufacture of other general purpose machinery	0.44	44	0.40	12.38	Machine building and metal equipment
	2926	Manufacture of machinery for textile, apparel and leather production	0.02	19	0.23	7.62	Machine building and metal equipment
	2929	Manufacture of other special purpose machinery	0.21	24	0.27	8.65	Machine building and metal equipment
	3110	Manufacture of electric motors, generators and transformers	1.18	30	0.92	46.62	Machine building and metal equipment
	3120	Manufacture of electricity distribution and control apparatus	2.11	45	0.52	28.35	Electronics
	3140	Manufacture of accumulators, primary cells and primary batteries	0.43	7	0.09	23.17	
	3150	Manufacture of electric lamps and lighting equipment	0.19	25	0.21	20.84	Electronics
	3190	Manufacture of other electrical equipment not elsewhere classified	1.08	27	0.37	19.65	Electronics
	TOTAL		**11.28**	**340**	**5.46**	**25.22**	
Medium-low tech sectors	2520	Manufacture of plastics products	2.70	182	1.92	55.11	
	2699	Manufacture of other non-metallic mineral products not elsewhere classified	0.24	4	0.11	25.92	
	2893	Manufacture of cutlery, hand tools and general hardware	0.88	60	0.58	61.74	Machine building and metal equipment
	2899	Manufacture of other fabricated metal products not elsewhere classified	1.42	135	1.35	78.11	Machine building and metal equipment

Table 1.7. **Specialisations of the manufacturing industry in Istanbul (2000)** (*cont.*)

	Four digit code of ISIC classification		Share in Istanbul value added (%)	Number of firms (2000)	Share in Istanbul exports (%)	Ratio of imports covered by exports	Sector/cluster
	3511	Construction and repair of ships	0.21	18	0.66	116.25	Machine building and metal equipment
	TOTAL		**5.45**	**399**	**4.62**	**64.72**	
Low-tech sector	1543	Manufacture of cocoa, chocolate and sugar confectionery	1.37	31	0.96	421.86	
	1729	Manufacture of other textiles n.e.c.	0.58	58	1.87	219.56	Textile
	1730	Manufacture of knitted and crocheted fabrics and articles	3.02	220	17.28	1676.98	Textile
	1810	Manufacture of wearing apparel, except fur apparel	11.95	830	23.84	1930.29	Textile
	1911	Tanning and dressing of leather	0.63	51	0.10	14.22	Textile
	1912	Manufacture of luggage, handbags and the like, saddlery and harness	0.17	14	0.22	90.38	Textile
	1920	Manufacture of footwear	0.80	88	0.74	93.70	Textile
		Other sectors*	7.95	232	3.83		
	TOTAL		**26.46**	**1 524**	**75.96**	**52.39**	
High point totals			**61.44**	**2 363**	**62.4**	**81.61**	

Notes: * Other sectors include codes 2102, 2109, 2211, 2212, 2221, 3691, 3699

The definition by level of technological sophistication is based on the classification adopted by the OECD. The table only shows *high point industries*, *i.e.*, those sectors with a location coefficient of at least 1.25, and a minimum share in regional industrial employment of at least 0.2% of total Istanbul employment.

Source: Based on data from on regional manufacturing statistics (Turkish Statistical Institute, Manufacturing Industry Statistics, 1995 and 2000).

High and medium-high technology activities accounts together for less than one-third of Istanbul's economy. From a technology content perspective, the most technologically advanced sectors in Istanbul (such as pharmaceuticals or TV sets) accounts for more than 18% of the total value-added whilst medium-high technology sectors (such as electrical equipment or chemical products) accounts for only about 11%. From a clusters perspective, there are three main clusters in Istanbul (though this list is by no means exhaustive):

- (1) The ***electronics cluster***[8] contributes 8% of value added, 6% of the number of establishments and 3.7% of total exports generated by the city. In theory, this is a sector with some potential in dealing with the city's ambitious vision to become a regional hub within the international flow of information.
- (2) The ***chemical and pharmaceuticals cluster,***[9] mainly present in the high-tech segment shows a surprisingly high participation in the overall industrial value added generated in Istanbul, (17.8%), while it makes up 3.7% of the number of establishments and 2.6% of the total volume of exports. In light of its potential to trigger high positive technological externalities on the development of such sectors as biotechnology, the sector can be considered a strategic niche of scientific and research driven industrial development. It is also one of the clusters featured as a high development priority on the agenda of the Turkish Scientific and Technological Research Council (TUBITAK). Considering the relatively small number of establishments, and its relatively high concentration of value added, the sector is characterised by a dominance of large national and international enterprises.
- The ***machine building and metal equipment cluster,***[10] which holds important links with car manufacturing and textiles, contributes less in value added (5.6%) and in volume of exports generated (5.18%), but this segment concentrates a substantial number of the total formally registered establishments in the Istanbul economy (18.4%).

A productive restructuring process of Istanbul's manufacturing sector seems to be ongoing. A comparison between sectors of overall manufacturing employment levels in 1995 and 2000 in Istanbul shows that employment is expanding in chemical activities. More precisely, employment shares grew in plastics, pharmaceuticals, as well as detergents and soaps. In the latter, growth in specialisation is also notorious (but not in plastics or pharmaceuticals). In textiles, there has been a mixed effect, employment has grown in apparel while it has decreased in knitting (Figure 1.19). Analysis of location coefficients (LQ)[11] shows the evolution of sectoral specialisation levels over the same period, supporting the hypothesis that Istanbul's activities are continuously upgrading towards higher technology content activities. More precisely:

- *Restructuring process in the textile cluster*. This is a sector that displays substantial differences in size, productivity, formality and technology levels. Apparel and knitted fabrics, which intensively use low technologies, account for the largest share of employment in Istanbul (Figure 1.19). While the apparel market has shown a slight decline in specialisation (LQ values) and increased employment (from 24.3 in 1995 to 26% in 2000), the knitted fabrics market has displayed a high increase in specialisation in spite of a decline in employment. There seems to be an ongoing process of restructuring within low-tech activities that could be related to an expansion of employment in apparel and a contraction in knitted fabrics in Turkey at large. Turkey is also experiencing the same restructuring in textiles, but the process has meant a greater loss of employment in knitting than in Istanbul – thereby leading to an increase in specialisation in knitted fabrics in Istanbul even while losing employment in the activity. This restructuring process could be linked to global trends. Apparel growth may be linked to global market demands and perhaps even FDI, while knitted fabrics are related to the traditional crafts in the nation. The main implication is that while the tradition in knitting is still strong, Istanbul seems to have started to use the expertise in the sector to seize global markets in apparel.

- *Specialisation and employment growth in higher-technology sectors*. High-tech activities are not only becoming an important source of employment in Istanbul, but also of specialisation. High-tech activities such as pharmaceuticals, which had the largest share in Istanbul's value added (13%), has emerged as a promising sector with the highest increase both in share of employment and in specialisation. Together with apparel and knitted fabrics, pharmaceuticals were the most important clusters[12] in terms of the share of employment in 2000, accounting for 35% of Istanbul's total manufacturing industry employment.

- *Other medium-low technology activities* are also important sources of employment in Istanbul. Electrical equipment and electric devices, soap and detergents, cleaning and polishing solutions, as well as perfumes, are all important for Istanbul's economy not only for the employment opportunities they provide but also for the positive trend in specialisation that may constitute a source of competitiveness. These activities have registered the greatest increase both in terms of employment growth and specialisation in Istanbul. One important implication linked to the changes in textiles is as Istanbul based companies begin to compete in global apparel markets they move towards hosting higher value-added activities with more intensive use of technology.

Figure 1.19. **Change in specialisation in Istanbul**

Manufacturing employment shares and specialisation changes (1995-2000)

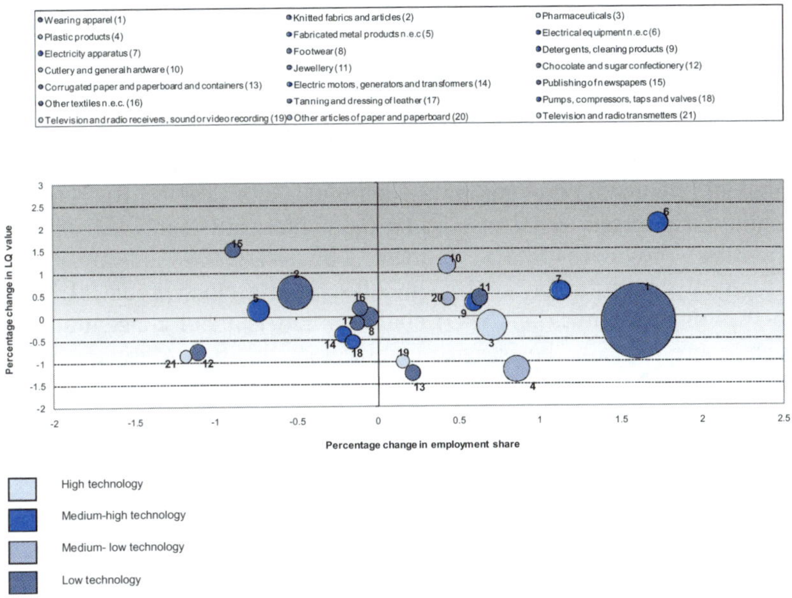

Source: Own calculations based on data from Turkish Statistical Institute, Manufacturing Industry Statistics, 1995 and 2000.

The ongoing productive restructuring will, however, require time and is moving at a slow pace. The participation of employment in the more traditional and labour-intensive sectors such as textiles remains not only substantial, but has been shifting only gradually to other complementary segments (in particular the production of other general purpose machinery, cutlery, hand tools and general hardware). There is no abrupt shift – or crowding out – of employment and investment patterns from traditional production towards the high-tech activities such as electronics, chemicals and the medical sectors. As a matter of fact, and this is a hypothesis that can only be corroborated by means of more detailed studies, it can be expected that this transition from a low-cost to a *higher-end* regional economy will be gradual, and will also benefit from the export surpluses and savings that have been accumulating – and will continue to be generated – through the continuous competitive upgrading of the textile and related labour intensive sectors. In a way, the generation of these export and savings surpluses in textiles has the potential to foster a continuous upgrading and learning process in the overall economy of Istanbul, which will gradually move in the direction of higher-value-added production and distribution niches within the global economy.

Clusters development throughout Polycentric Greater Istanbul

On a wider scale, a traditional pattern of relocation of activities within the larger Polycentric Greater Istanbul has been ongoing. Provinces outside Istanbul still maintain an important agricultural sector (Table 1.8). The share of employment in services is also by far the highest in Istanbul as compared with other provinces (53.5% followed by 34.8% in Yalova). The geographical concentration coefficient of service sectors produced by the State Planning Organization (SPO) confirms that Istanbul concentrated the highest share of all the service sub-sectors in the Marmara region (Figure 1.20).[13] More generally, there is evidence that the core of the city has been re-orienting toward financial services and some high-value-added activities, notably to branches of high-tech manufacturing, but also to the design-side of more labour-intensive activities such as textiles. In contrast, the rest of the textiles value chain, as well as the assembly plants in automotive and electronics have moved away from costly central locations. Textile establishments have predominantly settled in new locations in Çorlu and Çerkezköy (Tekirdağ province). In addition, a substantial number of firms in the sector have not relocated yet, but have acquired land for future expansion plans. Regarding car manufacturing, important companies like Ford and Fiat have moved from Istanbul to Bursa. In a subsequent stage, a large number of suppliers were directly attracted to Bursa. The development of Bursa as a site of car manufacturing was also stimulated by explicit policies of decentralisation within the Marmara region. Other large investments in car manufacturing were concentrated in Gebze and Kocaeli. Whilst such spatial development is typical during the urbanisation process of a large metropolitan area as labour and land costs increase in the area of the CBD (Central Business Districts), it has also been the result of explicit relocation policies aimed at removing manufacturing activities out of the city centre through instruments such as the Organized Industrial Zones (especially in Tekirdağ).

Table 1.8. **Sectoral share of employment in the Polycentric Greater Istanbul (2000)**

Provinces in the Polycentric Greater Istanbul	Agriculture (%)	Industry (%)	Services (%)
Istanbul	8.1	38.4	53.5
Kocaeli	39.0	28.6	32.3
Yalova	38.4	26.7	34.8
Bursa	33.5	33.1	33.3
Sakarya	51.9	19.6	28.5
Tekirdağ	38.8	30.3	30.9

Figure 1.20. **Concentration of services sector in the Marmara Region**

By NUTS 2 regions

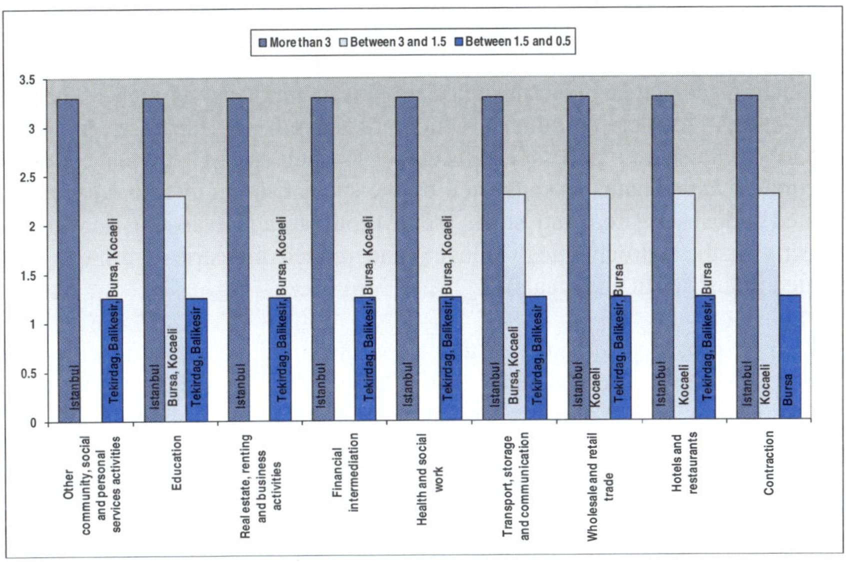

Note: According NUTS classification at level 2, Istanbul includes only Istanbul province; Tekirdağ includes Tekirdağ, Edirne and Kırklareli provinces; Balıkesir includes Balıkesir and Çanakkale provinces; Bursa includes Bursa, Eskişehir and Bilecik provinces; and Kocaeli includes Kocaeli, Sakarya, Düzce, Bolu and Yalova provinces.

Source: State Planning Organization.

An overall assessment of changes in employment and specialisation in manufacturing industries for Polycentric Greater Istanbul, *i.e.*, including the other five other provinces, seems to highlight similar trends towards a slow and progressive process of productive restructuring. More specifically, the following trends can be observed:

(1) ***Kocaeli***, with a higher GDP per capita than Istanbul, is mainly specialised in petroleum and car manufacturing, and their related supply chains. With 1.3 million inhabitants, Kocaeli is actually an industrial centre, specialised essentially in medium-high technology activities. In 2000, the automotive industry accounted for 14.5% of value-added (Figure 1.21). The province also concentrates car manufacturing related activities such as iron and steel, metal products, and plastic products that together amounts to 14.1% of the province's total value-added. The refined petroleum industry remains the most important sector, representing 31% of Kocaeli total value-added in 2000, due to localisation of the biggest refinery of Turkey, TUPRAS. Despite declines in both employment and the specialisation's share, the refinery sector seems to have favoured the production of related industries such as plastic products, as well as paints and other chemical products which displayed an increase in both employment shares and specialisation. Kocaeli seems to have more integrated value chains as suggested by the specialisation in automotive and related industries (iron and steel, metal products and plastics) as well as directly in the petrochemical industry and related industries (refinery and related industries in chemicals).

(2) ***Yalova***, located on the eastern side of Istanbul, is mainly a residential area with some low-tech, mainly textile, activities (Figure 1.22). With only 182 000 inhabitants, Yalova is the smallest province of the Istanbul Metro-Region, which was actually part of Istanbul until 1995. While spinning and weaving of textile fibres dominated the Yalova economy accounting for more than two-thirds of the total employment in 1995, the share has dropped sharply to half of total employment. Yet, one-fifth of the provincial value-added is still generated by the sector. The province seems to have found a niche market in basic chemicals, a medium-high technology sector that registered the largest increase in both employment shares and degree of specialisation.

Figure 1.21. **Change in specialisation in Kocaeli**

Manufacturing employment shares and specialisation changes (1995-2000)

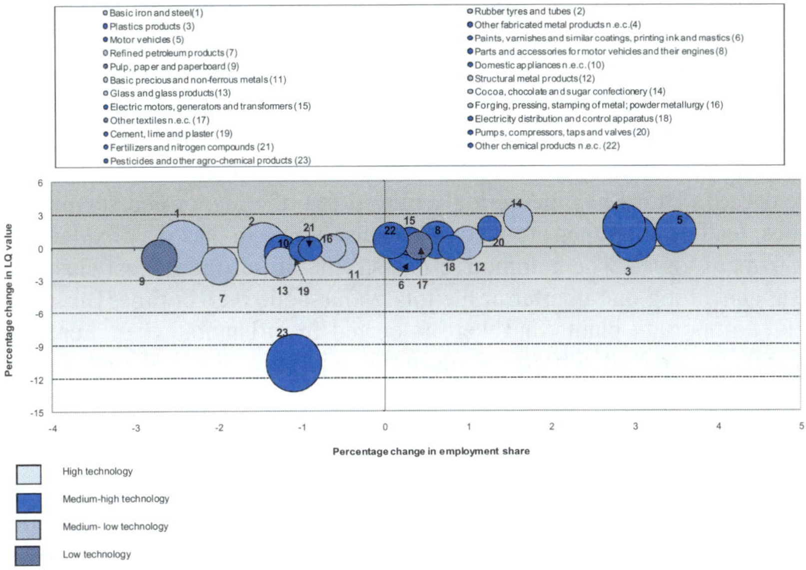

Source: Own calculations based on data from Turkish Statistical Institute (TURKSTAT), Manufacturing Industry Statistics, 1995 and 2000.

Figure 1.22. **Change in specialisation in Yalova**

Manufacturing employment shares and specialisation changes (1995-2000)

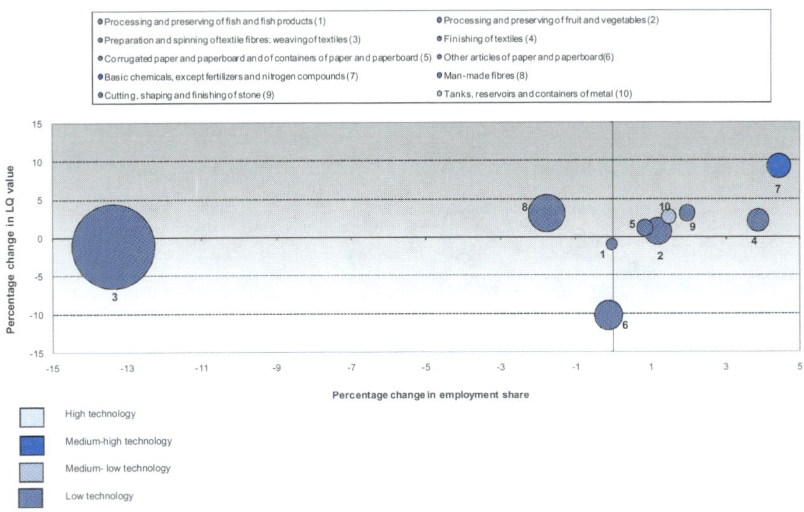

Source: Own calculations based on data from Turkish Statistical Institute (TURKSTAT), Manufacturing Industry Statistics, 1995 and 2000.

(3) ***Bursa***, the second most populated province in the Polycentric Greater Istanbul, is mainly specialised in textile industries, and to a lesser extent on the medium-high tech automotive industry. Bursa has 2.36 million inhabitants and is located to the south of Kocaeli. In 2000, textile represented 37% of employment in Bursa, as well as one-quarter of the total value-added. Although spinning and weaving of textiles reported the largest – but decreasing – share of regional employment, it also displayed declining specialisation levels. Nevertheless, in the last three decades Bursa has increasingly moved into the higher-end segment of textiles, leading to higher productivity levels, which in part may explain the employment losses. The automotive industry is the second largest cluster in Bursa, generating one-quarter of the total value-added. Over time, Bursa has received important plants that were relocated from Istanbul (*e.g.*, Ford and Fiat), which attracted subsequent clustering and networking of first, second and third tier part suppliers. This cluster has experienced losses of employment and dwindling levels of specialisation. However, in related industries such as iron and steel casting needed for auto-parts and car assembly, the trends are positive in both employment shares and degree of specialisation (Figure 1.23). In addition, the production of furniture has also become an important activity in the region and has had the best performance in employment share growth in the province.

Figure 1.23. **Change in specialisation in Bursa**

Manufacturing employment shares and specialisation changes (1995-2000)

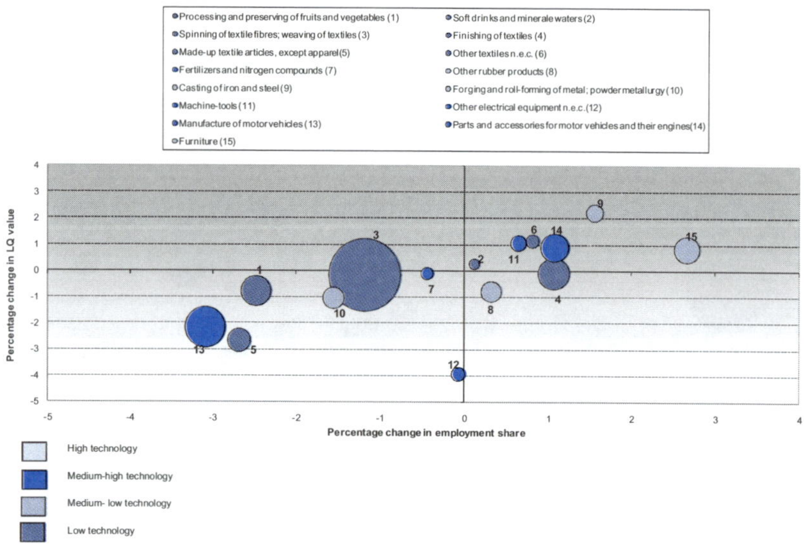

Source: Own calculations based on data from Turkish Statistical Institute, Manufacturing Industry Statistics, 1995 and 2000.

(4) ***Tekirdağ*** (693 000 inhabitants), the adjacent province to the west of Istanbul, is specialised in low-technology industries as well, including textile activities in apparel, knitted fabrics and textile fibres. Its spatial development cannot be analysed without taking into account the impact of official policies aimed at decentralisation outside Istanbul, especially in its early stages of growth in the 1970s. For example, in that period, the so-called Çerkezköy Organised Industrial District was created, which provided special financial and regulatory incentives for industries. This proved to be quite attractive considering the relative proximity of the area with Istanbul. However, the excessive concentration of textile in the subsequent growth stages seems to have reduced the attractiveness of the area for other investments. In 2000, apparel, knitted fabrics and textile fibres represented 40% of regional employment, as well as 30% of value-added. (Figure 1.24) Although specialisation on apparel has remained stable, its employment share increased from 9% to 16.5% between 1995 and 2000. The share of the provincial value-added in high-technology industries, mainly the production of TVs and radio receivers, is relatively low (3.3% in 2000) and even declining (from 7.6% in 1995). As the employment level was unaffected during the same period, it is possible that the activity (manufacturing of TV sets and radio) has moved elsewhere, leaving low-value-added processes within Tekirdağ.

Figure 1.24. **Change in specialisation in Tekirdağ**

Manufacturing employment shares and specialisation changes (1995-2000)

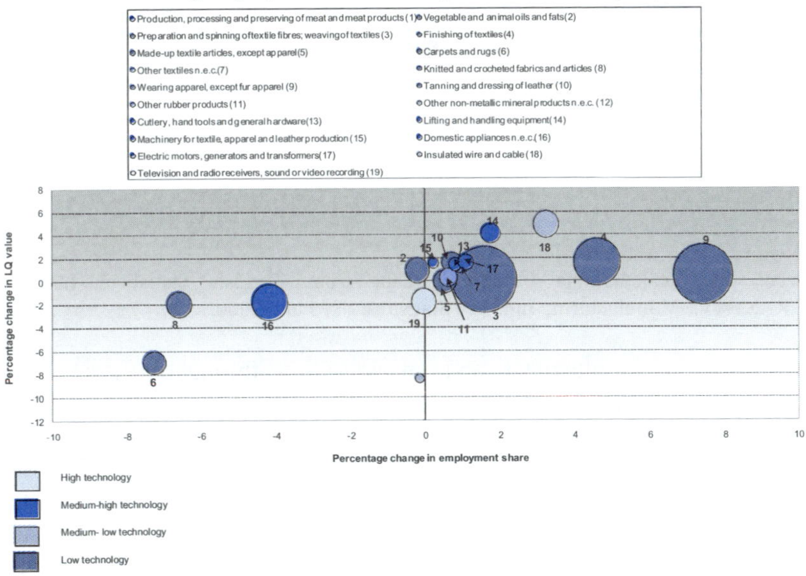

Source: Own calculations based on data from Turkish Statistical Institute (TURKSTAT), Manufacturing Industry Statistics, 1995 and 2000.

(5) Specialisation patterns in ***Sakarya*** (771 000 inhabitants) in the car and chemical industries are more similar, and linked, to Kocaeli, its adjacent province to the east of Istanbul. The production of motor vehicles and related sectors in Sakarya experienced an increase in specialisation as in Kocaeli. Like in Istanbul, Sakarya also exhibits high levels of specialisation in high-tech industries such as pharmaceuticals and other chemical products. Sakarya's medium-low technology activities such as the production of harnesses and other insulated cables and wires, although not the largest sector in the province, has experienced the greatest expansion in employment shares and in specialisation levels (Figure 1.25).

Figure 1.25. **Change in specialisation in Sakarya**

Manufacturing employment shares and specialisation changes (1995-2000)

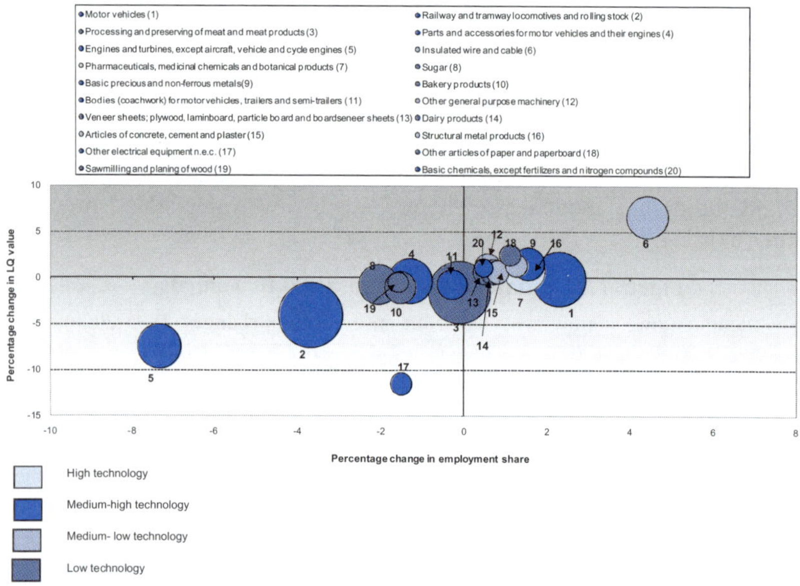

Source: Own calculations based on data from Turkish Statistical Institute (TURKSTAT), Manufacturing Industry Statistics, 1995 and 2000.

Changes in employment and specialisation throughout Polycentric Greater Istanbul suggest an increasingly dense pattern of relational and socio-economic networks between the city of Istanbul, on the one hand, and the outskirts of its larger functional metropolitan area (specifically Tekirdağ and Kocaeli), on the other hand. Nevertheless, and although some of the larger manufacturing establishments have moved out of the inner CBD, the locational pattern also indicates a continuing need for proximity with headquarters of larger firms, and small and medium-sized industrial enterprises showing a preference to remain within the city centre. Moreover, part of the business services located in Istanbul, such as finance and logistics, are directly linked to the manufacturing activities taking place in distant, and relatively self contained, provinces such as Bursa. The transition in segments such as textiles towards more design and fashion-intensive patterns of specialisation tends to reinforce the continuing need for a central location, where qualified labour, interpersonal contacts, the presence of university and training centres and institutional networking can be obtained with relatively low transaction costs. Within this overall process of structural restructuring, the tendency will be for the province of Istanbul to have a relatively higher concentration of business development services, headquarters and regional offices and smaller industrial establishments, in its core area, while the outskirts of the functional area, in areas such as Tekirdağ and Kocaeli, will have higher concentrations of manufacturing. Bursa will become increasingly self-contained and only loosely connected to Istanbul, with the exception of the linkages through the financial sector, which is concentrated in Istanbul. Finally, a relatively larger part of the purchasing power generated by the overall functional metropolitan area will be channelled to the more sophisticated consumer services that are present in the city of Istanbul itself, leading to a dynamic multiplier of the supply of services within retailing, shopping centres, supermarkets, restaurants and hotels.

1.3. Istanbul on the international market place

The opening of the economy of Turkey to the international market, combined with its advantageous geographical location have created new opportunities for Istanbul to compete more effectively with other metropolitan areas, especially those belonging to the so-called "Eurasia Region". With its proximity to east and south-east Europe Istanbul has the ability to reach the relatively newly formed market economies of Ex-Soviet European countries, offering a good platform for international actors to extend into Central Asian markets, not only because of geographical proximity but also due to existing cultural linkages. By concentrating the main headquarters of Turkey, Istanbul can extend its role as a gateway to regional and international markets. A careful assessment of Istanbul's international competitiveness position, particularly in those fields in which the city intends to position itself as a regional hub, is, however, necessary.

International competitiveness, exports and FDI

Despite being one of the OECD metro-regions with the lowest level of per capita income, Istanbul is also an urban area displaying high levels of growth. One of the plausible reasons for such a positive performance may lie in increasing openness to trade and FDI. Indeed, the increasing opening of metropolitan economies to international markets gives new opportunities to less developed metro-regions and might in certain cases represent a threat to some dominant metro-regions. For instance, from 1995-2002, Istanbul, like some relatively lower-income metropolitan regions in Korea (Busan, Seoul), and Eastern Europe (Prague, Warsaw), registered higher average annual growth rates than some richer metropolitan areas in Japan (Tokyo, Aichi), Germany (Frankfurt, Stuttgart, Munich) and France (Paris) (Figure 1.14).[14]

Turkey, and thus Istanbul, has increased its openness to the international economy. Although Turkey is still less open than the average of OECD countries, it has registered one of the highest trade-to-GDP ratios among OECD countries between 1990 and 2003 (OECD, 2006c). Exports in Turkey started to increase as soon as the early liberalisation reforms of the 1980s, which put an end to protectionism. Macroeconomic stabilisation and the structural reforms carried out after the 2000-2001 crisis, along with the real depreciation of the exchange rate in the 2000-2001 accelerated exports, outstripping export market growth by a cumulative 30% between 2000 and 2005. Turkey achieved – together with Ireland and the Slovak Republic – one of the largest gains in export market shares among all OECD countries during this period (OECD, 2006b). In 2004, Istanbul's share of total exports for Turkey accounted for nearly one half, *i.e.*, almost double its share of national GDP, whilst its share of total national imports amounted to almost 40%.

Istanbul, like the rest of Turkey, has been facing mounting competition from other countries like China or India, particularly in labour-intensive industries such as textiles. Domestic producers of both consumption and intermediate goods have seen their market shares reduced as imports thrive, resulting in the recent increase in Turkey's trade deficit. Strong real currency appreciation in recent years (2.5% in 2004 and 14.5% in 2005) has weakened the competitiveness of many business activities in Turkey, particularly labour-intensive firms that have not been able to raise productivity and increase their specialisation (OECD, 2006b). This concerns mainly the textile and clothing sector, which accounts for nearly 40% of Istanbul's total exports. International trade agreements and instruments will have an important impact on the future of this sector. In this regard, Turkey has been the first country to invoke a China safeguard for its textile and clothing sector when the total elimination of quotas entered into practice in January 2005. According to the WTO, Turkey could lose 8% of its share of the European market for textiles, especially to China and India.[15] Whatever the outcome of international agreements or effectiveness of domestic sectoral policies, this stresses the need to speed up the adjustment process.

FDI flows to Istanbul have recently witnessed a significant increase. Between 1995 and 2004, Turkey was not able to attract more than USD 1 billion per year, and thus ranked low among OECD countries for

FDI stocks (Figure 1.26). The metro-region gets the lion's share of total FDI in Turkey. Since the 1980s, Istanbul City received the largest number of foreign firms (60%), especially in the service sector, where the proportion of foreign companies grew from 8.49% to 28.91% between 1980 and 1990.[16] This represents 80% of the total value of FDI flows to Turkey. The largest share of the total FDI capitalisation went to manufacturing industries located outside the city in surrounding provinces. More recently, net FDI flows in Turkey picked up to 2.2% of GDP in 2005, following just 0.6% in 2004, with USD 9.8 billion.[17] A historical record was registered for 2006 with a total amount USD 20.2 billion.[18] The majority of these investments are concentrated in financial intermediation (USD 7 billion in 2006) and transport, storage and communications (USD 6.3 billion in 2006). There are also substantial investments in manufacturing (USD 1.4 billion), wholesale and retail trade (USD 1.5 billion) and construction (USD 0.5 billion). Net FDI flows to Turkey, however, remain low in comparison to those of Turkey's key competitors, such as China and some OECD countries from Central and Eastern Europe (Figure 1.27). The recent increase in FDI is driven in large part by the restructuring process in the banking sector, characterised by mergers and acquisitions, and large privatisation operations in telecommunications. The increase of the consumer market in Istanbul has also leveraged the entrance of foreign investment in shopping malls, wholesale and retailing, and real estate and construction projects.

Figure 1.26. **FDI stocks in a selection of OECD and non-OECD member countries**

FDI stocks in billions of USD in 2004

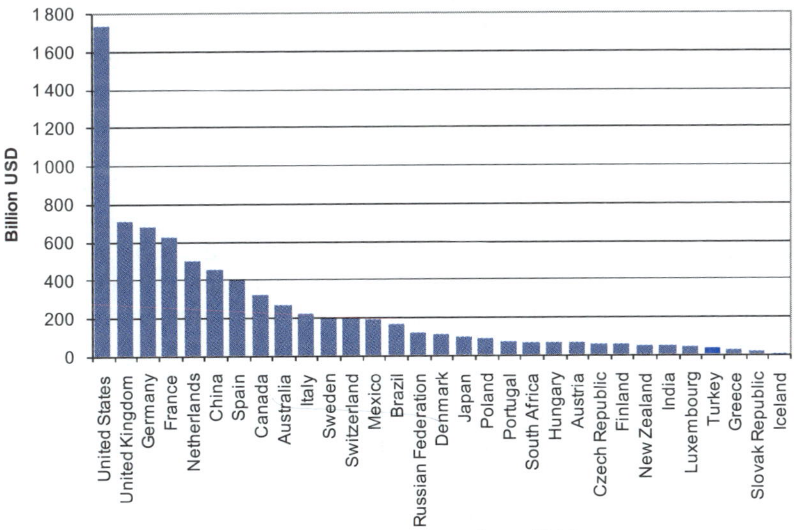

Source: OECD, International Direct Investment Database, 2006.

Figure 1.27. **Net FDI flows as % GDP among Turkey's main competitors**

%

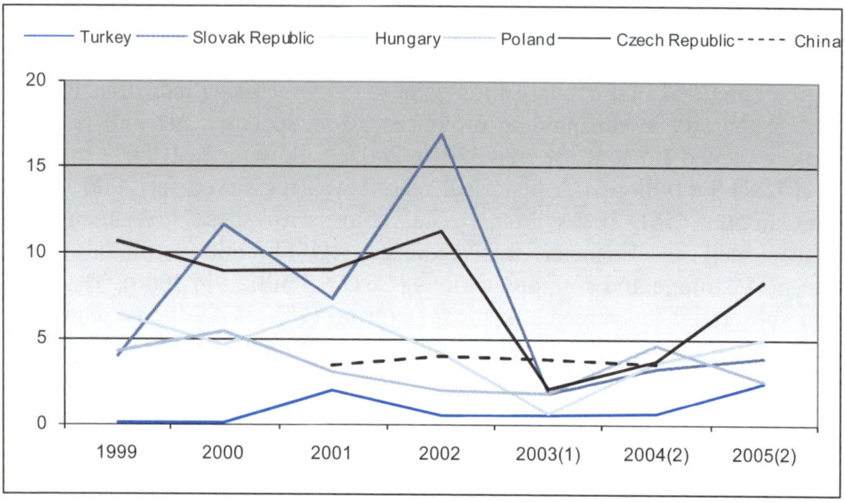

Note: 1. Preliminary; 2. Estimation.

Source: Central Bank of Turkey and OECD International direct investment database.

Foreign investment flows into the banking sector have opened up new opportunities for the City of Istanbul, particularly with respect to its wish to become a regional hub in financial and logistics services. Most FDI in Istanbul is concentrated in trade, real estate and, to a lesser extent, manufacturing. This also includes a wide range of mergers and acquisitions (M&As) that took place in the banking sector. The fresh capital injection that has occurred as a result of M&As has increased the capital adequacy ratio of the sector, which had been critically low following the 2001 financial crisis, and has strengthened Istanbul's position as an international financial hub.[19] Moreover, the substantial FDI in transport, storage and communications indicates the increasing attractiveness of Istanbul as a logistics and communications hub. In addition to privatisations in the telecommunications sector, the logistics and transportation segment is going through a rapid process of modernisation, which is characterised by an increase in scale and entrance of foreign operators in what can still be characterised as a relatively traditional small-scale sector. Finally, foreign investment in real estate has soared up with the rising consumer potential, the stabilisation of the investment climate and the introduction of a series of regulatory reforms. The Act 4916 in July 2004, for instance, facilitates the acquisition of property by foreigners. Moreover, a capital gain from a real-estate sale that was held back from the market by the same owner, for a period of four years, has become tax-exempted. Ongoing and prospective infrastructure-related projects, including housing renovation within the risk prevention programme, urban transformation, relocation and development of industrial zones, large-scale tourism complexes, and extensions of shopping centres, increasingly attract foreign interest. Although these types of foreign investors can (along with implementation of a mortgage system) help to accelerate the formalisation of the domestic housing market, they have also pushed up the housing prices by inflating the fear of a housing market bubble.

An emerging regional hub?

Istanbul enjoys a particular advantage in its geographical position between Europe and Asia. Turkey's geographical position grants easy access to markets on three continents with over one billion people and markets of nearly USD 13 trillion. Turkey is a neighbour of south-eastern European countries such as Bulgaria and Greece and it is within easy reach of the rest of Eastern Europe and other EU countries, a market that represents 576 million people and an economy as large as almost USD 12 trillion (about the size of the United States). Having access to the Black Sea, Turkey is also well situated to reach Russia, and the Central Asian countries of Georgia, Armenia, Azerbaijan, Kazakhstan, Kyrgyzstan, Turkmenistan, Tajikistan and Uzbekistan, with a combined population of 180 million people and almost half a trillion USD. Turkey can also access markets in the Middle East and North Africa among which are Morocco, Algeria, Egypt, Saudi Arabia, Israel, Jordan, Iran, Lebanon and Syria that represent around 250 million people and nearly USD 700 billion.[20]

Istanbul would like to take advantage of this strategic location and its cultural assets and dynamic economic base to position itself as a regional hub within a large macro-region, the so-called Eurasia region in three main fields: (1) finance and services; (2) logistics; and (3) tourism and culture. Both as a result of higher land and labour costs, and pro-active industrial relocation policies, there has been a marked shift in land use patterns in the inner city historical districts of Istanbul, establishing a potentially positive and mutually reinforcing dynamic between a growing sector of business services (such as banks and financial intermediary services, insurance, real estate, advertisement companies and logistics) and tourism and hotel functions.

Istanbul as a financial services provider

As the financial capital of Turkey, Istanbul has become an important player on the international financial market, largely outstripping other countries belonging to the Eurasia region. Turkey stands as the 6th most important emerging stock market after other global players such as Korea, Taiwan, India and China (Figure 1.28). In 2005, the total value of stock trading amounted to a USD 200 billion market in Turkey, *i.e.*, exceeding all Latin American countries, most of south-east Asian (except for Korea), Eastern European and Middle Eastern countries. This record represents more than twice that of Greece and more than four times that of Israel or Egypt. Istanbul is also home to the 4th largest bond market in the world, after the Spanish, English and OMX markets (Figure 1.29).[21] The total value of bond trading is around USD 531 billion, largely exceeding that of other big players like Korea, Germany and Euronext.[22] Yet the share of market capitalisation of the Istanbul Stock Exchange in relation to the national GDP is still low compared to well-rooted stock markets, though still higher than most emerging economy markets like Argentina and China (Figure 1.30). Actually, the lack of financial instruments and big institutional investors along with a low level of saving prevent the Istanbul Stock Exchange from reaching a higher capitalisation rate. The city's strength in finance and banking is complemented by a tradition of specialisation in segments such as insurance, brokerage, real estate and holding companies.[23]

The dramatic development of the Istanbul Stock Exchange (ISE) is a significant contributor to Istanbul's potential of becoming a financial hub within the Eurasia region. Thanks to high technological and human capital investment, the ISE is currently capable of matching EU requirements with slight difficulties. The electronic technology employed by ISE matches that used by NASDAQ, and it uses this infrastructure to manage a transaction volume of USD 1 trillion; an amount that is nearly four times the size of Turkey's GDP. Until 2006, the ISE benefited from the deepening of reforms after the 2000-2001 crisis. Its outstanding securities have increased from YTL 43.7 billion in 2000 to YTL 280.7 billion in 2005. The market capitalisation rate has shown a modest increase from USD 98 million in 2004 to more than USD 162 million in 2005. Likewise, the stock, bonds and bills markets show a growing tendency. For example, the volume of daily average trade value in the stock market has increased from USD 593 million in 2004 to USD 794 million in 2005. Istanbul also hosts one of the largest international organisations of stock exchanges, the Federation of Euro-Asian Stock Exchanges (FEAS), that includes 31 countries from Central and Eastern Europe and the Middle East. The total daily volume in stocks in the region covered by the FEAS reached

USD 1 822.6 million in 2005 and the average daily volume in other instruments USD 5 486.7 million, representing an increase of 334% and 119.2% respectively since 2001. This is an important opportunity for Istanbul, which features the highest average daily trading volumes in stocks, bonds and other instrument ratios within the FEAS. The ISE is also one of the most profitable stock exchanges in FEAS, with a monthly real return of 9.5% in December 2005 ranking Istanbul the 5th most profitable member among all FEAS members.

Figure 1.28. **Total value of stock trading in emerging markets**

Million of USD (2005)

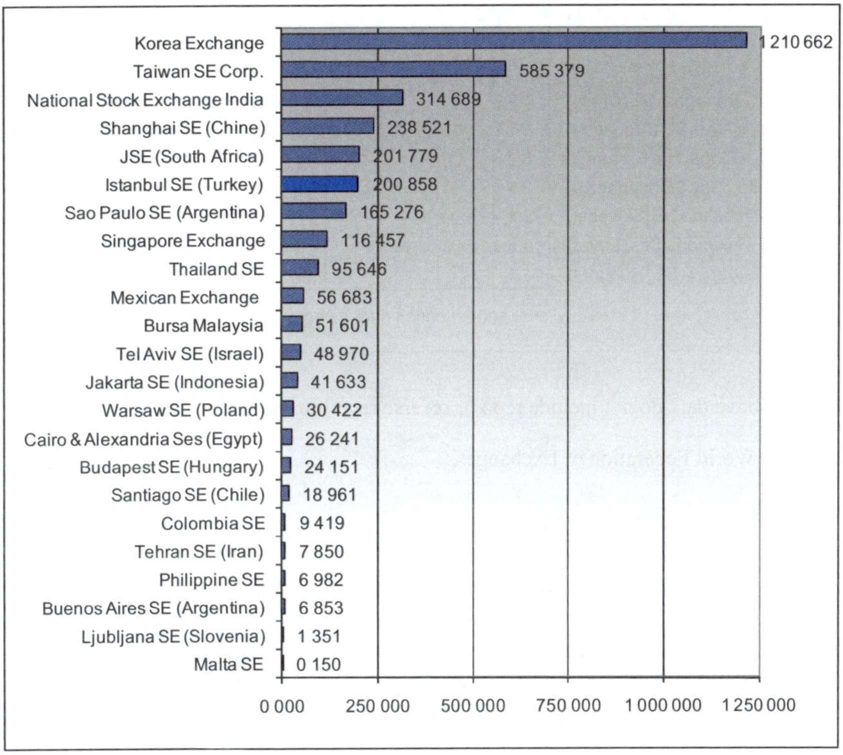

Source: World Federation of Exchanges.

Figure 1.29. **Total value of bond trading**

Billion of USD (2005)

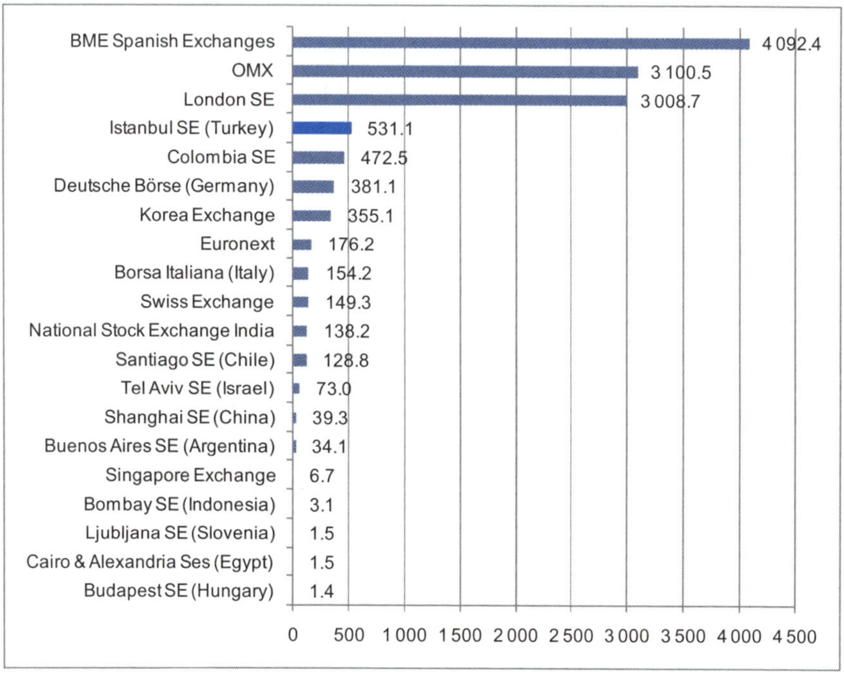

Note: Above data do not include repo or reverse repo transactions.

Source: World Federation of Exchanges.

Yet, Istanbul has to further develop its financial instruments to attract foreign sources and become a financial hub. Currently one of Istanbul's major weaknesses is that most of the capital markets are dominated by securities whilst stocks and other financial instruments remain limited. Security markets are in turn dominated by public securities, which represented almost 90% of total securities as of 2005 (Figure 1.31). The main reasons for the predominance of securities over stocks, and public over private securities, are the high borrowing requirements from the government and highly restrictive environment for issuing private securities. In contrast, the share of foreign investors in the stock market is 65%, showing ISE can attract international investors (Figure 1.32). Therefore, ISE is attracting a good share of its stock markets from foreign sources, but the size of this foreign influx remains small as compared to the amount of securities financing the public sector (Figure 1.33). It is important to bear in mind that a financial hub should stress the former rather than the latter.

Figure 1.30. **Stock market significance in the national economy**

Market Capitalisation / GDP (2004)

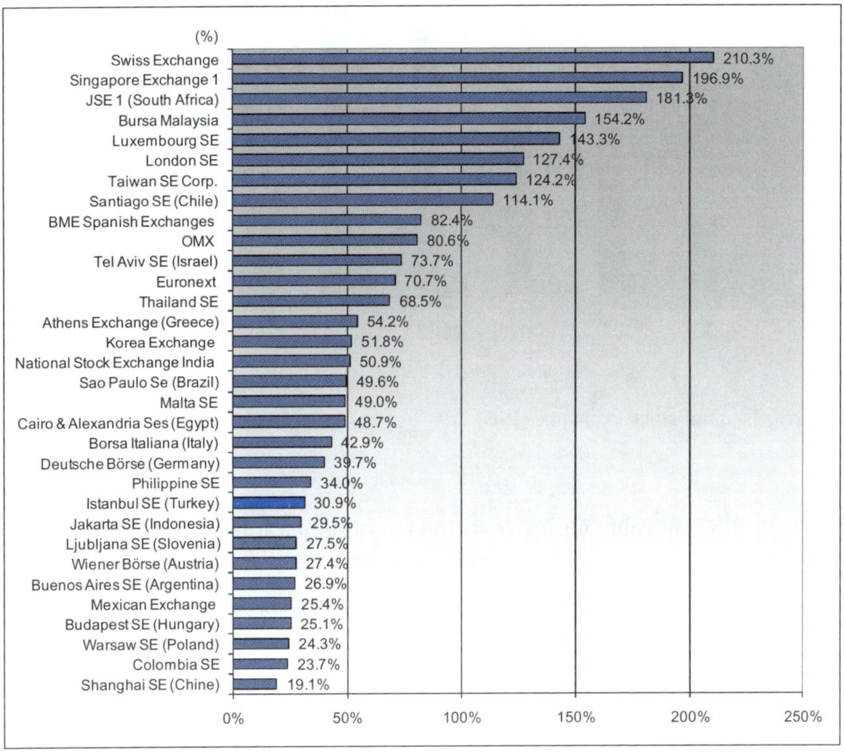

Note: Singapore Exchange and JSE market capitalisation data include also foreign listed companies.

Source: World Federation of Exchanges.

Figure 1.31. **Outstanding securities in the Istanbul Stock Exchange (2000-2005)**

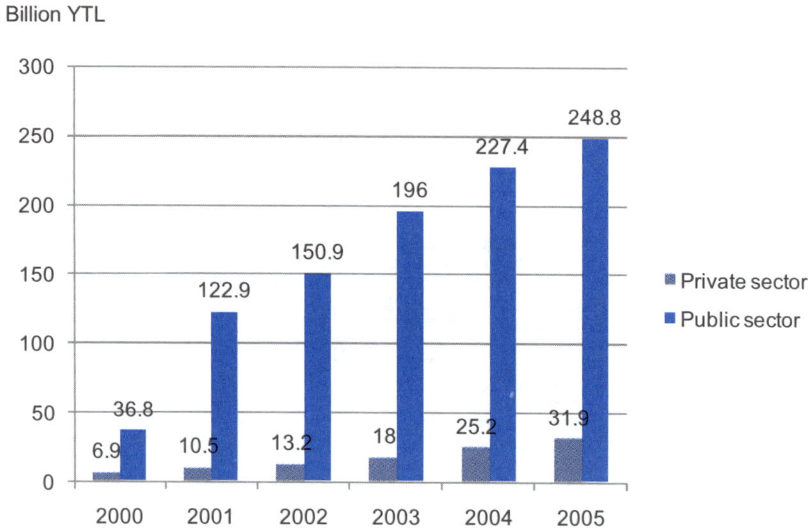

Source: Istanbul stock exchange (ISE).

Figure 1.32. **Foreign equity investments in the Istanbul Stock Exchange (1989-2006)**

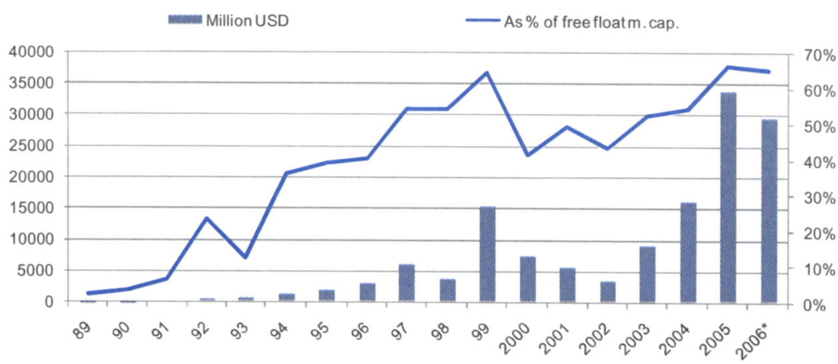

Note: * As of May.

Source: Istanbul stock exchange (ISE).

Figure 1.33. **Size of the capital in the Istanbul Stock Exchange (1999-2006)**

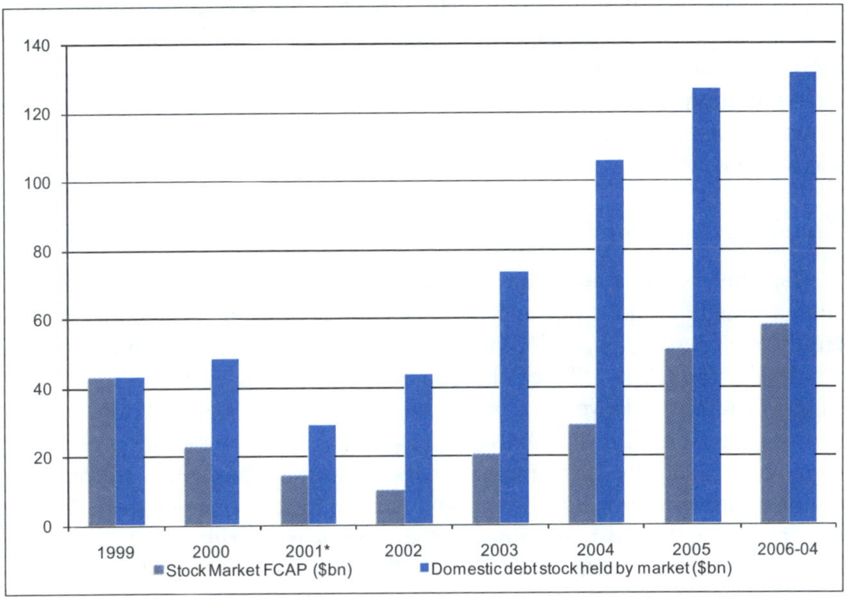

Note: * 3 and 5 year fix linked swap bonds pulls up the average maturity in 2001, in fact borrowing maturity in 2001 had dropped as low as 1.7 months.

Source: Bender, Deutsch Bank Group.

The banking sector in Istanbul is also more experienced than in other places in the Euro-Asia region but it needs further restructuring to become a regional services provider. Banking activities account for almost 90% of total financial activities in Turkey, and Istanbul concentrates the bulk of it: 46 out of 48 banks in Turkey are in Istanbul; more than 41% of total deposits and 46% of total credits. This reveals that a considerable portion of the income earned in Turkey is being moved to Istanbul's financial institutions. The size of this sector remains relatively small as compared with most OECD countries but above the average of developing countries. A major restructuring process happened after the 2001 financial crisis, including an important consolidation, which resulted in a drop in the deposit-to-credit transformation ratio in Turkey from 58.4% in 1998 to 51.9% in 2004. Yet competition in the banking sector – and the oligopolistic structure – remains rather weak (Yetim and Gülhan, 2005). Throughout 2005 and the beginning of 2006 a wave of mergers and acquisitions occurred in the banking sector in Istanbul. Although, the share of foreign banks increased only from 3 to 5% of the sector, this gave a new impetus to a more competitive environment. There are also some indications that the banking sector in Turkey may move towards a structure of relatively few but larger banks capable of competing with other important banking hubs. If sustained, this process may well pull down the current high intermediation spreads (difference between credit and deposit interest rates), a major obstacle for Istanbul's transformation into a regional banking services provider.

Istanbul as a logistics hub

Istanbul is the trade gateway of Turkey, with international transport connections to both Europe and Asia. Istanbul is the country's industrial and largest transportation corridor, processing around USD 15 billion per year in wholesale trade, *i.e.*, 60% of the country's volume (Çancı, 2006). In 2004 Turkey's retail trade volume was estimated to reach USD 50 billion, with approximately 35% in Istanbul. The city is gradually becoming a centre of commercial activity for international companies targeting surrounding regions: Eastern Europe, Caucasus and Middle East. It benefits from the fact that Turkey is linked to Europe by the motorway corridor stretching from Berlin to Istanbul (Berlin/Nuremberg – Prague – Budapest – Thessaloniki – Istanbul) called Corridor 4 by the EU Transport Corridor Europe–Caucasus–Asia (TRACECA) Programme.[24] Launched in 1993, the TRACECA programme also includes a ring motorway around the Black Sea and into Europe through Istanbul as well as sea routes in the Black Sea that connect to the Mediterranean by the Strait of Istanbul. Turkey also connects Europe through Istanbul to the Middle East through motorways from Ankara to Iraq, and also with railroad lines from Istanbul. There are also a number of international co-operation projects aimed at increasing international transport connections (see Chapter 2).

The potential for Istanbul to become a logistics hub is subject to certain necessary conditions. Competitive logistics hubs around the globe nowadays require the efficient combination of different transportation modes. Istanbul is quite well equipped with ports (air and sea). It has two international airports, the Atatürk International Airport located 24 km from the city centre and the Sabiha Gökçen Airport located 20 km east of the Asian side and 45 km east of the European city centre. The latter, in operation since 2001, has sufficient capacity to function as a new import/export hub. There are, however, chronic congestion and accessibility issues for both airports. Istanbul also has four ports. The Haydarpaşa port and the large Ambarlı port complex, both located on the European side of the Strait of Istanbul, are the most important in terms of logistics.[25] The two others ports, both located very close to the business centre are Zeyport and Galata, the latter used only for passenger vessels. The Marmaray project, an underground tunnel railway expected to be operational by 2010, should contribute to increased Turkish usage of the European Ro-La system. During peak hours only metro trains will be allowed, and during non-peak times, both passenger and goods trains will be allowed to pass in an effort to improve logistical flows and accessibility to the city. With several private piers and oil platforms, the Ambarlı port has registered increased capacity and is now well positioned among the top Mediterranean gateway ports, ranking fourth after Valencia, Barcelona and Genoa, surpassing Marseilles in France, thanks to recent intensive private investment in the port (Figure 1.34) (Ferrari, Parola and Morchio, 2006). Overall, it is crucial for Istanbul to develop multi-modal transport and better connect roads, motorways, railways, airports and seaports. Moreover, the logistics hub will require the development of a broader range of services to guarantee delivery times, regularity and frequency of services and direct service without trans-shipment or warehousing en route (Devacı, Cerit and Tuna, 2002). Finally, the logistics sector, still characterised by relatively small-scale operations and fragmented ownership, has not been able to implement processes of managerial and technological modernisation. Thus, the sector urgently needs to increase its scale and to connect with international best practices in port and logistics management. In that sense, the recent increase in FDI and efforts undertaken in international networking are promising signs (see Chapter 2).

As part of its strategy to become a logistics hub, Istanbul would like to play a role in the international transport of energy, an industry on the rise in Turkey. Turkey's privileged geographical position is likely to play an increasing role in integrating the European and Asian gas markets. Oil and gas pipelines have been set up primarily to cover internal demand as Turkey produces less than 8% of its oil demand and 3% of its gas demand. While oil pipelines are being built to meet increasing domestic demand, the natural gas network is also being developed to connect the Turkish network to other countries and integrate the European and Asian gas markets. By transporting Caspian and Middle Eastern gas to Europe, Turkey benefits from sales of gas that pass through its transit system. The strategy to seize this opportunity is based on three main cross-border pipelines:

1. The Turkey-Greece Natural Gas Pipeline Project has kicked off with the construction of 300 kilometres of gas pipeline between the two countries (200 kilometres of which are in Turkey) under the "South European Gas Ring Project", and BOTAŞ – the fully Turkish state-owned pipeline company – will start selling gas to Europe in 2006. Just a small part (17 km) of the pipeline will be constructed under the Marmara Sea away from Istanbul. The project became the Turkey-Greece-Italy Inter-Connecter on 4 November 2005.

Figure 1.34. **"Mediterranean gateway ports" throughout 2000-2004**

TEUs

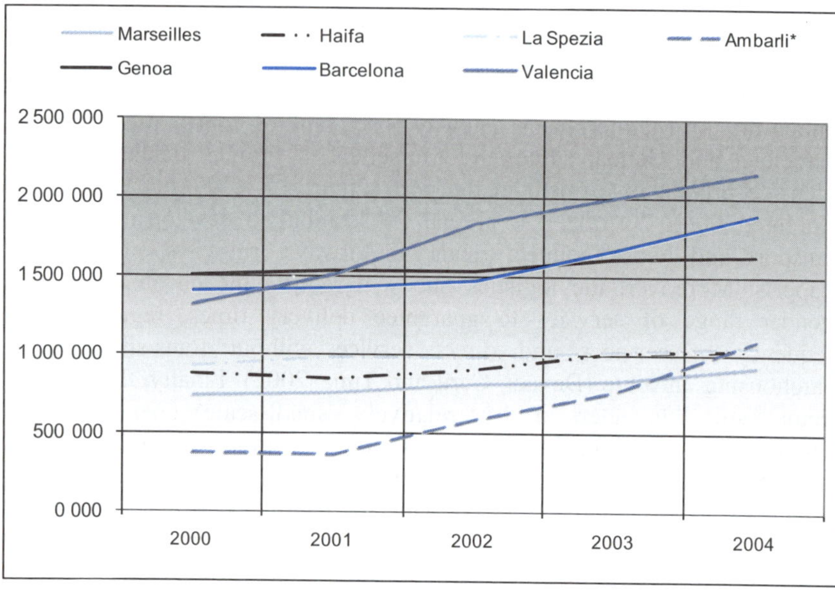

Note: Ambarlı's data referred to 2000 and 2001 are the sum of Armaport, Kumport and Mardas.

Source: Ferrari, C., F. Parola and E. Morchio (2006), "Southern European Ports and the Spatial Distribution of EDCs".

2. The Turkey-Bulgaria-Romania-Hungary-Austria Natural Gas Pipeline Project (Nabucco) will stretch for almost 3 000 kilometres and will be finalised by 2009, aimed at connecting European gas markets through Austria and Turkey.

3. The South Caucasus Pipeline (Baku-Tbilisi-Erzurum) project completes the Turkish transit system by enabling Turkey to receive gas from Azerbaijan.

Yet, Istanbul is unlikely to benefit from this opportunity for natural gas exports into Europe and it is in fact, undesirable for the urban area. Energy pipelines like other sources of energy such as nuclear or coal entail risks for the population. Istanbul is not only divided into two continental urban areas (European and Anatolian), but also divided by a geological fault line running along the Strait of Istanbul. The perennial risk of seismic activity makes Istanbul an undesirable location for an oil or gas pipeline. Moreover, the commercial and logistic activity already in place in Istanbul making intensive use of the Strait emphasises the need to maintain safer urban spaces, not only for navigation and cargo manoeuvre, but also for liveability reasons. The Strait of Istanbul is already facing risks with oil tankers using the Strait to reach the Mediterranean; indeed, a pipeline would add to the risks the city already faces.

Istanbul as a tourism and culture city

Turkey is one of the top tourism destinations in the world. Thanks to its cultural and natural assets, combined with a successful branding strategy to promote its coastal areas, and a relatively weak currency, Turkey stands as one of the top second-tier world travel destinations with the largest number of both tourists and tourism receipts (Figure 1.35).[26] In 2004, Turkey received almost 17 million tourists and nearly USD 16 billion, which made it the 12th top destination in terms of tourist arrivals and the 8th in terms of tourism receipts. The country registered one of the highest average annual growth rates in number of tourists over the period 1998-2004 among a selection of the top destinations in OECD countries and other non-member countries such as China, Brazil and South Africa (Figure 1.36). Not only have the numbers for arrivals increased over time, but also tourists arriving in Turkey are spending more money in Turkey than in other destinations.

Figure 1.35. **Second-tier world top travel destinations and expenditures**

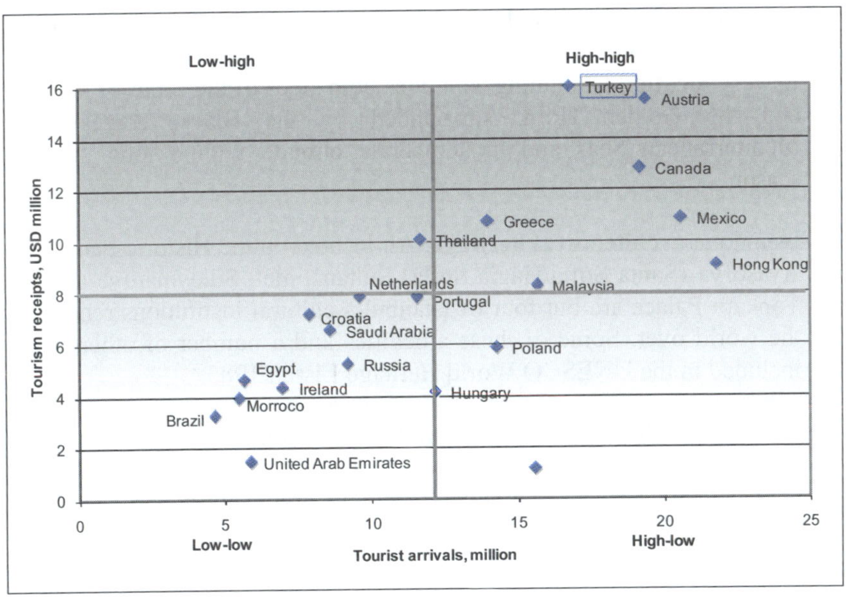

Source: World Tourism Organization.

Figure 1.36. **Arrivals of non-resident tourists staying in hotels and similar establishments**

Average annual growth in percentage, 1998-2004 or latest available year

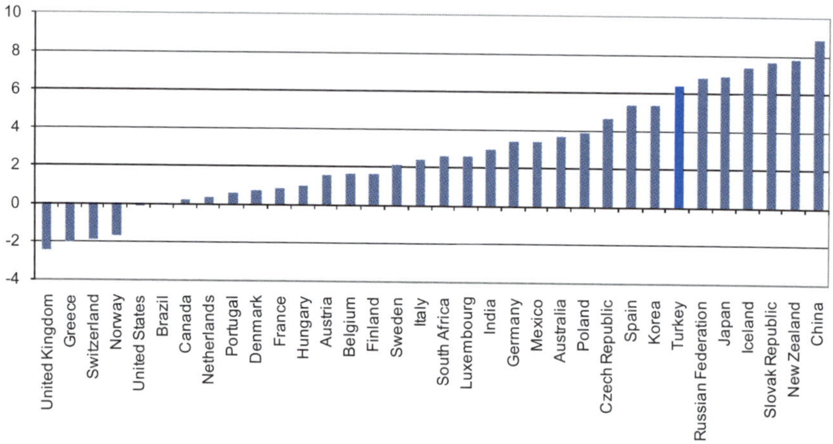

Source: OECD (2006), *OECD Factbook 2006*, OECD Publications, Paris.

Like Turkey, Istanbul enjoys significant cultural and natural assets that make it an important tourism destination. Its strengths are many and varied:

- Its very **location**, straddling as it does both sides of the Strait of Istanbul and the Golden Horn, surrounded by the Black, Aegean and Mediterranean Seas and its temperate climate with a long summer season.
- Its unique **architectural heritage**. All located on the Historic Peninsula, Ayasofya (Santa Sofia/Hagia Sofia) Sultanahmet, Süleymaniye and the Topkapı Palace are but four of Istanbul's cultural institutions renowned the world over. Some of these amenities and a number of others were included in the UNESCO World Heritage List in 1985.[27]
- Its **built patrimony**, including whole neighbourhoods in different parts of the city, especially on the Historic Peninsula and in Galata, that offer distinct characteristics that define Istanbul's architectural heritage. Some buildings, like the Pera Palas Hotel in Istanbul's old French quarter, are renowned across Europe and North America for their historical significance.

- The legacy of its **historical heritage** as a centre of several ancient civilisations with the presence vast array of mosques, synagogues, Roman and eastern churches, with some dating back thousands of years.

- Its wide range of **other attractions**, including a huge array of restaurants and small cafés, particularly those near the water, which prepare Turkish dishes using the freshest local produce, and Istanbul's Grand Bazaar and spice market, along with its trademark sweets, from Lokum to Helva, further contribute to its attractiveness.

Despite its assets, Istanbul could probably better leverage its existing potential to attract tourists. Tourism arrivals in Istanbul grew at a 14.4% annual rate over the period 1999-2004 (Figure 1.37). Moreover, one of the limitations to increasing the amount of revenue that Istanbul receives is the relatively short nature of the average stay, with average visits lasting only 2.5 days. Considering the extent of cultural, historical and natural assets, the stay duration could certainly be further increased. Yet, **weaknesses** are equally varied:

- **Hotel capacity** is insufficient. Quality hotels have developed in around the Historical Peninsula and Taksim as well as in proximity to the Istanbul Congress and Exhibition Palace in the Beşiktaş and Beyoğlu sub-provinces districts. However, the number of 5-star hotels still remains low compared to 4 and 3-star hotels. More generally, a severe lack of hotel rooms at all price levels further contributes to a rapid "churn" in tourist flows and is not conducive to enticing visitors to stay more than a few days.

- **Urban cultural amenities** remain low as compared to the major European, Asian and North American cultural centres with which Istanbul can potentially compete. Istanbul has two main public theatres[28] but for a city its size, it possesses a remarkably low number of small theatres, and other purpose-built spaces for arts, literature and music. It also seems to under-exploit its huge cultural assets. For instance, Istanbul has a some important state museums, such as Ayasofya, Topkapı Palace Yıldız Palace, Dolmabahçe Palace Museums and the prestigious Istanbul Archaeological Museum as well as a large number of private thematic museums (a total of 68; most are small with the exception of the Istanbul Modern Museum, Pera Museum, the Sabancı Museum and the recently inaugurated culture and arts centre, Santralistanbul). However, Istanbul has only 14 relatively small public museums compared with 134 in Paris, 148 in New York and 300 in London.

- **Associated infrastructure** challenges cannot be underestimated either. Congestion and relatively poor air quality, due in large part to a severe lack of mass rapid transit, threaten to choke access to the very cultural institutions that are key to attracting foreign tourists. For instance, the Historic Peninsula, with its concentration of cultural assets whose significance reaches far beyond the country's borders, is highly congested and remains poorly connected via public transport to the rest of the city.

Figure 1.37. **Tourism arrivals in Turkey and Istanbul (1999-2004)**

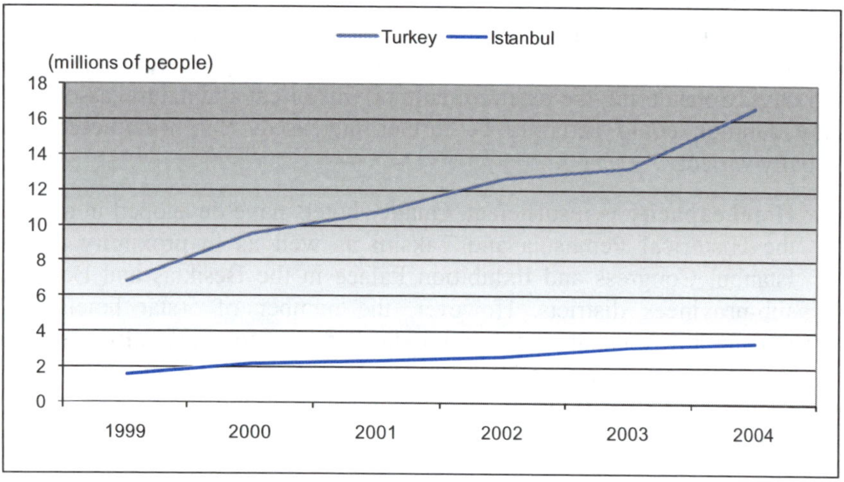

Source: World Tourism Organization (2005) *Tourism Market Trends.*

One of the market niches in tourism is that of Meetings, Incentives, Conferences and Exhibitions (MICE as dubbed by the World Tourism Organization). Istanbul has been promoting itself as a centre for exhibition, fairs and conventions through the Istanbul Convention and Visitor's Bureau (ICVB). The number of events has been steadily increasing since 2001 (Figure 1.38). In 2005 Turkey hosted 68 international meetings,[29] 44 of which took place in Istanbul (International Congress and Convention Association, ICCA).[30] With this capacity Turkey ranks 28 out of 73 countries, and Istanbul 25 out of 263 cities (big cities in 78 countries from around the world, including significant international destinations for meetings, *e.g.*, Vienna, Singapore, Barcelona, Berlin, etc.). There are currently several main areas for exhibitions and conventions in the city.[31] Istanbul has the potential to be amongst the top 10 cities, yet the focus of domestic organisers as well as a weak "international familiarity"[32] with its convention centre impede Istanbul's potential.

Figure 1.38. **Conferences and exhibitions tourism**

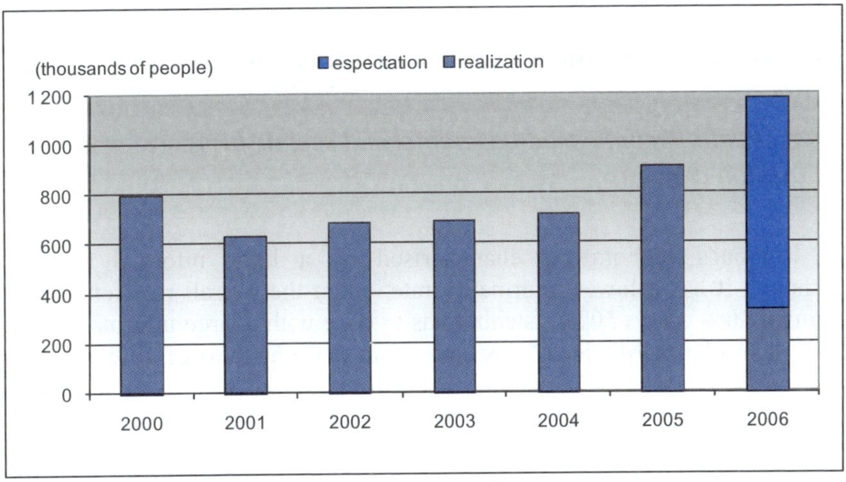

Source: Istanbul Convention and Visitor's Bureau (TUYAP), *www.tuyap.com.tr.*

1.4. Towards a competitive and sustainable mega-city: the challenges ahead

The economic base of Istanbul is at a crossroads. The metro-region has reached the limits of its industrial activities, especially in textiles and clothing, increasingly challenged by low-cost and labour-intensive emerging economies in Asia. Unemployment is high and the capacity of the formal sector to absorb newcomers in the labour market is limited. Instead, the informal sector is developing rapidly, especially with small and medium-sized firms, a trend that is not conducive to increasing the skills and producing the innovation that are necessary to upgrade Istanbul's productivity and growth. This stagnation in skills and innovation generates large income disparities within the metropolitan area accompanied by increasing spatial polarisation. Moreover, rapid urbanisation and over-migration are putting strains on land use and infrastructure in an already highly vulnerable environment threatened by earthquake risks and other environmental threats, such as heavy pollution and the over-use of the Strait of Istanbul for international trade cargos. These environmental and social concerns will certainly have a long-term impact on the metro-regional competitiveness and economic growth if they are overlooked by the economic development strategy.

Obstacles to a competitive business environment

Weakness in the industrial base: informal sector, firms size and innovation capacity

Istanbul's economy is characterised by a large informal sector.[33] Although it has a lower informality rate[34] than the overall rate for Turkey (around 30% *versus* 50%), Istanbul has to cope with a large informal sector. This is similar to Mexico City where about one one-third of all employees work informally (OECD, 2005h). The informality of the labour market in those metro-regions demonstrates that the transition from manufacturing to services is not always synonymous with the city's economic upgrading. Although the decline in manufacturing is often accompanied in such cases, as elsewhere, by an increase in service sector employment, the ability of the formal labour market to absorb former factory workers in such contexts is often limited. The forms and causes of an informal market are varied (Box 1.2). Activities involved include casual day labour, petty trading, street hawking, letter typing, knife sharpening, load carrying, street vending, and shoe shining. It is reported that there are about 500 000 street vendors in Istanbul,[35] one of its largest sectors.[36] Informal activities also include many small sub-contracting firms that work for formal enterprises as a part of their unregistered activities. For both Istanbul and Marmara Region, informal activities are particularly high in the construction, wholesale trade and manufacturing sectors (Figure 1.39).

Figure 1.39. **Informality by sector**

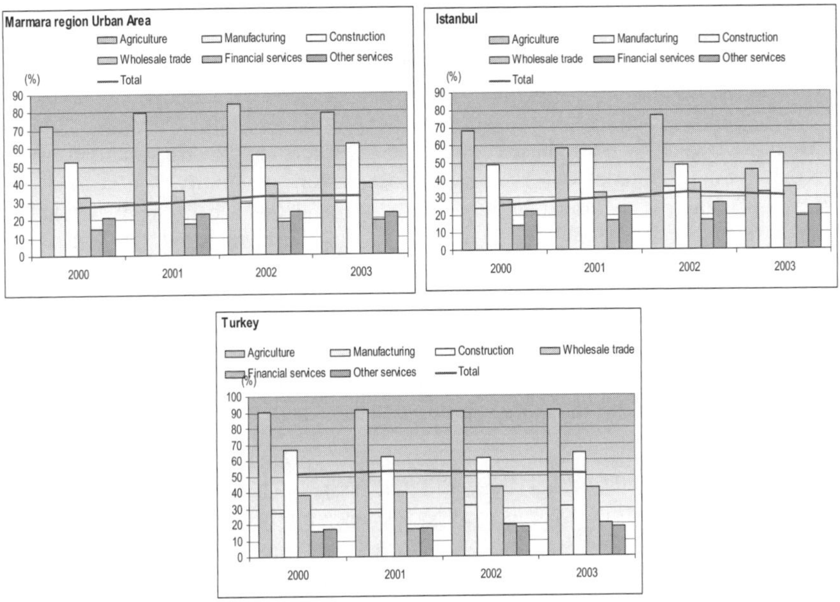

Source: TUIK, Household Survey database.

The extent of the informal sector imposes several costs that impede Istanbul's productivity and growth potential. There are some positive arguments in favour of the informal sector in that it can help relieve both urban employment tensions and the short-term transition costs related with macroeconomic adjustment programmes. However, in the long run, the informal sector impedes access to adult education, on-the-job training, and other human capital development mechanisms for upgrading skills to increase productivity and innovation potential. Informality also tends to exclude workers from social security and health benefits, thereby reducing productivity levels even further. Actually, Istanbul's low ranking in GDP per capita as compared to other OECD metro-regions is mainly explained by a lower productivity level, a result of both specialisation in low-value-added activities and of a low-skilled labour force. In turn, the lower level of educational attainment in Istanbul is related, to some extent, to the large informal sector in which nearly half of the workers has only primary education (Figure 1.40).

Box 1.2. Forms and causes of informality

The term "informal sector", coined by an International Labour Organization mission to Africa in the early 1970s, was invoked to refer to street vendors in Bogota; shoeshine boys and rickshaw pullers in Calcutta; garbage collectors in Cairo; home-based garment workers in Manila, Montreal, Madeira, and Mexico City; and home-based electronic workers in Leeds, Istanbul, and Kuala Lumpur. Some observers feel the sector is simply too varied or heterogeneous to be meaningful as a concept. However in many cities in developing countries, due to a high burden on the business sector and weak enhancement mechanisms, combined with high in-migration from rural areas, the informal sector presently accounts for a significant share of employment and output and cannot, therefore, be dismissed or disregarded. In addition, given its large size and diversity, as well as the increasing ties and overlaps with the formal sector, many have expressed the opinion that it is not a "sector" at all and that informal "economy" is the more appropriate term.

A large part of Turkey's economy is not properly registered with the authorities. Informality takes three different forms: 1) entire companies fail to register as legal entities; 2) registered companies employ undeclared workers; and 3) registered companies declare lower wages than those actually paid to their registered workers. The extent of informal activities varies across sectors, with unregistered employment being particularly widespread in agriculture (more than 90% of workers are unregistered) and construction (more than 60%). About 35% of private manufacturing and service sector employment is not registered. The reasons companies remain outside the formal economy are complex and multi-dimensional (Farrell, 2004). First, informal firms gain a cost advantage by evading fiscal and regulatory obligations. They do not pay income and value-added taxes, they avoid social security contributions and minimum wage requirements, and they circumvent product market regulations, including quality standards, copyright obligations, and intellectual property laws. Second, informality prevails if the enforcement of legal obligations is weak. Insufficiently funded and staffed enforcement agencies, ineffective judicial systems, and insignificant penalties for non-compliance thereby contribute to enforcement slippages. And third, social acceptance of informality removes the stigma of non-compliance with legal obligations and makes it possible for unregistered activities to become a mainstream part of the economy.

Istanbul's economy is a typical mirror of Turkey's economy due to its large size, and there are currently four distinct segments: 1) a small, internationally oriented, highly productive sector with foreign investment; 2) domestically owned, formal enterprises that manage to achieve strong growth and remarkable export performance despite the heavy regulatory and tax burden; 3) a large, low-productivity informal sector whose viability depends largely on the avoidance of state controls and charges; and 4) a public sector, where recent attempts to lift productivity by privatising state-owned enterprises have shown mixed results.

Source: OECD (2004), *OECD Economic Surveys: Turkey*, OECD Publications, Paris.

Figure 1.40. **Informality by level of education**

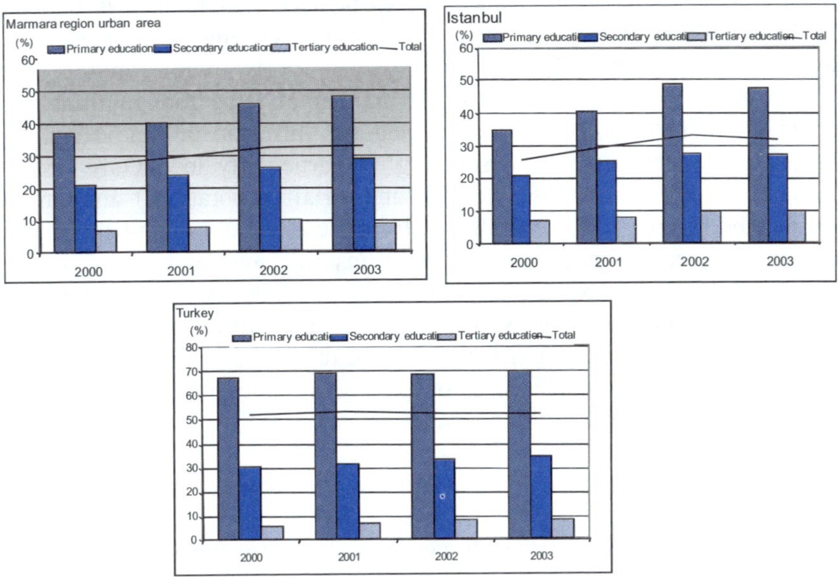

Source: TUIK, Household Survey database.

In order to move into niches that are characterised both by a higher value added content, and more knowledge-intensive production processes, Istanbul will have to make better use of R&D, and the potential linkages between the larger and smaller firms. Although data is not available at the local level, low expenditure on R&D and the number of patents in Turkey as compared to other OECD countries, and non-member countries like Brazil, Russia, India and South Africa, reflects Istanbul's performance in these fields (Figure 1.41 and 1.42). A recent study conducted by the Turkish Statistical Institute on process and product innovation, from 2002-2004, pointed out that only 34% of manufacturing enterprises, and 25.9% of services enterprises, engage in some form of technological innovation.[37] This weak innovation capacity is linked with the structure of the industrial fabric, composed of a large number of small firms operating mainly in the informal sector and with a limited number of foreign multi-national firms. In Istanbul, around 97% of the firms are SMEs, accounting for half of total employment and 30% of total value-added. The presence of a large number of SMEs offers the advantage of low operating costs and flexibility but in the specific case of Istanbul, their innovative capacity is comparatively low, due to their weak equity base, low capital stocks and lack of access to finance. One of the consequences of weak access to finance is that the 31.2% technological renewal ratio for small firms is much lower than it is for medium firms (46.2%) and large firms with more than 250 workers (56.3%). In addition, the number of large foreign firms that could facilitate technology transfers and the diffusion of innovation, for instance through domestic outsourcing, is particularly low. Only 17% of Istanbul's largest firms (the top 500 industrial corporations) are foreign companies (Figure 1.43).[38] Within Polycentric Greater Istanbul this figure reaches 26% as large manufacturing firms are mainly concentrated in Kocaeli, which also exhibits a higher level of productivity and output per capita. A detailed analysis on the strengths and weaknesses of different types of firms in Turkey, largely applicable to the case of Istanbul, clearly highlights the opportunity costs of having a large portion of business activities trapped in the informal economy (Box 1.3).

Figure 1.41. **Gross domestic expenditure on R&D**

As a percentage of GDP, 2004 or latest available year

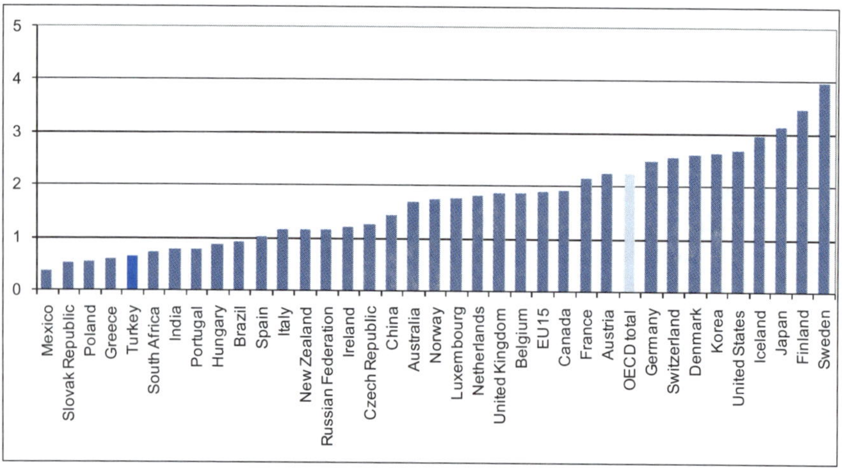

Source: OECD (2006), *OECD Factbook 2006*, OECD Publications, Paris.

Figure 1.42. **Number of triadic patent families**

Per million population (2002)

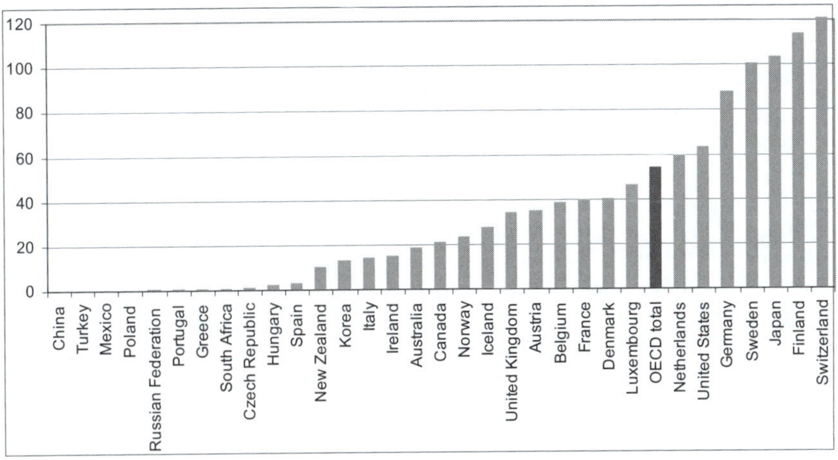

Source: OECD (2006), OECD Factbook 2006, OECD Publications, Paris

Figure 1.43. **Composition of large firms in Istanbul**

Source of investment in the largest 500 firms in Istanbul

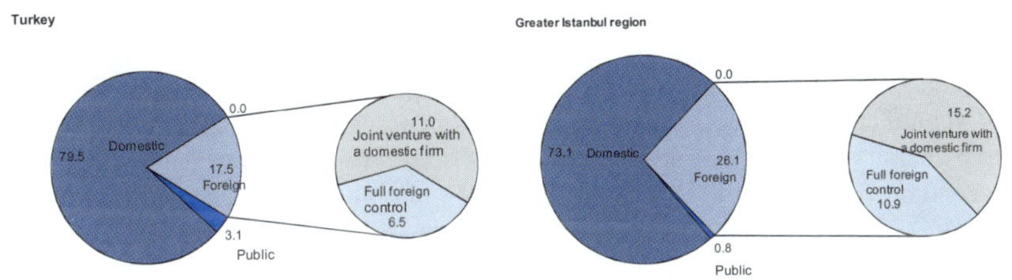

Source: Istanbul Chamber of Industry (2006), "The List of Top 500 Industrial Corporations 2005".

Box 1.3. Strengths and handicaps of Turkish firms according to their size

Small-sized enterprises (SSEs), including the self-employed and the so-called "micro" enterprises, are an important feature of the Turkish business sector. They operate for the most part informally. It is estimated that although less than 10% of value-added in Turkey is generated in this sector, these firms make up more than 30% of total manufacturing employment and 95% of the total number of manufacturing firms. These enterprises are found in large numbers in all manufacturing and service activities and many have only family members as employees. They are particularly numerous in clothing, metal-working and food industries. In services, they are widespread in retail trade, construction and transportation. The core strengths of SSEs are their very low operating costs and very high flexibility. They enter and exit markets at little cost and adjust employment quasi-spontaneously. Even if a minority of them, notably those settled in the "organised industrial zones" may be considered "half-formal", because they register some proportion of their sales, revenues and employment,[1] most of them remain entirely informal. The biggest handicap of the SSEs in Turkey is their weak equity base and their low physical and human capital stock, which pull their productivity down to much below industry averages. Essentially, these firms allow low-skilled workers to participate in the economy but they also face competition from imports from low-wage countries while not being able to reduce wages to such low levels. In some sectors, such as retail trade and construction, they also face more intense competition from larger domestic firms that have much higher productivity.

Medium-sized enterprises (MSEs) have been the most dynamic component of the Turkish business sector over the past decade.[2] Enterprises employing between 10 and 249 employees represented 34% of manufacturing employment and 35% of manufacturing value added in 2000, with expected increases over the last five years. One of the distinct features of these firms is that they are mostly owned and run by families (most of them of the first generation) and that – while being registered – they only partly comply with official regulations, thus permitting them to partly escape the *rigidities and costs of the regulatory and tax system.* These firms operate in all manufacturing and service activities, particularly in the tradable sectors such as textiles, clothing, metal-working, machinery, food, and furniture. They have grown in the traditional industrial centres of Turkey (Istanbul, Izmir and Bursa) but also, and more typically, in a range of Anatolian towns that have achieved exceptional industrial growth (such as Denizli, Gaziantep, Eskişehir, Kayseri – scattered through many different regions of Turkey). "Organised industrial zones" established in these towns have provided the infrastructure for this development.[3] The strength of these MSEs is their outstanding entrepreneurial spirit, and their engineering and technical

Box 1.3. **Strengths and handicaps of Turkish firms according to their size** (*cont.*)

competencies. Their equity-based capital structures have also made them less vulnerable to financial shocks than in the past. After the 2000-2001 crisis, as the domestic market contracted and currency depreciated, many of them sharply accelerated their openness to global markets,[4] by increasing exports and by diversifying their sources of know-how and technology.[5] These firms generally use special arrangements to avoid the full burdens of formality. A popular avenue is to employ their workers under *sub-contracting contracts,* outside company payrolls. This allows enterprises to remain below critical thresholds for the application of regulations concerning employment protection and other workplace rules.[6] Such avoidance is often achieved with the consent of workers who consider such flexibility a requirement for the survival of the firm. However, their financial and human capital constraints tend to limit their options in this regard. Semi-formal firms usually do not hire high-skilled managers. Firm owners would also rather avoid too much exposure to outsiders who may acquire sensitive information, and instead prefer to deal with family members.[7]

The ***formal sector*** in Turkey is characterised by mainly large-size enterprises that employ well-trained entrepreneurs, managers and workers, and are well equipped to modernise, invest and cut costs. The share of large-sized firms is smaller than in other OECD countries but they have been performing well over the past decade and have grown at an above-average pace. Large-size manufacturing firms employing more than 250 workers accounted for around 60% of manufacturing output and 30% of manufacturing employment in 2003. In addition to their good growth performance, the profitability of large firms has been better than in the rest of the economy and has continued to improve in the most recent period.[8] The key strength of these firms is their high level of productivity, which comes close to international standards, and contrasts with their relatively low labour costs in an international comparison.[9] The automotive industry epitomises the recent performance of the large-size formal sector. Car assembly facilities have been able to achieve international quality and productivity standards at relatively low costs. A larger share of car industry investment and production in Europe has consequently shifted to Turkey.[10] An important source of strength of formal sector firms (as compared to the informal sector) is their ties with multi-national firms, which include equity investments but also marketing, licensing and technology transfer agreements. Such ties are being developed with European, North American and Asian partners, frequently via joint ventures. Firms with foreign investors in their equity capital realised more than 40% of the total sales of the top 500 companies, and nearly 20% of the sales of the top 1 000 companies.[11] Contrasting with their important strengths, formal businesses face handicaps that can be binding constraints for their competitive performance and growth.

Box 1.3. **Strengths and handicaps of Turkish firms according to their size** (*cont.*)

Notes:

1. In the international literature "small firms" are those employing between 10-49 persons. However, in Turkey even firms employing less than 10 persons may be considered as "small firms" if they register part of their activities, pay social security contributions for some of their employees, and pay some taxes (in comparison to fully informal "micro-scale" units).

2. There are two statistical definitions of a medium-sized firm: 50-150 employees (Turkish) and 50-250 employees (international) both of which have shown strong growth in the past decade. In Turkey, many firms employing between 10-49 employees would also qualify as medium-sized firms if they demonstrate a robust capital base and operational stability.

3. "Organized industrial zones" provide physical facilities at low costs and offer standard energy, transportation and logistical services.

4. Dynamic medium-sized firms' performances have not been thoroughly analysed, as information about them is limited. A long-time observer has recently offered a number of observations on ongoing changes in their behaviour. See: Rüştü Bozkurt "Küçük ve Orta Ölçekli Aile Işletmelerinde Dönüşüm" (The Transformation of Family-Owned Small-and-Medium Sized Enterprises), in Tamer Koçer (ed) (2006), "Aile İşletmeleri ve Girişimcilik Uygulama ve Araştırma Merkezi 2. Kongresi Tutanakları", Istanbul Kültür Üniversitesi. The author bases his findings on monographic research he has completed on behalf of the Eskişehir Chamber of Industry, Konrad Adenauer Foundation and the financial daily Dünya.

5. Without necessarily infringing on existing intellectual property rights, they often duplicate the basic designs of the models, and the inputs and materials utilised, rather than directly counterfeiting.

6. Firms employing less than 30 employees are not subject to employment protection legislation – but remain liable to severance payments - and firms employing less than 50 employees are exempt from obligations to hire "socially assisted" employees (handicapped, ex-convicts etc.) and to provide mandated health, recreational and social facilities.

7. See "Corporate Governance in Turkey", Institute of International Finance, 2005.

8. According to the Turkish Central Bank's Enterprise Balance Sheet database the profit margins of large firms increased from an average of 3.1% in 2002 to 4.6% in 2004, while they remained stable at 2.3% for medium-sized firms, and declined from 0.1% to – 0.7% for small firms.

9. Domestic and foreign formal sector firms have access to high-quality human capital trained at the top Turkish and international universities. This helps them to absorb international management, technical, and finance know-how. A 2002 study by McKinsey of 11 manufacturing and service sectors found that formal-sector firms reach around 70% of the benchmark productivity level of US counterparts.

10. According to data from the International Organisation of Motor Vehicle Manufacturers, Turkey's automotive output increased form 298 000 vehicles in 1999 to 823 000 in 2004 (a 176% increase), while it decreased from 16 900 000 to 16 854 000 in the EU-15 (a decrease of 0.4%) and from 2 544 000 to 1 680 000 in Central and Eastern Europe (a decrease of 34%).

11. Istanbul Chamber of Industry (ISO) "Top 1000 Corporations" database.

Source: OECD (2006), *OECD Economic Surveys: Turkey*, OECD Publications Paris.

Burdens on the business environment framework

The difficulties to reduce the large informal sector in Istanbul and to attract more foreign firms are partly linked with a number of obstacles to a favourable business environment for formal firms. These obstacles are related in particular to: (1) product market regulations; (2) the tax system; and (3) the labour market legislation framework.

(1) *Product market regulations*. Formal sector firms in Turkey are exposed to a plethora of product market regulations more detailed than in other OECD countries in spite of the simplification efforts undertaken from 1998 to 2003. Turkey ranks second after Poland among OECD countries on a number of product market regulation indicators (fourth for state control, third for barriers to trade and investment and first for barriers to entrepreneurship) (OECD, 2006b). The complexities of regulations along with shortcomings in the commercial justice system are particularly discouraging for foreign firms. State involvement in the economy has decreased, but it still dominates important sectors such as energy, telecommunications, transportation and banking. One of the main consequences is that Turkish firms have to pay high fees for energy and telecommunications.

(2) *The tax system*. Tax avoidance is a driving motivation for firms to operate informally. Tax rates also stand as the leading obstacle for attracting FDI to Turkey, as identified by a Foreign Investment Advisory Services' survey (FIAS) (Figure 1.44).[39] Although improved by a recent reform, the corporate tax system remains very opaque, with relatively high standard tax rates and an excessive number of exemptions and loopholes. Large labour tax wedges have also led to an increase in formal employment costs. Labour costs in Turkey are low relative to OECD countries but stand higher than most of the Eastern Europe and Balkan countries, which are direct competitors of Turkey as export markets and in attracting FDI. With rigidity in tax rates and high social security contributions, the fiscal burden on worker earnings reaches 42.7% (the tenth highest rate among the OECD countries) of total labour cost in 2004.

(3) *Labour market legislation*. Formal employment is hindered by a high legal minimum wage and rigid labour market legislation. Turkey features one of the highest ratios of employers' labour costs for minimum wage workers among OECD countries with statutory minimum wages. In 2005 the government decided to raise the gross minimum wage by 45% as part as its social policy to tackle poverty, especially in less-developed areas. Istanbul features lower wage levels than the national average due to the fact that it concentrates fewer public employees who typically get higher wages

in Turkey (Table 1.9). Yet, the above employment cost for a minimum wage earner relative to the average labour productivity is an obstacle for small manufacturing firms in Istanbul looking to join the formal sector. The formal business sector also has as a barrier one of the most rigid employment protection legislations among OECD countries, especially in temporary employment (Turkey ranks first).

Figure 1.44. **Major obstacles to FDI in Turkey**

Percentage of firms identifying problem as "major" or "very severe" obstacle

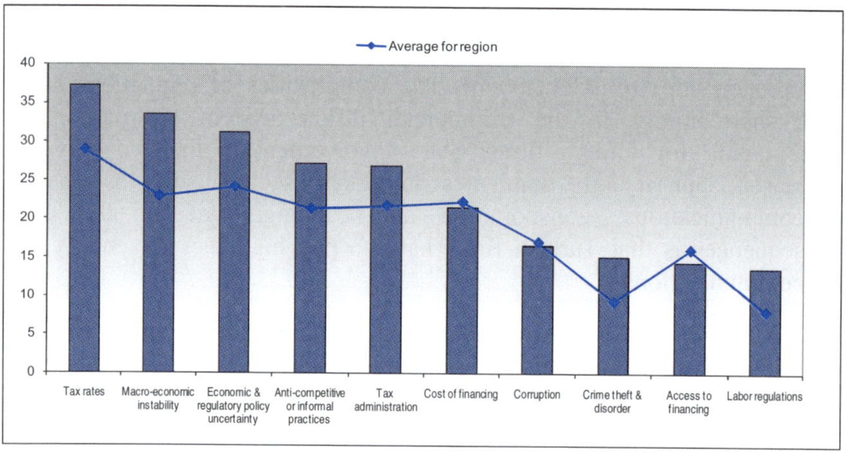

Source: FIAS filed survey 2005.

Table 1.9. **Wage evolution in Istanbul and Turkey**

	2001	2002	2003	2004
Minimum wage (USD)	152.195	236.438	306.000	433.575
Turkish Lira	123.6	156.0	204.0	303.4
Gross wage (Istanbul) (thousand of USD)	594.553	709.941	790.755	1.030.270
Turkish Lira	482.3	468.3	527.1	720.9
Gross wage (Turkey) (thousand of USD)	667.568	762.894	847.643	1.083.500
Turkish Lira	542.2	503.4	565.9	758.1
Turkish Lira/USD Exchange rate	1.2313	1.5154	1.5003	1.4292

Source: Turkish Statistical Institute (TURKSTAT) (*www.turkstat.gov.tr*).

Poverty and human capital

Human capital improvement and poverty alleviation are necessary to reduce the informal sector and to offer a better environment for business development. The ongoing structural change of Istanbul's economic base, *i.e.*, the transition towards a post-industrial, more advanced services oriented city, has created a new employee group of highly educated professionals earning high wages (Erkip, 2000). Meanwhile, increasing competition from low-labour-cost countries has impacted the real income of workers engaged in labour-intensive activities, with a large number operating in the informal sector. This process is common to any economy experiencing a major shift of its industrial mix but the effects in Istanbul have been magnified by a large influx of low-skilled migrants in a relatively short period of time. A main consequence has been increased social disparities with increasing wage differentials between services and manufacturing. In 2003, the *Gini Coefficient* for Istanbul was calculated as 0.43, which is above national average of 0.42 (UNDP and SPO, 2005). Although data on poverty level is not available at the local level in Turkey, there are some indications that the number of poor is high and has increased over time even if poverty rates are lower than in other parts of Turkey, especially as compared to rural areas.[40] Whilst laws and regulations are necessary to promote greater formality, equal importance should be given to other policies that will raise the income of the poorest segment of the population (Sojo and Villarreal, 2004).

Strengthening the educational sector will be crucial, specifically in light of some of the structural deficiencies that Turkey and Istanbul are facing. First, despite the fact that Istanbul is doing relatively better than other provinces, there are still substantial illiteracy rates in the peripheral areas (*gecekondu*), particularly for women (more than 10% are illiterate). Second, early childhood education, provided by the Ministry of Education, a series of social service institutions, nursery schools and NGOS, is relatively under-represented in Istanbul. According to data provided by the municipality, from 2004-2005 only 16% of 4-6-year-olds in Istanbul benefited from early childhood education. This is in light of the fact that the OECD is increasingly considering early education a crucial factor for the effectiveness and efficiency of the overall learning process. Third, there seems to be a rather low collective appreciation of the potential role of vocational education and training. Consequently, students are only oriented to strive for entrance to university, preventing them from making a vocational choice before entering university. This situation renders vocational schools ineffective and stimulates educational mismatches. Finally, there seems to be little strategic planning for matching vocational school profiles and labour market needs, resulting in a vocational education structure that fails to meet the rapidly changing demands for intermediate-skilled labour in Istanbul.

Impact of over-migration

Rapid urbanisation growth and a large influx of domestic and foreign migrants to Istanbul in a relatively short period of time have created huge congestions costs, notably traffic congestion, and other forms of air, water and soil pollution. Poor quality public infrastructure and basic service provision have arisen due to the difficulty of maintaining a high-quality physical environment and responding to the growing needs of such concentrations of people and activities. This impacts the spatial and socio-economic structure of Istanbul, now confronted with increasing spatial polarisation. Meanwhile, Istanbul is physically at risk: first because of the probability of earthquake, but also because the over-use of the Strait of Istanbul for international trade and the potential environmental impact of industrial sites. Addressing all these issues is certainly not an easy task, particularly in light of the fact that they all contribute to the city's sustainability, social order and ultimately its economic attractiveness.

Congestion: transport, water and housing

As with most metro-regions, especially fast-growing mega-cities, Istanbul is facing severe congestion. Traffic is made even more difficult by Istanbul's geological structure. Since the central city is split by the Strait of Istanbul and the northern part of the city are green areas, at present the only available connections are two bridges and ferries. Chronic congestion is reported not only in the city centre, but also on the two bridges on the Strait of Istanbul (the Boğaziçi Bridge and the Fatih Sultan Mehmet Bridge). As many people commute from the more residential eastern side to the western side, every day more than 380 000 vehicles cross over the two Strait of Istanbul bridges, much higher than their designed capacity of some 270 000 vehicles per day. In other terms, the bridges run, on average, at 40% over their capacity. The two bridges are also used to connect two main highways.[41] Currently, an undersea rail tunnel across the Strait of Istanbul is under construction, the “Marmaray Project" will eventually connect the existing rail system with an interchange station and the metro system.[42]

Low mobility within the metro-region is due to an over-use of roadways. Car ownership has swelled more rapidly than road capacity. The number of motor vehicles has increased by 647% while population has increased by 142% between 1980 and 2005. By comparison, the number of persons in Istanbul per car is 4.2 against 4 in New York, 2.5 in Paris and 2.2 in Tokyo, whereas mass transport in Istanbul is only 36 km of underground and light rail system, compared to 171 km in London, 200 km in Paris, 219 km in Tokyo and 438 km in New York.[43] Current trips are split between automobile (30%), public transport (50%), taxi (9%), and company and school buses (11%). Meanwhile, newly developed urban transport (tramways, LRT [Light Rail Transit] and metro) is so short and insufficient that modal shift has not been achieved effectively. Tramways and LRT have aggravated traffic flows particularly along the narrow and crowded streets. Further increases are estimated to range between 150 and 240% in vehicles while a 40 to 100% increase in population is expected between 2005 and 2020.

Rapid motorisation has created economic, environmental and health costs. Traffic congestion has increased time loss and unreliability. One estimation of the total economic losses due to congestion is USD 7.2 billion per year, assuming that 1 million cars travel per day with an average two hour idle period in traffic, and considering gasoline losses, manpower losses, and depreciation.[44] Another calculation of indirect economic losses by traffic congestion at the two bridges of the Strait of Istanbul is USD 5.6 billion per year[45] (Tezcan, 2002). Moreover, current use of the transportation system, which depends heavily on motor vehicles, has caused a lot of CO_2 emissions (52.6% increase from 1990 to 2000) as well as other damaging emissions (Table 1.10). Finally, road safety has also become a concern. Although no data is available for Istanbul, it is noteworthy that Turkey's road fatalities per vehicle are the worst among OECD countries (Figure 1.45).

Table 1.10. **Emissions caused by road traffic in Istanbul**

Emissions	Tons per day		
	1990	2000	Increase (%)
CO2	3 288.4	5 017.3	52.6
CO	21.0	31.5	50.1
NOX	4.7	7.6	62.5
SO2	0.7	1.0	55.7
Particulates	0.5	1.0	82.5
Methane	1.0	1.4	47.9

Source: Haluk Gerçek.

Figure 1.45. **Road fatalities**

Per million vehicles and per million population (2004)

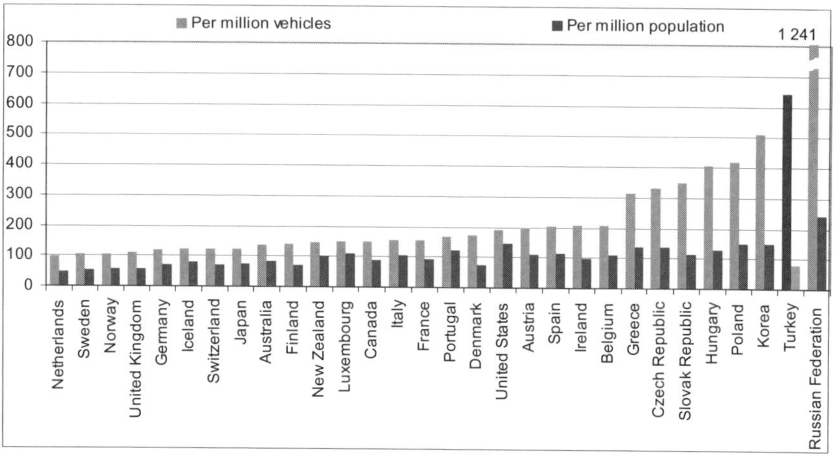

Source: OECD (2006), *OECD Factbook 2006*, OECD Publications, Paris.

Rapid influx of migrants to Istanbul has gone hand in hand with the proliferation of informal settlements and slums, a phenomenon seen throughout Turkey over the second half of 20th century. Due to the complexities of getting exact figures on the size of informal housing,[46] the 1995 Master Plan produced by Istanbul Metropolitan Municipality used estimates to calculate that around 55% of Istanbul's settled areas are composed of several types of informal settlements, with the potential to rise to 75% in areas of uncontrolled urban sprawl. These squatter buildings are also called *Gecekondu*, which in Turkish literally means a "house built overnight". According to the official definition in the Gecekondu Act of 1966, these neighbourhoods are typically built on abandoned land or on land owned by others, without the permission of the landowner, and do not comply with building rules and regulations. This spatial development pattern has raised serious concerns for Istanbul's environment, particularly over the last 20 years as the development of these informal settlements has spread towards water reserves and preserved forest areas in the north-east periphery of the city. These new settlements have since been recognised as official sub-provinces.

Growing population and squatter settlements raise important concerns for the provision of basic services, including water supply and treatment. In the early 1990s Istanbul experienced severe water shortages as in-migration (14.6% annual growth in 1980-85) had surpassed the projected water demand. Then huge investments (USD 3.6 billion in 1994-2004) were made to improve and expand water and wastewater systems (Altınbilek, 2006). Currently, there are enough water resources in Istanbul and there are large-scale water supplies projects, including new pipelines for transporting water from the Asian side to the European side, which meet projected demand until 2040. The main issue is that supply is not appropriately delivered everywhere in the city as the unplanned areas all around the city are not always equipped with water supply and other basic utilities, giving rise to increasing informal and parallel planning circuits. Moreover, although water quality has improved recently by a sharp increase in wastewater treatment (95% in 2004) and new treatment plants, a 2004 survey shows that only 35% of customers drink tap water (Altınbilek, 2006). Since a large portion (97%) of water supply of Istanbul is from surface sources, public authorities have designated water protection zones to preserve watersheds from increasing pressure from population inflow.

Proliferation of informal settlements has gone hand in hand with increasing spatial polarisation within the metro-region. A main difference arises between the centre and the periphery. Some of the congestion costs are reflected in high prices for land, labour and other resources, which make the cost of living in the centre of the metro-region high, making life particularly difficult for the low-wage populations. Distressed areas have also developed in some parts of the historic city whilst high-income groups are increasingly moving to the forestry areas in the north. Immigrants consider the poor neighbourhoods in the historical centre temporary shelters rather than as their permanent homes, as their longer-term plan is to move to the newly emerging squatter districts. This pattern of spatial polarisation has caused security concerns with a rise in crime level even in the city centre. The number of reported crimes against persons is higher than that of crimes against property; however it is still low compared to many OECD metro-regions (OECD, 2005f). Moreover, rapid transformation of the composition of the local population has resulted in a loss of collective identity and an erosion of social capital.

Major environmental risks

Istanbul has experienced one of the most damaging earthquakes in the world. On 17 August 1999 an earthquake struck the Marmara region causing significant material damage and a high number of casualties. Over 18 000 lives were lost, more than 50 000 serious injuries and an estimated 600 000 people became homeless. More than 51 000 buildings were either heavily damaged or totally collapsed and another 110 000 buildings were moderately or lightly damaged. According to the initial assessment by the

World Bank, between USD 1.1 and 3 billion were lost in the housing sector, one-quarter of a billion USD in infrastructure (municipal infrastructure, roads, bridges, highways, telecommunications and electricity) (World Bank, 1999). The ratio of damaged buildings was at least four times higher than that in the 1995 Hanshin-Awaji Earthquake in Japan and 12 times higher than that in the 1994 Northridge Earthquake in the United States. The disaster had major consequences for Turkey's economic performance as a whole: when the indirect and long-term effects are properly considered, the damage totals approximately USD 20 billion, which was about 9-10% of GDP for 2000 (OECD, 2004b).[47] The impact on Istanbul's economic activity has also been considerable.[48] The epicentre was so close to the nation's industrial heartland, Kocaeli and Düzce, that many industries suffered heavily and were forced to go out of business or incurred costly restoration.

Earthquake disaster prevention is a major challenge for Istanbul and for Turkey. The probability of facing another earthquake in the future is high, as historical records clearly indicate that along the great Anatolian Fault earthquakes occur periodically, and costs are great considering the estimates of huge human and economic costs. Different studies have provided estimated parameters of the earthquake risks posed to the population, buildings, transportation system and urban services. A recent study conducted by the Japan International Cooperation Agency (JICA) stresses that the likelihood of having a major earthquake with its epicentre as close as 10 km to Istanbul in the next 30 years is extremely high. Depending on different scenarios, this study indicates estimates of huge human casualties, ranging from 73 000 to 87 000,[49] and of economic loss (direct and indirect) of approximately USD 30.4 billion (24.5% of Turkey's GDP) to USD 34.5 billion (equivalent to 27.8% of Turkey's GDP), *i.e.*, one-fourth to one-third of Turkey's annual GDP (JICA, 2002). The same study warns about the crucial challenge of urgently dealing with the high informal building stock vulnerable to earthquakes. In a recent study with a different scenario, based on current real estate property prices in Istanbul and estimates of the fraction of the GNP that depends on businesses based in Istanbul, the direct and indirect costs of the damage is estimated at USD 60 billion and USD 80 billion, respectively (JICA, 2003).

Istanbul's environment is also challenged by a number of threats. Almost half of Turkish industry is located around the Marmara Sea. Moreover, the Strait of Istanbul is considered one of the most hazardous, crowded, and potentially dangerous waterways in the world.[50] As the sole water route between the Black Sea and the Mediterranean, the Strait of Istanbul is highly congested with the freight ships, coasters, fishing vessels and local traffic. Every day, 1.5 million people are on the move at sea by intra-city ferries and other shuttle boats, crossing from one side to the other (Turkish Statistical Institute, 2000). This strait is one of the narrowest in the world with many winding/sharp points, and rapid and complex currents all along densely populated shorelines. Frequent ship accidents produce important human, economic and environmental costs for the city – around 72 accidents have occurred over the last three years – including oil spills, large-scale fires and explosions.[51] It is reported that there is one vessel failure every 2.5 days on average (Directorate General of Coastal Safety). Meanwhile, vessels carrying dangerous goods such as crude oils, chemicals, gas, etc., are increasing in number and size (10 027 tankers out of 54 627 commercial vessels in 2005). Turkey, having full respect of the principle of freedom of navigation and legal responsibilities arising from the Montreux Convention, has taken measures in accordance with internationally accepted maritime standards to enhance the safety of navigation, life, property and environment in the Turkish Straits. One of such measures is the "Maritime Traffic Regulations for the Turkish Straits", dated 1998. Furthermore, the Turkish Government established and activated a modern Vessel Traffic Services system as of December 2003 in the Turkish Straits. However, the risk of a possible disaster as a result of a continuous increase in maritime transportation of oil and other dangerous cargo remains.

Projections for population growth are posing tremendous challenges for urban development planning in Istanbul. More specifically, the 2005 population is expected to grow from its present level of 12 million to 16 million in 2017, and to 23 million in 2023. This will result in intensified pressure on industrial and residential uses in the northern part of the metropolitan region, where the natural protection areas and the watersheds are located. In addition, *ceteris paribus*, *i.e.*, without substantial changes in the planning approach, the implication of these population projections is that the already intense commuting patterns between the Anatolian and European parts will only increase, accelerating the growth of pollution and congestion levels, and thereby threatening the sustainability of the metropolitan region. Although the recently approved Master Plan stipulates that alternative axes are to be developed through the provision of special industrial zones with infrastructure, especially in the western areas, the difficulties and complexities of such an approach cannot be underestimated. The recent experience of the Ikitelli, for example, which was planned as a logistics hub, has only been able to attract investments with a lower value-added in textile and furniture.

Notes

1. At the provincial level, there are both a provincial special administration (local government) and a provincial government (central government entities at the local government). Both entities are headed by the same governor (see Chapter 3).

2. After Tokyo, Seoul, New York, Mexico City, Osaka, Rhine-Ruhr in Germany and Los Angeles. In the international literature the definition of mega-cities differs within the spectrum from 5 million to 10 million inhabitants. While the United Nations defines mega-cities as metro-regions with a population over 8 million, the OECD has used 6 million (OECD, 2006a).

3. This figure reflects migrants before 1970.

4. Istanbul still concentrates a relatively large part of labour-intensive low-productivity activities such as textiles and clothing. This pushes down the average productivity levels of the city, making the productivity differential between Istanbul and Turkey in other (non-textile) sectors higher than 50%.

5. Real GDP per capita: GDP per capita with 1987 constant price in national currency.

6. More specifically, OECD urban regions featured an activity rate of 44.3% against 49.7% and 44.5% in intermediate and rural regions respectively in 2003.

7. EMBI spreads in Turkey increased by around 150 basis points and the increase in TRY dominated benchmark bond yields reaching about 800 basis points in June 2006.

8. The electronics cluster includes: the manufacture of electronic valves and tubes (code 3210), television and radio transmitters (code 3220), television and radio receivers (code 3230), instruments and appliances for measuring, checking and testing (code 3312), electricity distribution and control apparatus (code 3120), electric lamps and lighting equipment (code 3150) and other electrical equipment not elsewhere classified (sector 3190).

9. The chemical and medical cluster includes the manufacture of pharmaceuticals (code 2423), soap and detergents and the like (code 2424).

10. It should be observed, however, that the machine building and metal equipment cluster has a substantial number of unregistered firms and employees, thereby giving it a somewhat mixed character. The segment includes the manufacture of pumps, compressors, taps and valves (code 2912), lifting and handling equipment (code 2915), other general purpose machinery (code 2919), machinery for textile, apparel and leather production (code 2926), other special purpose machinery (code 2929), electric motors, generators and transformers (code 3110), cutlery, hand tools and general hardware (code 2893), other fabricated metal products (code 2899), and building and repairing of ships (code 3511).

11.

$$LQ = \frac{\dfrac{E_{ij}}{\sum_i E_{ij}}}{\dfrac{\sum_T E_{iT}}{\sum_i \sum_T E_{iT}}}$$

E_{ij} denotes the employment of a given industry (i) within a given Istanbul region.

$\Sigma_i E_{ij}$ denotes total employment of manufacturing industry of a given Istanbul region.

$\Sigma_T E_{iT}$ denotes the total national employment of a given industry (i).

$\Sigma_i \Sigma_T E_{iT}$ denotes the total employment of all industries of all regions.

12. Manufacture of apparel except fur apparel (1810), manufacture of knitted and crocheted fabrics and art and knitting industry (1730) and manufacture of pharmaceuticals, medicinal chemicals and botanical products (2423).

13. Geographical concentration coefficient = (Eij/Ej)/(Yi/Y)

Eij: total number of workers in region I sector j

Ej: total number of workers in sector j in Turkey

Yi: surface area of region I Y: surface area of Turkey

14. One should note, however, that when many lagging regions grow they do so at high rates, due to the magnitude of the change from the steady-state level.

15. For these two countries, the tariff equivalent for quotas was 12% for textiles and 15% for clothing; cf. (Nordas, 2004).

16. Prime Minister's Office, Under-Secretary of Treasury of Turkey, General Directorate of Foreign Investment and Istanbul Metropolitan Municipality.

17. Such an increase in FDI represented approximately 40% of the current account deficit (Turkish National Economic Outlook, 2005). FDI flows, therefore, have led to a more stable economic outlook as the trade deficit and more broadly the current account deficit is now significantly financed by FDI flows.

18. Data from the Central Bank of Turkey.

19. The capital adequacy ratio (CAR) is a measure of a bank's capital. It is expressed as a percentage of a bank's weighted credit risk exposure. This ratio is used as an indicator of the stability and efficiency of financial systems around the world.

20. Under-Secretary of Foreign Trade, *Uluslararası Doğrudan Yatırımlar*, 2005.

21. OMX Exchanges include Copenhagen, Helsinki, Stockholm, Tallinn, Riga and Vilnius Stock Exchanges.

22. Euronext figures include data from Belgium, France, Netherlands and Portugal Stock Exchanges.

23. The Levent and Maslak financial districts are home to the headquarters of Turkey's largest companies and banks. Both Levent and Maslak have a continuously growing and changing skyline with several new skyscraper projects proposed, approved and initiated every year. In addition, the headquarters of 136 of the 144 brokerage houses are located in Istanbul, mainly in the Maslak and Levent districts. All of the 11 individual pension fund firms are also located in Istanbul.

24. In recent years, the Corridor 10 (Salzburg-Ljubliana-Zagreb-Belgrad-Nish-Sofia-Istanbul) has also been used.

25. Ambarlı port complex is located on the north shores of the Marmara Sea. Ambarlı Port Complex port is divided into two regions. Region No. 1 Ambarlı New Port, located to the west of the oil terminals, consists of privately owned dry, bulk and container terminals. Region No. 2 consists of the oil platforms, jetties and mooring buoys. Region No. 1 includes: Kumport, Akçansa Cement Pier, Mardas, Armaport, Anadolu and Set Cement Pier, Soyak; and Region 2 includes: Çekisan (BP Amoco/ Mobil/Shell) Jetty, Offshore Platform and Mooring Buoys, BP Amoco Mooring Buoys, Aygaz Offshore Platform, TEAS/Petrol Ofisi Platform and Mooring Buoys, Total Offshore Platform. The Pendik and Ambarlı

ports of İstanbul registered a total of 80 000 TIR shipments to Trieste-Italy. The number for Pendik Ro-Ro port is 57 692 TIR for 2006.

26. World tourism is dominated by six large countries receiving 40% of tourists in the world and nearly half of the world's revenues in the sector, namely the United States, France, Spain, Italy, Germany, China and the United Kingdom. The second-tier destinations are dominated by countries such as Turkey, Austria, Canada, Mexico and Greece.

27. They include the Topkapı Palace, Yıldız Palace, Süleymaniye Mosque, Zeyrek Mosque (Pantocrator Church), City Walls, Bozdogan Aqueduct, and the Golden Horn.

28. One is financed by the State (Ministry of Culture and Tourism) and the other by the Istanbul Metropolitan Municipality.

29. International meetings are defined by the UIA to include either one or both of the following criteria: (1) Meetings organised or sponsored by "international organisations"; (2) Other meetings of significant international character, which meet the following criteria: minimum 300 participants, minimum 40% foreigners, minimum five nationalities, minimum three-day duration.

30. *www.iccaworld.com.*

31. The so-called Conference Valley is located in the heart of the financial district. Its centrepiece is the Istanbul Lütfi Kırdar Convention and Exhibition Centre (ICEC) with capacity for 2 000 people, but the Rumeli Fair and Exhibition Centre and a series of five-star hotels with a capacity of around 6 000 guest rooms increases Istanbul's capacity. For larger events however, the so-called CNR Expo, located near the international airport and the major road system, has a capacity of more than 2 000 people with hotels, catering services and security facilities. A third location for events in the city of Istanbul is the Grand Cevahir Hotel and Convention Centre, with auditorium capacity for 1 013 people. Finally, TÜYAP, located in the Büyükçekmece/Beylikdüzü area on the western side of the city, some 20 km from the Atatürk International Airport, is the largest fair and congress centre of Istanbul. It has 120 000 m^2 of exhibition space, evenly divided between indoor and outdoor areas. Since its foundation in 1979, TÜYAP has gone through successive stages of growth and expansion in capacity, a clear indicator of the potential of industrial and business exhibitions in Istanbul. Presently, the organisation has domestic offices in Bursa, Ankara and others, and international contact offices are in Moscow, Tbilisi, Sofia, Aleppo and Tehran.

32. International familiarity is a criteria in the business survey "European Cities Monitor" (Cushman and Wakefield, 2004), to assess the familiarity of international business with cities as a business location.

33. The informal economy (also known in the literature as the "Non-Structured Sector", following statistical conventions and definitions fostered by the United Nations Organization since the Nairobi Conference held in the 1970s) takes both highly visible as well as less apparent modalities, and is related to (here you might also say "and impacts") important economic, social and juridical matters.

34. Informality rates were calculated using Turkey's household survey; thus, informality is considered as the ratio of employees without any social security to total employment. One important reason for higher informality rates in Turkey than in Istanbul is the fact that rural areas are inclined to rely on agricultural activities which are typically informal. Around 90% of workers in the agricultural sector were working informally in Turkey.

35. See *www.ntv.com.tr/news/144050.asp*.

36. Results from the Istanbul Chamber of Commerce's (ITO) survey show there are 5 500 African immigrants in Istanbul, half of them working as street vendors.

37. Turkish Statistical Institute, innovation statistics, *www.turkstat.gov.tr*.

38. Ranked by total sales.

39. FIAS, the Foreign Investment Advisory Service is part of the World Bank.

40. Regarding 2004 figures of three poverty levels in the urban areas of Turkey, food poverty ratio is 0.92%, food and non-food poverty ratio is 21.95% and finally absolute poverty ratio 0.03%, which are lower than Turkish averages (1.35%, 26.95% and 0.2% respectively). (Turkish Statistical Institute, 2004, *www.turkstat.gov.tr*).

41. The E5, E90 and Trans European Motorway (TEM) are the three main roads leading to Turkey from the European border and the inner city borders to the east. The E5 is mostly used for inner city traffic while the more recent TEM highway is mostly used by intercity or intercontinental traffic.

42. The project includes a 13.6 km crossing the Strait of Istanbul with four new underground stations and the upgrade of 63 km of suburban train lines to create a 76.3 km high capacity line between Gebze and Halkalı. It has been constructed by quake-resistant engineering against magnitude 7.5 level earthquakes. The scheduled completion is by 2010.

43. Data from the IMM's Istanbul Metropolitan Planning and Urban Design Centre.

44. (1) Gasoline losses USD 986 million (*i.e.*, 1.8 litres per hour, USD 1.5 per litre); (2) manpower losses USD 3 750 million (*i.e.*, 1.5 persons per car,

250 days, USD 5 per hour); and (3) depreciation USD 2 500 million (*i.e.*, USD 5 per hour).

45. (1) Gasoline losses USD 864 million; (2) manpower losses USD 3 600 million; and (3) depreciation USD 1 200 million. Assumptions are based on the current situation as follows: 120 million vehicles cross the two bridges per year, total two hour delay (one hour in the morning and one hour in the evening), composition of vehicles: cars 79% (1.8 litre loss per waiting hour), buses 3% and trucks 18% (4.2 litre loss per hour), 1 million passengers using the bridges per day.

46. In general, it is quite difficult to get exact data on the size of informal settlements. First, there are several possible sources of informal housing, for example, related to land tenure, the legal status of the area, the subdivision procedures, the zoning laws, building codes, and standards or environmental legislation, to mention a of few possible scenarios of informality. Second, it is also difficult to find a common denominator to analyse informal housing, either in terms of the physical standards of the units, or the socio-economic profile of its communities. While there is informal housing that comes close to completely consolidated housing, we also find deteriorated slum housing, with a lack of basic services and badly in need of upgrading. Informal housing is not the equivalent of slum housing inhabited by low income people in the outskirts of the city as it also includes some middle income apartments and even luxury units that are built in more central parts of the city. Third, a distinction should be made between illegal/irregular housing, on one hand, and informal housing and urban development, on the other hand. More specifically, and in light of the frequent *ad hoc* amnesties that have been given over time to illegal construction and land use occupation, it is quite difficult to trace down the accumulated net effect of these frequently haphazard legal changes on the state of the total housing stock in Istanbul.

47. The overall estimated cost both in terms of income loss and national wealth loss ranges between USD 9 and 13 billion according to the State Planning Organization and from USD 6 to 10 billion according to the World Bank. A study by the Turkish Industrialists and Businessmen Association (TUSIAD) estimates a total loss of more than USD 15 billion. When the indirect and long-term effects are properly considered, it would be around USD 20 billion, which was about 9-10% of GDP for 2000.

48. The costs to the business sector was initially calculated from USD 1.1 to 2.6 billion, hitting especially hard the small and medium-scale enterprises which were undercapitalised and had little insurance coverage (World Bank, 1999).

49. JICA made an estimate of damages by possible earthquakes, with a magnitude of 7 to 7.5, providing four models. The worst scenario is

involving 87 000 deaths (1.0% of total population) and 135 000 serious injuries, while even the least damage scenario predicted 73 000 deaths (0.8% of total population) and 120 000 serious injuries (JICA, 2002). Sources include The Study on Disaster Prevention/Mitigation Basic Plan in Istanbul including Seismic Microzonation in the Republic of Turkey, JICA and Istanbul Metropolitan Municipality, March 2002. Economic damage by an 7.5 earthquake magnitude affecting Istanbul is estimated at USD 30.4 billion (equivalent to 24.5% of Turkey's GDP), in case of an M7.7 earthquake it is estimated at USD 34.5 billion (equivalent to 27.8% of Turkey's GDP), see JBIC (February 2003), "Special Assistance for Project Implementation (SAPI) for Emergency Earthquake Recovery Loan – Final Report".

50. The Strait of Istanbul is approximately 31 km long with an average width of 1.5 km and at its narrowest 698 m. The Strait has many winding/sharp points (the maximum course alteration of 80 degrees and at narrowest part 45 degrees).

51. For instance, in 1979, a crude oil tanker, Independentza, had an accident at the south entrance of the Strait of Istanbul and 110 000 tons fuel-oil burned for more than two months causing very serious environmental problems at the heart of the city.

Chapter 2

Fostering Istanbul's International Competitiveness

Introduction

Despite the tendency for new industrial investments to locate in the surrounding provinces within Polycentric Greater Istanbul, Istanbul can be considered the industrial, financial and logistical centre of the country. Over the last few years, the broader reform processes underway in Turkey imply positive change for Istanbul's role in the national and international context, and open concrete prospects for strengthening its strategic position in the global economy. In this respect, it has become increasingly clear to policy makers, both at the national, provincial and metropolitan level, that it is crucial to leverage Istanbul as the major economic centre and the country node for international trade flows. Supplementing Istanbul's new strategic planning system, policy makers tend to agree on two related objectives to improve Istanbul's role in the national and global arenas:

- *Istanbul: a regional hub in the Euro-Asia region.* Istanbul will be a global gateway city between Europe, Asia, the Middle East and the former East European countries and serve as a regional provider of financial services, a logistic hub, and a tourism and cultural centre.
- *Istanbul: the information-based, innovation and business centre of Turkey*. Istanbul must be a dynamic economic learning system with a strong capacity to generate value added, quality employment, and innovation to better position itself to effectively compete with other metropolitan areas in the international marketplace whilst generating positive spillovers to the rest of the country.

Istanbul will however have to address a number of challenges to achieve this ambitious goal. They include:

1. *Accelerating the economic base upgrading.* Istanbul has to accelerate the transformation of its development model, now predominantly based on cost competition, towards an approach based on creativity, knowledge, innovation and a higher level of command and control over global production chain functions, such as finance, product and process design, quality engineering, marketing, distribution and differentiation. The current productive restructuring process is moving at a much slower pace shifting only gradually to other complementary segments. Without addressing the obstacles to reducing the large informal sector in Istanbul and to attracting innovative foreign firms, Istanbul will be hard pressed to generate the innovation and skills that are necessary to generate endogenous growth through improved productivity and growth. These difficulties are partly linked with a number of obstacles to a favourable business environment for formal firms (product market regulations, tax system and labour market legislation). In addition to these obstacles, a comprehensive approach to the informal sector should also address human capital development and poverty alleviation.

2. Building appropriate conditions for three related field of the regional hub strategy.

   - The prospects for Istanbul to become a logistics hub requires the efficient combination of different transportation modes and implies the development of services around it to guarantee delivery times, regularity and frequency of services and direct service without trans-shipment or warehousing en route. This requires a wise strategy that will take into account important sustainability concerns. Over 60% of Turkey's total trade flows through Istanbul, a figure only expected to grow in the coming years with increasing national and international trade.

   - The financial services hub strategy requires developing financial instruments (the securities market is currently dominated by the public sector and the stock market is not enough developed) and introducing more competition in the banking sector to push down the current high intermediary costs. Pressing reforms should be addressed as competition with other financial centres in the region is high.

   - Istanbul has the capacity to become a cultural and tourism centre but this requires increasing hotel capacity, better valorising and marketing historical and cultural heritage, and developing more urban cultural amenities (museums, theatres, etc.). Moreover, more local stakeholders should be actively involved in the development of a comprehensive tourism strategy.

3. *Addressing negative externalities that cast a shadow over Istanbul's attractiveness*. This includes improving physical infrastructure, especially for transport and stock building. Particular attention should be paid to the over-concentration of the population and its related consequences on the environment (congestion, illegal housing, and pollution) and on social cohesion. Finding a solution to reduce regional disparities in Turkey, is key to controlling population overflow into Istanbul. Earthquake risk is a major threat requiring a comprehensive prevention strategy, especially related to the proliferation of illegal settlements.

4. *Setting an integrated strategy and governance adaptation*. A comprehensive and explicit strategic vision for economic development in Istanbul is necessary to develop appropriate policy tools to reach the goal of becoming a regional hub. There is a relative absence of integrated policies that foster systemic territorial competitiveness for the metropolitan area. This is partly related to the deficiencies in the overall structure of governance, as the metropolitan area lacks a strong institutional framework that can guide the functioning of local and metropolitan markets as well as outline appropriate mechanisms for involving major stakeholders, including from the business sector.

2.1. Promoting Istanbul's international competitiveness

Upgrading Istanbul's economy

Istanbul needs substantial economic restructuring in its aim to transform the city into an innovative metro-region and a regional hub. As mentioned in Chapter 1, the region has a solid base in low-technology manufacturing industry, and is diversifying into relatively medium/high-technology segments as well as pharmaceutical and medical products. However, a lack of microeconomic adjustments and institutional bottlenecks are slowing the pace of industrial transformation. Traditional, labour-intensive sectors are struggling against increasing global competitive pressures. There is also a widening mismatch between average educational attainment and the needs of Istanbul in developing more, high-value-added activities. Traditional, labour intensive sectors (such as textiles) in particular are struggling with relatively low productivity and relatively high per unit labour costs.

Upgrading Istanbul's industrial mix will require tackling a wide range of issues, some of which could benefit from a territorial-based approach. The first step would be a comprehensive examination of ongoing economic restructuring, both in the province of Istanbul and throughout the Istanbul functional area, be it through commuting patterns or through the supplier relationships of the main production chains throughout the area. For example, although actual car manufacturing is concentrated outside Istanbul (mainly Bursa and Kocaeli), there are several supplier relationships that span a wider area outside these areas. As such, in order to analyse the ongoing restructuring process it is necessary to have a more detailed view of the spatial pattern of sub-contracting processes, and innovation and design taking place throughout the production chain. These more detailed studies could provide input for testing, for example, which part of the "command and control" of the production chain (in terms of process and product innovation, design, marketing, etc.) is still strategically concentrated in the city of Istanbul. The financial and trading functions, to mention two obvious examples, are predominantly concentrated in the city of Istanbul. The results of these studies might then produce a series of policy actions that should be introduced to support these efforts. Whilst many of these actions would be related to national macroeconomic policies, products and labour markets regulations, tax and national sectoral policies (*e.g.*, education, labour markets) to ensure productivity and growth, competitiveness of the business sector also depends on factors related to the regional environment. The following section includes a selection of the national and regional/local policies that affect Istanbul's enabling environment and its upgrading capacity: (1) innovation and cluster policies; (2) specific industrial policies; (3) business development and SMEs; (4) informal sector and poverty alleviation, and (5) FDI attraction policies.

Innovation and cluster policies

Istanbul benefits from the national government's increasing focus on innovation systems. In recognising the need to strengthen and increase the scale of innovation the government has introduced the National Development Plans calling for a more active government role in setting up a national system for innovation. The National Development Plan highlights the need for infrastructure development for e-commerce and faster data transmission for small to medium enterprises (SMEs). For example in the latest plan there is a special emphasis on improving training opportunities for SMEs and stimulating links between large companies, universities and SMEs to strengthen and speed up technological exchange. In its strategic plan, Vision 2023, the Turkish Scientific and Technological Research Council (TUBITAK) has identified goals and guidelines in the fields of science and technology, and it has also initiated projects that will move the country forward on this path. Then in November 2004 TUBITAK signed a protocol with primary and secondary schools to disseminate issues related to science and technology. The government supported the organisation with a EUR 250 million increase in TUBITAK's 2005 budget, and a EUR 25 to

54 million increase in its industrial support budget from 2000 to 2005. Moreover, the Turkish Research Area (TRA), the private and public institutions that execute, fund or demand research and development, provide an enabling environment for interaction between TUBITAK, the private sector, universities, the State Planning Organization, public institutions and NGOs. The targets for 2010 are ambitious, both in terms of desired increases in R&D expenditure (from its present 0.8% to 2% of GDP), and in the number of researchers (targeting 40 000). TUBITAK also provides funds to the Technology and Innovation Funding Program (TEYDEB), created in 1995,[1] aimed at the creation of an innovation-oriented environment amongst SMEs. Its operations are characterised by a flexible project-based approach aimed at increasing the effectiveness and efficiency of technology transfer and risk sharing between universities, private businesses and public institutions. Using this approach, several specific technology groups have been established in segments such as biotechnology, material engineering, information and communications technology and electronics, among others.

The Technology Development Foundation of Turkey (TTGV) is another institution active in enhancing innovation capabilities,[2] offering Technology Development Project Support explicitly aimed at supporting technological product and process innovation that translates into permanent knowledge accumulation for the supported firm. More than 50% of the firms supported to date within this framework are less than 10 years old and are primarily in the Marmara Region (which includes Istanbul). Nearly half of these firms have purchased services from universities, some of who are also supported by TTGV, such as Istanbul Technical University and TUBITAK Marmara Araştırma Merkezi (Marmara Research Centre/MAM). TTGV programmes extend to bringing entrepreneurs with new ideas and financial actors/capital holders together to facilitate venture capital distribution, providing financial support for establishing technology parks and technology centres. One important development in recent years has been the foundation of two Innovation Relay Centres (IRC) in Turkey. Both IRCs aim to bring together technology demands and supplies within their structures and to become productive members of the IRC network. However, such a centre has not been founded in Istanbul.

A particularly promising initiative is the creation of local and regional innovation systems through techno parks and the Technological Incubators system. Launched in 2002, this initiative aims to foster partnerships between the private sector, universities and SMEs to stimulate a higher quantity and quality of product and process innovation. Under the initiative, proposals for creating technology development zones are submitted to a government committee comprised of officials from the State Planning Organization, the Ministry of Public Works and Settlement and other offices like the Scientific and Technological Research Council of Turkey (TUBITAK), the Higher Education Council (YOK), the Union of Chambers and Commodity Exchanges of Turkey (TOBB) and the Technology Development Foundation of Turkey (TTGV), all presided over by the Department for Research and Development of the Ministry of Industry and Trade. The proposals include detailed descriptions of the site plan, infrastructure, buildings, partner organisations (at least one university) and expected spillover effects (new products, processes and multiplier effects on the economy). In its working plan, the consortium (also known as an incorporator committee) may also incorporate a proposal to obtain (partial) grants for land and infrastructure acquisition. Then once the zone has been approved, salary and value-added tax exemptions may be obtained for periods up to 10 years. Public university research personnel and staff may also benefit through financial rewards and salaries from work in the techno parks, compensation that would have previously gone directly to the university revolving fund. With approval from the University's Board of Directors, academic staff is also allowed to establish firms to commercialise the results of their work in the zones and can be management partners in related firms. This legal environment may prove to provide an important financial incentive to stimulate academic talent to work more closely with the private sector, and to do more research and development outside of the university. In countries such as Spain and Brazil, similar legislation was passed to stimulate collaborative networks between universities and the private sector (Box 2.1). Although the Brazilian experience in establishing these networks is quite recent, it should be noted that the legal reforms are the result of a broader discussion on the direction of technology and industrial policies in the country, which has been ongoing since 2001. Consequently, the present range of financial, tax and legal incentives aimed at stimulating interaction between the private sector and universities is quite broad, and relatively well articulated in these policies. In this respect, the Brazilian case could provide an inspiring example for Turkey.

ARI Teknokent located in Istanbul Technical University (ITU) is a good example of university-business partnership targeting innovation strategy and implementation. ARI Teknokent is strategically important as a unique techno-park located in Istanbul, and also due to its proximity to business centres.[3] This techno-city was established in 2001 on the ITU campus, with a limited capacity of 48 companies, six of which are foreign investments. The main focus of park is software development for business, specifically for the financial sector. As an owner of the techno-park, the university is responsible for physical infrastructure. On one hand, tax exemption and proximity to the business centre provokes office space demand, on the other hand the limited office capacity puts pressure on rents, for example the fixed office rate is EUR 15 per m^2; the highest price in Maslak (business district).

Box 2.1. The microeconomics of research partnerships: the case of Brazil's Law on Innovation and the Madrid Institute for Advanced Studies

In Brazil, most public universities, either state or federally financed, have respected post-graduate and PhD programmes that produce internationally recognised research and scientific publications. The challenge however is in transferring the good quality papers from the national and international scientific community into patents or practical recommendations for process and product innovation. Consequently, most of the research and development efforts of university professors never leave the university. As most of this research is state financed, this is an untapped resource both in terms of its financial potential and the value of knowledge transfer to the private sector.

In 2005, after years of debate, the federal government finally succeeded in having Parliament pass a law on innovation with the explicit objective of establishing stronger, more profound links between private enterprise and universities. The new law establishes an enabling framework for financially advantageous collaborative networks between universities and private businesses. University professors can open a business, participate in the financial rewards associated with patents or process and product innovations, and support the construction of portfolios of patents outside the university. The legal and administrative guidelines for economic exploitation of inventions and innovations are much more flexible, specifically when compared to the previous cumbersome public tendering procedures. The new law, inspired by the Korean experience, is expected to significantly bolster both R&D expenditures and the number of patents developed by enterprises collaborating with universities.

In Madrid, the regional government is creating the so-called Research Institutes for Advanced Studies in order to foster a more dynamic and result-based network of universities. The institutes, which are expected to be operating from next year onward on a pilot basis, are aimed at creating research teams of excellence, with participation from internationally renowned researchers in nine different areas in which Madrid might be developing a dynamic knowledge base (applied mathematics, energy, material engineering, chemical science, humanities, etc.). The partnerships are created on a competitive tender basis, while the organisational structure of the institutes follows a more flexible structure on the basis of a foundation, with a board of trustees that also allows international participation. According to the co-ordination of the programme, its main aim is to reduce the red tape within the university system, to introduce more performance oriented criteria of evaluating what universities do, and to stimulate knowledge and innovation alliances among university and private enterprise. Although it is of course still too early to evaluate such initiatives, its replication of programmes is likely to stimulate a change in culture and organisational structure within universities.

Source: Federal Government of Brazil, Ministry of Science and Technology, "The Law on Innovation", *www.planalto.gov.br/ccivil_03/_Ato2004-2006/2004/Lei/L10.973.htm*, accessed October 2005.

The GOSB[4] technology park located in Gebze (located in Kocaeli adjacent province) is also a good example of the possible synergy created by the techno parks initiative. With its starting capital of YTL 17 million and 35 000 m^2 location it has attracted a series of international firms, from Italy, Spain, Belgium, China and the United States. The park is focused on information technology for car manufacturing, logistics, the biomedical sector and financial data distribution. Though car manufacturing has been present in Istanbul since the 1980s, the GOSB Techno-Park offers companies research and development capabilities previously unavailable or less accessible. Two companies taking advantage of this new infrastructure are Fiat and Peugeot with their joint testing facilities. The synergy between large international firms and local firms is starting to bear fruit as the park begins to build up a portfolio of patents. All this contributes to making GOSB a more attractive car-manufacturing cluster, making it a prime candidate for future research and development investments.

The scale of the above-mentioned initiatives is still rather small and many challenges remain. For example, there is presently only one techno park in the city of Istanbul (under the umbrella of the Istanbul Technical University), and two in Gebze (one of them being the GOSB Park). The majority of the private sector representation seems to have a positive opinion of the role of Technological Development Zones, however the scale of the initiative needs to be further developed. A careful evaluation of site factors in the early stages of proposing a park is important in order to optimise the potential economies of agglomeration and ensure that the location matches the preferences of the businesses in the area. For instance, according to qualitative information obtained in one of the interviews, while there is a waiting list for the techno park located in the Istanbul Technical University, physical space is still available in the Gebze zones. Moreover, more attention should be paid to the sectoral profile of techno parks; for example Istanbul should prioritise design and fashion incubators, instead of focussing only on technological parks with a strict high-tech profile. There are 18 Technology Development Centres (TEKMER), or technological incubators, in Turkey providing common infrastructure for technological start-up firms. After their incubation phase, firms can be relocated to techno parks, aimed at a more mature target groups.

Under the technology parks initiative stronger links should be made to attract foreign direct investment (FDI), and to disseminate technology and management modernisation process knowledge amongst small and medium domestic enterprises in Istanbul. Though there is a promising number of incoming FDI joint ventures[5] the inflow of FDI alone does not automatically trigger dynamic learning and technology transfer for local firms. Several mechanisms could direct foreign investment toward facilitating the active, knowledge-generating participation of local firms in increasing Istanbul's innovation capacity and Turkish economic internationalisation such as creative forms of joint ventures, acquisition of foreign technology licences and turnkey projects.

Considering the fact that important intangible technology transfer and dynamic learning occur within production chains (*e.g.*, in function of supplier-buyer relations, processes of technical assistance and by exploring export markets), strategic opportunities could be better exploited within the Istanbul economy. There are no explicit policies that provide incentives for learning by doing and learning by using within the established production chains of the Istanbul economy. Technology parks could be instrumental to technology transfer as they provide an environment for catalysing strategic alliances among national and international enterprises of various size, university staff and the public bodies responsible for the direction and selection of projects. Direct financial incentives could be used to bridge the current gap between universities and the private sector. Rewards could be aimed at university professors increasing their portfolio of applied research (supplementing their base salary), or stimulating enterprises to fund research and development through university staff (through direct subsidies and/or tax incentives). The recent legislation on the technology parks sets a new framework for encouraging greater collaboration between university researchers and the private sector by allowing university researchers to work in enterprises, and to retain the financial gains associated with the work in the Technology Development Zones. An example of how this sort of programme could be further supported would be through initiatives that aim to increase the efficiency of existing businesses, and make full use of best-practice processes, techniques and work practices. This is a potential approach for a region where firms have been under-investing in technology, worker training, or skills development, and with a relatively high proportion of SMEs operating at the end of their product life cycle. This type of programme is aimed at establishing good practice in firms that need to modernise their production. The North East Productivity Alliance Project in the United Kingdom provides an example of this approach (Box 2.2).

Box 2.2. North East Productivity Alliance: United Kingdom

The North East Productivity Alliance (NEPA) is an alliance of academics, senior business people and government agencies. It was established in 2001 to improve productivity in manufacturing. The programme focuses on:

- Providing training for the existing workforce in key aspects of productivity improvement;
- Spreading best practices across the region's manufacturing businesses;
- Promoting the understanding and adoption of appropriate engineering software solutions, and increasing skill levels in the use and application of digital tools; and
- Providing the high-level engineering skills, and research in critical areas of engineering and manufacturing.

The alliance has worked with over 300 firms in the North East. Agreement from Nissan Motor Manufacturing UK Ltd. to champion the alliance has been critical to its success. The opportunity for other North East firms to benefit from the collective experience of Nissan and others has proved compelling. Nissan, also benefits indirectly from the upgrade of its supplier firms in the region.

Workforce training focuses on creating a positive workforce attitude toward undertaking productivity improvements. Manufacturing staff are encouraged to obtain formal qualifications in productivity improvement, accompanied by know-how and application of fundamental productivity improvement training programmes designed to provide staff with know-how in productivity improvement tools such as standard operations, 5C/5S – organising the workplace, skill control and *kaizen* (continuous improvement). A series of work-based qualifications involving innovative approaches in Performing Manufacturing Operations (PMO) and Business Improvement Techniques (BIT) are also delivered.

Best practice dissemination uses a productivity diagnostic tool to help determine the productivity and competitiveness issues within a company. The results of the diagnosis also provide a useful tool to help decide the breadth and depth of any productivity interventions that may be required. Specially trained improvement engineers from the NEPA industrial partner companies then work with companies to achieve the identified productivity improvements.

The software solutions focus in the programme is on increasing productivity by providing various levels of training in software products. The applications include product design, analysis, process planning, cost estimation, factory

Box 2.2. North East Productivity Alliance: United Kingdom (*cont.*)

layout, ergonomics, robotics, machining, inspection, factory simulation, engineering and manufacturing data and process management, supply chain collaboration and their link to an e-business strategy.

The project links closely to research carried out in the University of Sunderland and other universities and the expertise in the region's exemplar companies to develop existing programmes and to disseminate best practices. The programme also works closely with software developers, industry organisations, and in partnership with other regions.

The establishment of eight research fellowships in key engineering disciplines fosters high-level engineering skills. Senior personnel from the NEPA companies are appointed as fellows to undertake research that is intended to be subsequently implemented within the companies and disseminated across the region. The fellows are expected to champion their activity in other companies.

Source: OECD (2006), *OECD Territorial Reviews: Newcastle in the North East, United Kingdom*, OECD Publications, Paris.

This effort will also need to be complemented with programmes within universities focused on increasing research and development implemented in partnership with the private sector. Universities in Turkey in general, and in Istanbul in particular, will have to go through an intense process of managerial and organisational change in order to increase the portfolio of projects and programmes with the private sector. Regional universities should be targeted for opening research and business support centres that focus, at least partially, on collaboration with local industry or stimulating the development of new local enterprises. In fostering new business growth, SMEs' access to consultancy services is essential, and could be further promoted as SMEs face a range of barriers in accessing university knowledge resources. Internationally there are various mechanisms for managing consultancy and other links between universities and SMEs, such as university consultancy companies or providing problem-solving spaces for SMEs. International studies have shown that the exchange of ideas facilitated by academics often leads to intensified co-operation, joint initiatives by firms, and finally to innovation. It is true that the demand from small firms for interactions with universities is low. Nevertheless many examples have shown that if universities can bridge the gap, firm behaviour often changes with notable increases in regional social capital. Across the OECD countries non-university higher education institutions have been most active in this regard.

The lack of firms investing in innovation may be due to the fact that the benefits of investment in knowledge and innovation spillover are not fully retained by those making the investment. This reduced incentive leads to under-investment in innovation, which is often particularly acute in the case of SMEs. The policy responses to this issue are generally the provision of intellectual property protection, and subsidies or tax credits. The second problem, which is most acutely felt by SMEs, is the risk in financing innovation due to the sometimes highly uncertain value of the activity. Often firms either cannot find external capital before the innovation is commercially successful, or the cost of capital is such that it discourages firms from investing in innovation. In addressing this issue, an efficient financial services sector is important, especially for established firms.

Access to early capital is a major issue in Turkey and increasing the efficiency of the financial markets would be an important step toward creating a more vibrant venture capital market. The government might have special consideration for venture capital funds, in particular those aimed at early stage funding, as this funding is the most risky and difficult to obtain. In addition the government could consider initiatives aimed at educating investors and the recipients of investment. Increasing general awareness of the sector might stimulate greater interest and increase willingness to make investments. Education of those seeking financing would also facilitate the market by making firms aware of the expectations of venture capital and angel investors. Initiatives aimed at stimulating information sharing between venture capital sources and firms as well as encouraging the centralisation of venture capital in technology parks might also help stimulate the market. Finally, larger firms should be encouraged to establish venture capital funds as a form of technology filtering, reducing thereby their costs and risks associated with their technology developments. Particularly in sectors such as pharmaceuticals and biotechnology, larger firms could be used to provide support for the development of venture capital as an instrument for spreading the risks of technology development over a larger number of actors.

Specific industrial policies

Specific sectoral support measures, targeted at segments that are promising or are facing problems of productive restructuring, may be justified. Sector support could involve economic development actors creating sector strategies and action plans, or support delivery through the existing generic programmes. Alternatively, a sector-based approach could focus on generating strategic public and private collaboration, possibly facilitated, between sectors identified as having higher than average productivity and growth potential, or those facing productive restructuring problems. The process requires private sector commitment to engage with government, and it requires government to have the ability to add value by jointly developing a vision, strategy and action plans. Key to the success of such an approach would be political engagement – to raise the profile of the activity, to ensure co-ordination, oversight and monitoring of the government agencies involved, and to ensure political accountability. Also key to the success of such an approach would be to guarantee that the composition of the groups reflected the senior and relevant actors from the private and the public sectors (including relevant national government agencies), with a built in sunset clause for government engagement. Finally policy makers should be responsible for determining what resources are reallocated to which sector-specific activities.

An active sector approach should focus on new activities that have the potential for spillovers into the rest of the economy, or which provide demonstratable effects. Here the focus would be on encouraging transformation and initiatives that stimulate new activities: such as new technologies, new business models, specific human capital development, new markets, and, new goods or services. The focus is not on the sector *per se*, but rather on increasing the sector's potential for generating new areas of specialisation. In relation to sector-specific initiatives, there are several promising segments of the economy that might justify special attention. Pharmaceutical manufacturing, medical and surgical equipment, and soap and detergents and the like have the potential to trigger positive technological externalities on the development of such sectors as biotechnology. Therefore these sectors, that together sum up some 18% of value added of the Istanbul economy, might be considered a strategic niche in terms of science and research-driven industrial development.

The chemical and medical sectors, for example, have shown promising growth patterns over the last few years. The elaboration of sector strategies involving decision makers from business and local, provincial and national governments, would be relevant for strategic planning related to technology transfer, the improvement of Technology Development Zones, venture capital, and Technology Transfer to SMEs. The approach would be to establish a participatory appraisal of the main challenges and potentials of doing business in Istanbul. Subsequently, and on the basis of this appraisal, policy networks and strategic alliances could be mobilised to implement specific projects.

Health tourism and its related services provide another opportunity for such an approach. Although it is difficult to find hard data on the sector, in countries like England, Belgium, the Netherlands, Luxembourg and Germany, an increasing number of quality hospitals are active in attracting patients on public health system waiting lists. Good physical infrastructure, quality certified doctors, competitive costs and an aggressive market strategy represent an important potential currently being tapped by the more entrepreneurial hospitals. Informal evidence obtained through interviews showed that this is a growing sector, though lacking systemic organisation of business support systems. Some of these hospitals are also becoming increasingly active in trying to co-ordinate forward and backward links with businesses, such as visa arrangements, the logistics of patient transfer with air companies, strategic alliances with private health insurance companies in potential client countries, website and health tourism promotion, and lobbying efforts targeted at institutions and health providers in potential client countries.

Business development and SMEs policies

In principle, technological and industrial policies should focus trying to connect and insert smaller firms into the wider processes of technological and managerial change taking place in and around Istanbul. This is necessary to facilitate SME participation in the production chain strategies implemented by larger manufacturing firms (car assembly, electronics, telecommunications), in areas such as sub-contracting, flexible and modular production, decentralisation of risks and specific activities of component suppliers, etc. An active local economic development strategy may capture some of this positive spin-off for SMEs.

In Turkey, business development and SME support initiatives are delivered by a national agency, KOSGEB. KOSGEB is a semi-autonomous non-profit organisation linked to the Ministry of Industry and Trade, responsible for the growth and capacity building of SMEs. KOSGEB's Board is comprised of members of the central government and private sector representative organisations. The core activity of KOSGEB is the provision of business development services to SMEs, such as soft credits and grants, technical assistance and consultancy, information sharing, exploration of new market niches and export assistance. It is also involved in technological modernisation assistance through the creation of infrastructure for laboratories and the development of prototypes aimed at testing new products and processes. KOSGEB targets some 265 000 industrial SMEs in Turkey, approximately 67 000 of which are in Istanbul. Interested businesses submit a business plan, in either the standard paper or electronic format, which serves as their entrance point for all further dealings with the agency. In general, there are two stages of support. The first is a grant (up to a ceiling of YTL 200 000/USD 140 000), and the subsequent stage is a soft loan with the same ceiling, which can be used for such items as consultancy, marketing, R&D, equipment, market studies, investment in the creation of a new brand, infrastructure or expenditure for the development of e-commerce. KOSGEB is also exploring ways to use its SME application databank as a source of information for the elaboration of pro-active business development strategies. Of the 20 000 establishments that have filed KOSGEB electronic forms, the 30%, that were accepted are predominantly concentrated in and around the metropolitan area of Istanbul.

KOSGEB is also actively involved in the intermediation and allocation of structural funds, associated with Turkey's objective to become a member of the EU. A series of projects are either being implemented, or are in the pipeline, aimed at creating a number of European-Turkish Business Development Centres. More specifically plans range from business innovation centres, on-line information networks between local actors (the KOBINET project), and vocational training projects for specific sectors (*e.g.*, clothing), to cluster and small contractor development in car manufacturing in special industrial zones, and the elaboration of a Women's Entrepreneurial Management Support System. These are but a few examples of the useful strategic intermediary and buffering role of KOSGEB within projects involving technical co-operation with the EU.

Regional or local design and delivery of initiatives could extend KOSGEB's reach. The agency allocates support and grants to SMEs to fund managerial and technological upgrading by reviewing their business plans. While KOSGEB is in the process of doing a general overview of its clients to strengthen its database, a future alternative would be to give local partners greater responsibility for the management of programmes and client management. Experience in other OECD countries has shown that the use of local institutions in designing and delivering programmes is particularly effective for extending programme reach. In that respect, the role of many European regional development agencies have shown an effective track record in mobilising local stakeholders (such as local governments, labour unions, business associations and NGOs) in order to elaborate and deliver better projects with the available resources.

The challenges facing the textile and clothing sector are substantial, specifically in terms of its difficulty to implement strategies of technological and managerial modernisation. That said there are promising signs that this segment is transforming into a business development system in which local stakeholders are taking a relatively active role in management and decision-making. The sector is represented by the Turkish Clothing Manufacturers' Association (TGSD), a private voluntary participation organisation with approximately 4 000 members, and the Istanbul Textile and Clothing Export Union (ITKIB), a semi-public organisation under the Under-Secretariat of the Prime Ministry for Foreign Trade, with some 28 000 members (approximately 5 000 clothing exporters) as all textile and clothing exporters are required by law to be members. The number of firms in the industry quadrupled in the 1990s; a phenomenon fuelled by export incentives, a historical technical tradition of skills since the Ottoman Empire, a strong international demand and relatively low labour costs. According to a recent survey of 159 textile sector firms done by Riddle and Gillespie (2003), 60% of those interviewed confirmed that their firm had been created in the 1990s. The newcomers to the sector, with relatively little know-how of and experience with new export markets, highly appreciated ITKIB services (between seven to eight range out of ten) specifically those related to export-oriented market research and other information sharing mechanisms. New venture firms, and those exporting only to less developed markets (*i.e.*, non European segments) rated the role of ITKIB as even more important.

In the business development and SME support initiatives managed by KOSGEB, little attention was paid to the potential of regional and local clustering, or the role of collaborative stakeholders' networks of component suppliers, universities and business associations. The main advantages of clusters are seen in lowering transaction costs and in positive external effects through spatial proximity of relevant actors and other companies contributing to the production chain. Companies within clusters are considered to achieve higher productivity and innovation rates through closer information exchange, lowering costs through spatial proximity of suppliers and enhanced competitiveness through increased competition (McKinsey, 2003). In the context of Istanbul, strengthening the networks between firms, encouraging links up and down supply chains, and internationally should be a priority for regional economic development actors. International evidence shows a range of potentially complementary instruments, such as buyer and supplier fairs, the provision of real and financial services to early-stage clusters, financial and tax incentives to specific sub-contracting procedures and information sharing on production chains.

The concept of clustering and clustering policies is relatively new in Turkey. Considering the ambitious policy agenda for establishing an economic transformation towards high-end and niche sectors, it is surprising that little attention has been paid to clustering and clustering policies. The few clustering experiences have been largely driven by private sector initiatives. However, policy makers in Turkey have also increasingly become aware of the strategic role of public policies in the development and stimulation of clusters. For instance, in the context of the pre-accession programme to the EU, Turkey has signed the European charter for small- and medium-sized enterprises,[6] and had made progress with the formulation of a SME Strategy and Action Plan in 2003. In 2005, an EU-financed programme was started, which involved the Under-Secretariat for Foreign Trade (UFT), the Turkish Exporters Union, KOSGEB, the State Planning

Organization, the Under-Secretariat for Treasury, and a series of provincial chambers of trade and/or industry, and universities. The basic objective of the programme is to develop a comprehensive and strategic vision for a cluster policy in Turkey, and to build human and institutional capacity to set in motion the implementation of this vision. The project is organised in two different stages. In the first one, capacity building and institutional strengthening of UFT and related organisations will be undertaken through training, study missions and the elaboration of manuals and tool-books on clusters and cluster policy. In the second stage, ten priority clusters will be mapped and specific business plans and proposals will be developed, for example for the joint acquisition of equipment and common infrastructure.

A similar approach is being followed by another project that is financed by the EU for the textile and clothing sector. Its main objective is to prepare the sector for the growing international competition that is expected within the context of the increased liberalisation of the clothing and textile markets from 2005 onwards. The first phase of the project is aimed mainly at the institutional strengthening and capacity building of the sector. This will be done through the creation of a Cluster Co-ordination Agency, a Textile R&D centre and a Fashion Institute. Moreover, this phase will strengthen and update the role of ITKIB in providing collective services for stimulating clusters, *e.g.*, through joint business plans and investment proposals. In the second stage, collective investment proposals are elaborated, which could be forwarded and financed by the EU-Turkey Financial Cooperation Program. Although these initiatives are promising steps in the direction of a broad-based territorial cluster policy, more progress should be made in light of the rapid and intense restructuring that is taking place in clothing and textiles. Substantial challenges can also be expected in business segments characterised by a prevailing culture of low cost "cut throat" competition, and of triggering "a rat race to the bottom" in terms of cutting profit margins and overheads. Instead, clustering presupposes efforts towards collective action in order to establish positive synergic benchmarking for the sector as a whole.

Particular attention should be devoted to micro-firms. In many cities there is a wide technology gap between these firms and the sector of internationally competitive, export-oriented firms (in the wealthier metro-regions, the former sector is large; and the latter is quite small.) While lack of access to modern equipment is a clear problem for micro-firms, lack of information about production methods and processes also appears to undermine the productivity of individual firms and whole sectors. Strong co-operative production chains, including links between SMEs and larger more competitive firms are hampered by weaknesses in areas such as standardisation, quality control and just-in-time management. Addressing the technology and information gaps is critical to enabling small industries to achieve higher levels of productivity and reduce polarisation of the economy. The challenge for public policy is to reach these firms through a cost-effective enterprise development strategy. The difficulty is that the enterprise base is large and geographically diffuse, combined with the fact that firms can be informal or semi-formal and, as such, hard to influence through public policy. Facilitating access to financing and creating venture capital systems are the most effective policies for overcoming the low capital structure and lack of access to technology of micro-firms. Other policies include establishing research institutes that micro-firms can utilise without paying high fees. But some also argue that strict rules to protect intellectual rights also harm the ability of micro-firms to access new technology as these firms could otherwise imitate existing technology.

Informal economy

As mentioned in Chapter 1, there is a large and relatively vibrant informal economy that has developed over time in Istanbul. Estimates on the distribution of unregistered workers in different segments show that the informal economy may account for up to 30% of the overall metropolitan economy. In general, there is a need to get additional and more accurate information about the dynamics of the informal economy. Empirical studies on unregistered work have been undertaken in such sectors as luggage trading, street vending, home-based economic activities (largely carried out by women), self-help and self-construction in squatter settlements. These studies have shown that the sector performs an important role in compensating for the short-term negative effects associated with structural adjustment and crisis situations (Onis and Rubin, 2001). Traditionally, informal economic activity has been viewed as a concentration of negative externalities including taxation leakages, unfair competition, costs associated with the illegal inflow of immigrants, and deterioration of urban public spaces. Generally the informal economy is also less productive than the formal economy. Therefore, modernising it and integrating it into the formal economy would help to address the productivity challenge.

Substantively eliminating the informal economy is a long-term policy goal, involving actions from several sectoral authorities, at the local and national government levels, as well as combining experience and information from different sectors of society. To succeed, clear leadership should be defined at an appropriate government institution, representatives from the private sector should be invited to jointly define the best courses of action and an effective governance arrangement should be in place to push forward the overall strategy. Periodic reports to local and national authorities on the advancement and obstacles met along the process could be considered to secure that all actors are adequately presented with the right incentives to participate, as well as to secure the necessary support from the top authorities. There is merit in considering a more bottom-up approach to controlling (not "solving") the problem through greater involvement of local government and the private sector in collaboration with national policy makers. Local government could be effective at addressing issues of corruption by improving the capacity to provide or better co-ordinate local services such as licensing, permitting, zoning and land use regulation, parking, security, garbage collection, transportation. Local government can also promote formalisation through appropriate incentives, *e.g.*, by reducing local red tape, simplifying export rules and regulations, potentially creating a free trade zone or a tax cut, or more efficient and speedier tax rebates.

One of the most important actions to take is to address the legal framework for micro-firms, which constitute an important part of the informal economy. In general, the informal way of doing business in small economic units is not motivated by the will to infringe laws and regulations on behalf of their owners, but by the fact that those laws and regulations have been designed and prescribed in the past by legislatures or executive authorities, with larger economic units in mind. Simply, very small firms that struggle every day to keep in business struggle, or simply cannot, honour the rights and obligations included in those laws and regulations. Therefore, informality tends to arise in economic activities typically performed by very small firms, as is usually the case in services. In Istanbul, laws and regulations in place imply that firms must incur labour related costs that are about 50% of wages and salaries paid directly to workers. The economy of the metropolitan area is comprised to a very large extent of service activities, in which firms are usually of rather small size. Under these conditions, it is easy to understand why non-compliance with said laws and regulations is widespread (in other words, why the informal economy is large in the metropolitan area).

Efforts should be put towards moving to a more modern, realistic and effective legal framework adequately suited for very small firms. Merely strengthening local enforcement efforts of existing laws and regulations is not sufficient. There is instead a need for the combination of several legal and regulatory reforms by corresponding authorities. On labour and social security matters, reforms are called for to lower costs on top of wages for firms, so that they can afford compliance. The benefits that would spring out of this are twofold: employers would enjoy larger juridical certainty from compliance with legislation, and this would likely induce more investment and higher productivity; and workers would enjoy better legal protection from adequate labour contracts, plus access to practical levels of social security (health-care, pensions, etc.). In addition, reforms on the fiscal side should be considered to facilitate compliance for small firms. In the experience of other OECD member countries, this usually calls for: (1) reducing formalities and paperwork, by in depth simplification of tax declarations and the periodicity with which these must be made; (2) establishing flat taxing schemes, to free small firms from complex calculations (avoiding specific deductions, varying tax rates for a number of different income brackets, eliminating specific accounting practices, etc.); (3) improving tax collection efforts, for which more participation of local authorities can be effective, given that the cost/benefit of tax collection from small firms could be relatively lower for local than for national authorities (for example, collection of flat taxes from small firms can be delegated to local government and the resulting income largely or entirely allocated to it, based on contracts between the national and local governments). Meanwhile, simplification or deregulation on local matters, related for example with environmental and safety aspects, should also be considered for small firms. Usually, in the experience of many OECD member countries, complex or relatively opaque procedures linked to inspection by local officials, generate conditions that only marginally reach the fundamental objectives targeted, while they open opportunity for corruption and extortion that harms small businesses.

Policy makers could, in addition to the long-term goal, seek to build upon the entrepreneurial assets present in the informal economy with suited support programmes to enhance the productivity of small firms. The luggage trade, the informal construction and speculative activities in the squatter settlements and the informal home-based economic activities, show that the informal economy needs greater diagnosis, and tailor-made policies and strategies to integrate, rather than exclude or ignore, this segment of the economy. There is room for further effort through initiatives aimed at capacity building, micro-credit and support to co-operatives and home-based activities of women. Although there is evidence of successful experiences of NGOs in strengthening and empowering home-based-workers, for example through the formation of home-workers co-operatives, there is a need for a broader policy framework that supports these rather isolated initiatives. Overall, there are few if any initiatives to develop alternative delivery mechanisms for business development services for the informal economy (such as incubators for co-operatives, micro-credit systems, one-stop business shops and similar initiatives). Experience in other countries has shown that communities must be able to identify which institutions are providing the services that impact their business. Only then are institutions able to extend the reach of their programmes. In addition the programmes should be adapted to the specific limits and potentialities of the target group. Micro-credit schemes for example, operate best through specially trained credit officers that go into the field and visit potential clients, and usually help them fill out the relatively simple forms. Along the same lines, capacity building and incubator programmes are likely to need a far more detailed implementation and monitoring process than is the case for firms in the formal economy.

The absence of instruments such as micro-credit is particularly remarkable in Turkey. In Asia, and in Latin American countries like Bolivia, Colombia and, more recently, Brazil, the use of micro-credit instruments has gone through considerable development and growth. In its more classical forms, micro-credit has substantially improved access to credit for the more vulnerable segments of the society, those typically involved in the informal sector. Working initially with small amounts of cash, micro-finance institutions directly present in the community through so-called "community credit-agents" substantially reduce the costs and risks associated with loan approval, monitoring, and control of loan repayment. They also serve as an effective social control exercised by the community itself on strict repayment of loans, flexible and relatively simple forms of collateral and loan approval procedures, and, last but not least, the possibility of co-operative and collective forms of collateral. These factors all contribute to stimulating low default rates and replicating small micro-credit schemes on a much larger scale. In countries such as Bangladesh, this instrument has penetrated large segments of society, and provides alternative and accessible forms of credit to SMEs and low-income households.

The informal suitcase trade, for example, is evidence that policy makers are under-utilising the entrepreneurial potential of this sector. There is ample evidence of a vibrant entrepreneurial spirit among the informal businesses of Istanbul and its direct surrounding area, like that of the informal suitcase trade between the Laleli neighbourhood of Istanbul and the former Soviet Union and its surrounding republics. Studies reveal that this trade was characterised by a diversity of goods and services that peaked in the late 1990s until the 1998 Russian crisis, generating approximately USD 5 billion in annual sales from some 5 000 shops (Eder, 2003). The extensive chain of activities and actors related to this kind of trade, from shop owners, travel agencies, customs agents and service suppliers, implied substantial direct and indirect backward and forward linkages. After the 1998 rouble crisis the suitcase trade went through a dramatic downsizing with trade volume down from over 100 000 tons in 1996 to only 12 000 tons by June 1999. Likewise, the number of flights to and from the Russian federation and the CIS countries (Commonwealth of Independent States) dropped from an annual figure of 28 040 flights, and more than 2 million passengers, in 1997, to 5 301 flights, and 383 537 passengers, by June 1999. Finally, it should be noted that the official Russian governmental policy was aimed at reducing this type of trade flows.

The strength of the suitcase trade during the 1990s has revealed the remarkable entrepreneurial spirit of community networks aimed at income and employment generation. Surviving macroeconomic crisis has only reinforced these networks by forcing them to be more organised. Although at present there does not seem to be an overall strategy towards the sector, the entrepreneurial capacity could be reinforced and strengthened though intelligent formalisation strategies based on subsidised conditional forms of (micro) credit, capacity building, and information sharing on market segments and managerial modernisation. More specifically, a mechanism is needed to provide the sector with easy access to credit. For example, the research on suitcase commerce showed that the bulk of transactions were made in cash, to impede the government's ability to track informal transactions. At best, and only after the accumulation of sufficient levels of social capital and trust among buyers and sellers, alternative forms of consumer credit could be supplied.

The role of small and traditional street-corner commerce also requires special attention. These are typically employment-intensive sectors that face severe competition from the bigger (international) retailers. Both the ongoing spatial and sectoral restructuring show a tendency of internationalisation of the commercial areas (retailing sector), threatening the survival of the smaller commercial districts. In addition, entry of international retail networks and mall developments are also having a spin-off effect on the real estate sector, intensifying the crowding-out effects on traditional retail outlets and street corner commerce. The more recent data on FDI do indeed confirm the rapid entrance of larger internationally oriented shopping areas and retail outlets. Despite facing severe challenges that will likely continue, traditional forms of retailing persist all over the city. Unofficial estimates show that the number of traditional corner shops decreased from 16 527 in 1987 to 11 800 in 1992. While the administration is keen on relocating some of the commerce out of the inner city, the relocation projects have not resulted in desirable effects, as evidenced in the wholesale fresh produce market and the hardware/industrial spare parts district (located in the Beyoğlu district). As the restructuring and relocation process continues, the government could do more to facilitate the process by using associations such as retailer organisations to facilitate urban development. The Business Improvement Districts (BDI) programme in Michigan in the United States is an example of an approach for managing districts undergoing transformation. The scheme's objective is to finance and implement a series of small investments earmarked for specific territories. A special levy on the property tax is used to finance collective services such as business plans, mutual credit and guarantee schemes, parking facilities, renovation of building structures and facades of shops, marketing programmes, improved visual communication, street cleaning, lighting and security. Typically, the efforts of SMEs are reinforced by the local government, which also steps in with additional investments and maintenance. International evidence, specifically from the inner cities in Canada and the United States, show remarkable success in terms of diversifying and integrating districts into the overall urban and socio-economic fabric of cities through public-private partnerships (Box 2.3).

Box 2.3. **The role of business improvement districts in Michigan, United States**

Business Improvement Districts (BIDs) are an expansion of the Principal Shopping Districts Act of 1961. BIDs allow qualified downtown and commercial areas (including multiple units of government) of cities to levy a special assessment (in addition to *ad valorem* property taxes) for district improvement. Tax revenues may be bonded against to finance district improvements. Similar to Principal Shopping Districts, only cities (or groups of cities) may establish Business Improvement Districts.

Established BIDs or Principal Shopping Districts may do all of the following within the district (see statute for a complete listing):

- Open, widen, extend or realign highways, and construct, maintain, or relocate pedestrian walkways. Also, BIDs may prohibit vehicular traffic where necessary and prohibit parking on highways.
- Acquire, own, maintain and improve properties and off-street parking lots, and contract for the operation and maintenance of off-street parking lots.
- Construct and maintain malls with bus stops and information centres that serve the public interest.
- Promote economic activity in the district, specifically by initiating market research, public relations campaigns, institutional promotions and sponsorship of special events and related activities.

Concerning the terms and performance guarantees, upon appointment a district governing board may avail itself of a host of financing methods for district improvement. These include, but are not limited to: local unit general revenues, revenue bonds, general obligation bonds, special assessments, grants or gifts. Any bond, note or other obligation used for BID financing must not exceed an interest rate of 10% or be sold at a discount of more than 10%.

Box 2.3. The role of business improvement districts in Michigan, United States *(cont.)*

Business Improvement Districts are governed by a locally determined board consisting of the following representatives:

- One appointee from each city in the BID, as designated by the chief executive officer of each city in the BID, subject to the approval of the legislative body of each city.

- Business representatives of the BID as nominated by businesses and property owners in the BID.

If any single business or property owner is projected to pay more than 50% of the special assessment levied for district improvement, then that business or property interest shall constitute a majority of the total board membership. If a city or set of cities in a BID choose to levy a special assessment, then they must develop a marketing and development plan, and identify the different classes of property owners who are going to be assessed and the respective assessment amounts. For BIDs created after 14 July 1992, revenues from special assessments may not exceed USD 10 000 per parcel.

Successful Business Improvement Districts in other major cities (*i.e.*, New York, Philadelphia) led to the passage of the law on BIDs in the state of Michigan.

Source: Citizen´s Research Council of Michigan, "Survey of Economic Development Programs in Michigan", *www.crcmich.org/EDSurvey/financg-taxauthorities/bid.html.*

A promising approach made up of broad-based and integrated reforms aimed at the reduction of informality can be seen in Mexico. The Mexican federal government has become aware that the legal framework surrounding the many smaller enterprises has become inadequate. Considering the large number of smaller firms, there are insufficient instruments to guarantee enforcement of labour and social insurance legislation. In addition, the existing legislation is applied homogeneously, and does not allow for differentiation between smaller and larger business units, the latter typically having important economies of scale and facilities to comply with existing rules and regulations. Moreover, unionisation in smaller business units is typically less frequent in light of the direct bilateral negotiations between the small number of employees and the owner. Therefore, the Mexican approach aims to streamline and simplify the regulatory framework for smaller businesses, thereby creating the basic conditions for formalisation. At the same time, an integrated approach aimed at the *microeconomic* inclusion of the so-called "moderately poor" (a target group located in between the extremely poor and the non-poor segments, which has been growing over the last few years) is realised through programmes aimed at adult education, creation of school certification, labour training and the provision of child-care facilities. Finally, tailor-made complementary programmes are designed to increase the number of formal self-employed micro-businesses (*e.g.*, through micro-finance or insurance schemes), or the wage employment in formal establishments (through one-stop business schemes, incentives on sub-contracting or credit schemes, to mention a few examples) (Sojo and Villarreal, 2004). In Brazil, similar legislation aimed at simplifying the legal and tax environment of micro-enterprises is presently being discussed by the federal parliament. If approved in its present format, the law is expected to have a positive effect on the reduction of informality.

FDI policies

As part of the internationalisation of the economy, Turkey's ability to attract more foreign direct investment (FDI) has become a priority. As noted in Chapter 1, Turkey is becoming a more attractive investment option, particularly for European investors. Moreover, the recent trends of FDI inflow confirm Istanbul's attractiveness in sectors such as finance, trade, transport and communications. Providing an environment attractive to FDI has become important because production fragmentation has resulted in a growing importance of trade and investment flows between countries (and regions). Across the OECD, foreign multi-national affiliates are growing in importance. In addition to FDI as an important source of jobs, FDI can bring with it the opportunity for domestic firms to link into global value chains as suppliers, and opportunities for direct and indirect forms of technology transfer. Foreign affiliates are on average more labour productive than the average domestic firm. They also make a significant contribution to labour productivity growth. Multi-nationals also tend to encourage local capacity building, and FDI often results in movements of people, demonstration effects and increased competition.

In addition to the general macroeconomic structural adjustment programmes implemented in Turkey following the 2000-2001 crises, several specific measures for FDI promotion have been introduced. One is the Improvement of the Investment Environment Coordination Board (IIECB) a body chaired by the State Minister for the Economy and composed of both private and public sector actors whose aim is to provide advice on improving the investment environment, particularly in Istanbul. Formation of the IIECB represents a significant change in bureaucrats' and politicians' outlook towards foreign investment as bureaucracy and business gather on the same platform for the first time. This board has already achieved concrete results from 2003-2006 by legislating 30 new regulations. In addition, the new Foreign Investment Law, provide several facilities for attracting FDI. For example, the approval procedures – based on bureaucratic screening and evaluation – have been removed and substituted with a legal notification mechanism. In addition, no minimum capital is required anymore, which puts national and international firms on a level playing field and is still in line with international legislation. Turkey has also signed several international treaties that have created a more liberal investment climate. Moreover, the country has made progress in deregulating national product and factor markets, and reducing social security and tax payments, which are important steps toward increasing cost competitiveness. Recently, the Turkish Promotion Agency has been formed, and has started works for the formation of 26 regional development agencies (two have been already established, one in Izmir and the other in Çukurova).

Programmes facilitating links between domestic firms and multi-nationals in the region (backward links) are a means for capturing FDI benefits from the introduction of new technologies and management skills. Specifically in strategic sectors that are going through a rapid process of modernisation and development, such as tourism, logistics and finance, a more pro-active policy stance should be taken for capturing technological and managerial spin-off from FDI. The logistics sector, for example, is a typical example where FDI inflow can help to increase the scale of enterprises and upgrade managerial practices. As mentioned in Chapter 1, there is promising evidence of an increasing flow of FDI in this sector. Backward links are considered to be the strongest and most consistent forms of positive FDI spillover. An example of a successful programme for strengthening links between domestic firms and multi-nationals is Ireland's National Linkage Programme (Box 2.4).

Building a regional hub

Logistics (including port strategy)

Transforming Istanbul into a regional logistics hub will depend on the intensification of relations with existing and potential trading partners and the development of transnational transport infrastructure. Since the 1980s Turkey has been implementing an export-led trading regime, and is now becoming more pro-active in the co-ordination and harmonisation of economic and trade relations within the region. The National Development Plan is setting targets to facilitate integration with the Trans-European, Europe-Middle East and national road network, and to undertake detailed studies for the improvement of the sea and maritime ports. A number of international co-operation projects have also been initiated with strategic partner countries, including:

Box 2.4. National Linkages Programme: Ireland

Since the mid-1980s, Enterprise Ireland (EI) has been operating various linkage programmes to integrate foreign enterprises into the Irish economy. It pursues two tasks: first, to support Irish enterprise efforts to build capacity, and innovate and create new partnerships; and second, to assist international investors reach suppliers in Ireland. EI collaborates closely with foreign affiliates, their parent multi-nationals, and the various government agencies involved with local suppliers. Between 1985 and 1987, an estimated 250 foreign affiliates were actively involved in the linkage programme. During that period, affiliates operating in Ireland increased their purchases of local raw materials fourfold, from IEP 438 million (Irish pounds) to IEP 1 831 million, and more than doubled their purchases of services from IEP 980 million to over IEP 2 billion. In the electronics industry alone, the value of inputs sourced locally rose from 12% to 20%. On average, suppliers saw their sales increase by 83%, productivity by 36% and employment by 33%.

EI's matchmaking worked closely with foreign affiliates to ensure suppliers were capable of achieving the demand and quality requirements. One of EI's key criteria used for selecting local suppliers was their management team's attitude and potential to grow. Also noteworthy is that EI's matchmaking is no longer seen as so critical. The need diminished over time as the composition of affiliates, their motivations for locating in Ireland, and their local knowledge, changed. Ireland's competitive advantages in the global value chain became generally recognised.

Source: UNCTAD (2005), *World Investment Report 2005: Transnational Corporations and the Internationalization of R&D*, UNCTAD, United States.

- *The Transport Corridor Europe-Caucasus-Asia (TRACECA):* the project, signed in 1998, has as its explicit objective to stimulate the development of economic relations, trade and communication in Europe, the Black Sea Region, Caucasus, the Caspian Sea region and Asia. The project has been actively supported by the EU through funds for capacity building, technical assistance and infrastructure investments aimed at the improvement of roads, railways and commercial navigation in the region.

- *Organization of the Black Sea Economic Cooperation (BSEC)*: With the entry into force of its Charter on 1 May 1999, BSEC acquired its international legal identity and was transformed into a full-fledged regional economic organisation. It is composed of Albania, Armenia, Azerbaijan, Bulgaria, Georgia, Greece, Moldova, Romania, Serbia, Russia, Turkey and Ukraine. It came into existence as a unique and promising model of multi-lateral political and economic initiative aimed at fostering interaction and harmony among the Member States, as well as to ensure peace, stability and prosperity encouraging friendly and good-neighbourly relations in the Black Sea region. The BSEC Headquarters is in Istanbul.

- *The Trans-European Networks (TENs).* In order to promote the interconnection and interoperability of national networks as well as access to such networks as a key element for the creation of the internal market and the reinforcement of economic and social cohesion, the EU has developed guidelines covering the objectives, priorities and identification of projects of common interest for the transport, energy and telecommunications sectors. The rationale behind the Trans-European Networks Policy is that it makes little sense to talk of a single market with freedom of movement within it for goods, persons and services, unless the various regions and national networks making up that market are properly linked by modern and efficient infrastructure. As a negotiating candidate country to the EU, Turkey is working with the EU Commission to jointly develop the technical specifications of the extension of the Trans-European Networks to Turkey. More specifically, as part of the accession process to the EU, policy makers in Turkey have started to move toward the European Spatial Development Perspective, which implies a common framework for transportation, land use and spatial planning. Here expectations are that Istanbul will perform a crucial role. For example, the Trans-European Motorway, designed to trigger more intense trading links between Turkey and the countries of the Mediterranean and the Adriatic Sea was allocated substantial funds in order to improve the transportation axes.

A number of actions have also been taken to promote an efficient combination of different transportation modes. The government's latest National Development Plan acknowledges the importance of increasing capacity to manage increasing trade demand, both through expansion and shifting the modal transport split away from trucks to other transportation modes (railways, maritime and seaports). Actually, the disequilibrium in the modal split is an issue when evaluating urban transport: almost all of the domestic logistic operations arrive and leave Istanbul by road, with negligible sea and railway transportation participation. The disequilibrium has obvious negative externalities on the overall efficiency of the transportation system in terms of congestion, pollution and environmental deterioration for both the city and the country. An explicit effort is being undertaken by the city to increase the rail travel for passengers from the present 7% to 28% in the medium run (2010), and to 43% in the longer run (2023), by extending the railway network. The government of Turkey has also been active in implementing measures aimed at reducing overlapping competencies and encouraging competition among the many public bodies responsible for planning, operating and regulating urban transportation. At the municipal level, Istanbul has been investing in better integration and co-ordination between the different modes of transportation through "intelligent systems", and physical investment in the port and railway network.

Istanbul needs to address several bottlenecks to increase the competitiveness of its logistical hub. While the physical capacity of the ports needs to be augmented, the managerial and financial approaches of the sector also need to be streamlined in line with international best practice. The business segment is characterised by a large number of small family-based enterprises with relatively traditional managerial practices, and a lack of scale. Moreover, the sector needs to speed up the introduction of multi-modality and "intelligent" integrated logistical management in order to provide more value-added to the cargo that is being handled by the city. Transportation modes by rail, road and water need to be better connected and storage and warehousing capacity for containers developed. In practice, container depots are scattered throughout the city, which increases fragmentation and logistical challenges. Finally, and thereby contributing to the modernisation of Istanbul's logistics hub, new actors, such as the private sector and foreign investors, have recently entered the sector. This process needs to be accelerated, however, for example, by efficient information sharing on the prospects of the sector, regulatory and managerial reform and investment in macro-infrastructure.

Transforming the city of Istanbul into a logistical hub does not necessarily involve increasing capacity. Logistics hub capacity should be measured in terms of value-added, and not only incremental volume or throughout. Currently, Istanbul's ports, especially Ambarlı, have the greatest capacity in Turkey. Part of the planned capacity expansion of the Turkish port system will also take place outside Istanbul, with TEU 5 830 000[7] after 2010, TEU 3 200 000 of which will be concentrated in Istanbul. Nevertheless, on the international scale, the most competitive ports are not necessarily those with the highest volume of cargo, but rather those that possesses the most "intelligent" port systems, *i.e.*, capable of planning and managing a chain of activities for their clients (just-in-time management, insurance, economies of scope, distribution, finance, etc.). "Intelligent" port systems tend to be more sustainable, generate higher value added and, in general, are working with several smaller, flexible – and networked – retro ports that specialise in specific products. Given the important environmental concerns in Istanbul, especially related to the over-use of the Strait of Istanbul, such an approach would be even more appropriate.

Several actions could be taken to improve the management and operation of Istanbul's ports. This will require increased participation of the private sector in investment, operations and maintenance of new ports (for example through Build Operate and Transfer [BOT] schemes), and the dissemination of new information technology aimed at more effective port management. The Turkish Republic State Railways (TCDD, Türkiye Cumhuriyeti Devlet Demiryolları) – the owners and operators of part of the Turkish ports – are increasingly transferring responsibilities for operations and maintenance to the private sector, like the planned transfer of 99 depots in an effort to create employment and improve service delivery. However, there is a need for continued decentralisation of efforts in this area since in Turkey it is still by and large a national affair. International experience shows that productive restructuring is often accompanied by bringing in a city's active stakeholders in the transformation of port systems (local governments, trade unions and business associations, infrastructure operators, freight companies, etc.). At the same time, local stakeholders in port management (freight forwarders, businesses) should also be actively involved in setting up new market and product combinations in order to position ports in the global economy. In that sense, ports (and their hinterland territories) need to become more pro-active players in terms of redefining their roles in the international economy.

Istanbul's port strategy also has to fit into a broader strategy for urban development. At the moment, there are several ports in Istanbul: Ambarlı, Zeyport, Haydarpaşa, Salıpazarı and the newer Derince and Pendik. While it has proven difficult to obtain detailed information on specific projects, the overall strategy in recent plans seems to be aimed at relocating port activities out of the city centre, specifically in light of the limited available space and the potential nuisance and pollution generated by the port. Broadly speaking, while the Salıpazarı and Zeyport ports are important for passenger transportation, Pendik and Ambarlı are expected to play an increasingly important role in logistics for the city. For instance, the Haydarpaşa port and railway complex, located within the city limits (residential part of the city), will be abolished as a port and returned to the city authority who is currently reviewing proposals to transform it into a hotel complex with office towers. Likewise, an ambitious project for the Salıpazarı complex is to transform it into a cruise port for luxury vessels. Meanwhile, the Ambarlı complex, managing predominantly container and international rural goods trade, has been expanding with substantial private investments but has some infrastructure deficiencies. Although it is not located right in the centre of the city (it is 34 km away) it is still within the metropolitan area, and the debate over the extension of the port continues to raise concerns among those that seek to further relieve the congested metro-area by investing instead in Izmit (located further away in the Kocaeli neighbouring province) and other stakeholders, especially from the private sector that have increased their stake through joint-ventures in the newly built terminals of the Ambarlı port complex.[8]

A good illustration of some of the ongoing challenges facing the transformation of port systems, and the insertion of an obsolete port area into the overall strategic urban development policy, can be found in Salıpazarı harbour. Over time, it has increasingly lost its cargo functions to the Haydarpaşa port, and more recently to the Zeyport area (the latter has better connectivity with the land transportation corridors) causing much debate and speculation. After declaring the port a "special tourism area" in 1993, the central government launched a proposal from the Ministry of Culture and Tourism to transform the area into a nodal point for international cruise ships with an adjacent international luxury shopping, hotel and business area. This designation meant that virtually all decision-making processes would be centralised, with little room for local stakeholder involvement. Moreover, from international experience it is well known that projects aimed at the transformation of former harbour areas into commercial and tourist destinations are in general quite polemic, and receive a good deal of critical feedback from professional organisations and NGOs. In the particular case of the Salıpazarı harbour, the local neighbourhood association forwarded an alternative project, providing mixes of residential use, preservation of high-quality public space, hotels and restaurants. Local transportation options also proved to be a limiting factor, as access would be largely limited to public lines and second tier arterial roads resulting in traffic congestion and an overload on the local infrastructure. In addition, the proposal included several contradicting options for the future role of the district that was being planned as a thriving area for finance, retail and tourism.

International cases provide important lessons for how the city of Istanbul can combine its initiatives to strengthen its international passenger function, and create good quality public space, residences and recreational value for the local inhabitants. Projects such as the one in the Salıpazarı harbour show several differences specifically in terms of the smaller size of the project, and the plan to retain the central business districts (CBD) (contrary to the typical American case). Like in other cases Istanbul must also elaborate and find new uses for obsolete land in and around the inner city port. In these respects a couple of lessons can be drawn in relation to this type of urban transformation project. First, it is important to apply an overall comprehensive planning approach, and to avoid a fast track implementation of specific projects, without consideration of their impact on the overall urban development pattern. Second, the involvement of local governments and community actors is strategic in order to bring more local information to the table, and to avoid false dichotomies.

Istanbul can learn from other OECD metro-regions that have been successfully transforming their inner-city ports into wise urban development projects. In competitive and successful port regions, public and private actors are collaborating in projects such as creating decentralised policy networks structured around themes such as the technological and logistical modernisation of port infrastructure, or the planning and implementation of special purpose projects. In that sense, the revitalisation and transformation of obsolete inner city port areas into mixed-use quality areas has become a logical consequence of this paradigm of pro-active involvement of local governments in the future of their ports. The Kop van Zuid Area, located in the city of Rotterdam, is a good example of such an approach (Box 2.5).

Box 2.5. **Linking cities and their ports: the example of the "Kop van Zuid" project in the city of Rotterdam, Netherlands**

In the 1970s, the port of Rotterdam started to lose part of its competitive position to the Asian ports and European cities such as Hamburg and Antwerp. Rotterdam's focus was on maximising the volume of cargo and transit through its port, with limited effort dedicated to developing capacity to add value through logistics and additional services for its clients. The more dynamic parts of the port system had also increasingly been relocated to the outskirts of metropolitan Rotterdam, more specifically to meet the need for larger storage areas and more profound waters, neither of which were in the older inner city port areas.

At the same time, many of the older inner city port areas had become obsolete, and transformed into problem areas characterised by high levels of unemployment, social exclusion of the local (immigrant) inhabitants, and an overall deterioration of the urban public space. The socio-economic stigma within the overall urban fabric of Rotterdam was only further aggravated by the fact that the course of the river separated the port area from the CBD, generating serious challenges in terms of accessibility to and from the area.

While previous social housing programmes had been developed for the area, they were never implemented. By the end of the 1980s, the city of Rotterdam started to implement – together with actors from the private sector and the civil society – a series of strategic planning exercises aimed at developing a vision for the future of the city and its port. According to the Rotterdam 2045 scenario, the city would have to create more value added out of its port by upgrading its logistical and informational infrastructure. Moreover, it would have to increase its flexibility through the implementation of smaller networked retro-port systems.

Box 2.5. **Linking cities and their ports: the example of the "Kop van Zuid" project in the city of Rotterdam, Netherlands** (*cont.*)

Ironically enough, and quite similar to other port cities around the world, this scenario would open a concrete incentive for re-establishing the link between the city and its port by relocating some of the more high-tech components of port management back to the city. Likewise, according to this vision, Rotterdam would also have to work on its somewhat negative image as having a low degree of liveability in terms of the lack of quality urban public space, options for leisure, hotels and restaurants.

Therefore, the vision for the future included a series of innovative urban projects, generating good quality urban public space, interesting urban design and an attractive environment for new business and residents. This strategic scenario also re-opened the debate over the future of the obsolete inner city Kop van Zuid Area. Through a competition of ideas with the participation of various international architects, a more detailed concept for the area was developed, according to which green areas and high-quality public space, tourism (hotels, restaurants, and cinemas), high-quality residential areas and logistical economic activities aimed at the port were combined. One of the flagship elements of the project was the highly attractive Erasmus Bridge, which connected the formerly isolated Kop van Zuid Area with the inner CBD. In a way, the bridge represented a symbol for the future of the city according to which the port and its area had found a new equilibrium.

The project is expected to be completed in 2010 and has contributed to the effective revitalisation of the area. Of course, a huge urban transformation project like this was not without its problems. Initially, also as a consequence of the lack of community participation, there was a widespread criticism on the lack of social housing in the overall project. As a consequence, developers had to buy the right to build extra apartment units through the mixing of lower income units and the preferred number of apartments units.

Source: Rotterdam City Development Corporation (1993), "Metropolis in the Making", Rotterdam.

Financial and service centre

As mentioned in Chapter 1, Istanbul has become an important player on the financial and banking markets, within the Eurasia region, but still confronts significant challenges to truly become a regional financial hub. The Istanbul Stock Exchange (ISE/İMKB) has registered a significant increase in the total value of both stocks and bonds trading but the lack of financial instruments and big institutional international investors along with a low level of saving prevent it from reaching a higher capitalisation rate. Weaknesses include the large dominance of the capital markets by securities (mostly public) over stock and other financial instruments. The banking sector, more experienced than other places in the Eurasia region needs further restructuring to become more competitive. For the moment, competition remains limited, large banking groups are lacking and thus high intermediary costs are not attractive.

The Istanbul Stock Exchange (ISE/İMKB) is expected to continue to play an increasingly strategic role contributing to the city's competitiveness on the financial markets. Although the 2000-2001 crisis took a toll on the credibility of the financial sector in general, and the banks in particular, the post 2001 reforms have been relatively successful in gradually rebuilding confidence, and expanding the role of intermediary financial institutions and the ISE. First, establishing a more centralised Banking Regulation and Supervision Agency (BRSA/BDDK), and the creation of a Savings Deposit Insurance Fund (SDIF/TMSF), with its own Board of Directors, has lead to a more solid regulatory framework, which was considered to be one of the key elements lacking at the time of the 2000-2001 crisis. Second, new legislation like Law No. 5411 contributes to bringing the regulatory framework into compliance with EU directives and international standards. Third, the role of public banks and the political influence on the financial sector performance has been gradually diminishing. Finally, the ISE has become increasingly aware of its international strategic role in harmonising and standardising regional capital markets. For example, in 1985 it became a member of the World Federation of Exchanges (WFE). ISE is also a founding member of the Istanbul-based Federation of Euro-Asian Stock Exchanges (FEAS), an organisation aimed at integrating capital markets and harmonising the framework of financial regulation.

Further reforms are needed to strengthen the banking sector and consequently the financial sector (Box 2.6). With new disinflation policies the high burden of transaction and intermediary costs on the banking sector increasingly became a significant obstacle to achieve the goal of creating an international hub. While the economy has begun to experience macroeconomic stability, private savings have decreased and a serious increase in current account deficit has occurred. Lacking the resources to finance the growing economy, the banking sector needs to increase shareholder equity to meet potential increases in credit demand. However, even if an increase in shareholder's equity has been realised, high transaction costs may force domestic firms to turn to foreign sources for financial resources (İnan, 2004). Thus the Turkish banking sector may be on the edge of facing serious competitive pressure in the short and medium run. Reducing the high transaction and intermediary costs must be the objective of policy makers to promote Istanbul's goal of becoming an international financial hub.

Box 2.6. Banking sector reform in Turkey

The banking sector's contribution to the economic growth performance of Turkey remained very limited in the past because of general economic instability and an inefficient public banking sector with revenues lost in hidden accounts. This undesirable structure was a contributing factor to the November 2000 and February 2001 crises, and has motivated a series of structural reforms, also meant to make Turkey a more attractive candidate for EU consideration. The Banking Sector Restructuring Program, enacted in 2001, was intended to strengthen the sector, specifically by contributing to financing economic growth. With the help of economic recovery, the restructuring programme brought about significant improvements in various fields, including the asset size of the sector, capital adequacy ratio, volume and quality of loans, etc. The sector's risk management capacity also improved as a result of legal regulations. However further prudential regulations, in line with international best practices, are needed to sustain improvements in the banking sector such as:

- Establish an efficient early warning system to detect open position and balance sheet mismatches in the banking sector.
- Maintain public banks operation at arms-length from government with explicit budgeting of their policy missions.
- Continue recapitalisation of private banks according to Basel rules and limit intra-group lending.
- Improve transparency and accountability through the Banking Supervision Agency.
- Minimise systemic risks arising from the non-bank foreign exchange exposure of bank borrowers.

Source: Republic of Turkey, (2004), *Pre-accession Economic Programme 2004, National Report of Turkey, Ankara* and OECD (2006), *OECD Economic Surveys: Turkey*, OECD Publications, OECD

The policies that are necessary for increasing the financial competitiveness of Turkey are mostly regulatory in nature. Effective licensing of financial market workers, and the resultant increase in the capabilities of the people who advise investors, has proven to have considerable positive effects during the last few years. Formation of strong and competitive intermediary institutions in financial markets is crucial in reaching out to investors. Currently, 85% of the activities of intermediary institutions are on stocks. Were these institutions to deal only in other activities, they would be able to cover only 16% of their operation costs. This clearly shows how dependent the financial intermediary institutions are on the stock exchange and emphasises the need for a deeper market for a stronger financial system. Deepening the financial market will require further amendments to the current legislation as well the issuance of different types of financial instruments like private equity investment, corporate bond in foreign currencies, etc.

There have been positive signs towards improving the competitive environment in the financial sector. The Banking Sector Restructuring Program, that went into effect in 2001, was intended to strengthen the sector and with the help of economic recovery, the restructuring programme brought about significant improvements in various fields, including the asset size of the sector, capital adequacy ratio, volume and quality of loans, etc. There has been considerable improvement especially in capital adequacy ratio that increased to 25.4% in June 2004 from 20.8% in 2001. Similarly, the share of loans of deposit banks in assets, which was at its historically lowest level with 17% in 2002, reached 28% in August 2004. The risk management capacity of the sector improved as a result of legal regulations and the share of non-performing loans in total loans, which was 17.6% in 2002, declined to 6.3% in June 2004. The competitive pressure is also expected to increase with Basel-II, a programme that is designed to improve risk measurement and management techniques. Continued fiscal reforms, principally aimed at the generation of prudent primary surpluses, will be crucial in cutting the vicious cycle between increased public sector borrowing requirements, high interest rates and the "public banking" of private sector banks (Akçay, 2003). If successful, the banking sector will become less dependent on public debt securities, and increase its portfolio towards its core business as a financial intermediary. In this virtuous scenario, increases in productive investment, financial and managerial modernisation of enterprises and higher economic growth figures will lead to a growing role of the ISE within the regional financial networks of the Eurasia region. As mentioned in Chapter 1, the large recent inflow of FDI in the segment of financial intermediation (USD 7 billion in 2006) is a strong sign of an ongoing restructuring process of the banking sector into the direction of a system with a larger scale, and a strengthened capacity to operate in an increasingly demanding and competitive international scenario.

These reforms are even more pressing since Istanbul will face tough competition, particularly from cities like Dubai. Over the last few years Dubai has made extensive efforts to foster its development into a regional financial hub in the Middle East (Box 2.7). Dubai's ongoing experience is particularly striking because it shows the potential of an aggressive and pro-active "differential branding" strategy: in a relatively short period it has transformed one of its impending economic threats – the excessive dependency on oil reserves within a scenario of fast depleting reserves – into an opportunity for sectors such as finance, urban development, real estate and business services. To compete more effectively, Istanbul needs to make more progress on integrating its marketing, urban and local economic development policies into a comprehensive strategy aimed at the transformation of the city.

An important development in Turkey's financial markets will be the introduction of a mortgage system. The public sector has a high debt stock that keeps the interest rates high and turning the financial system of the country to finance debt rotation. However, this cycle has been broken by the implementation of the last stabilisation programme. Given the decrease in interest rates and dissolution of factors that have prevented long-term low-interest opportunities to finance expenditures – one of which is the double digit inflation rates that have been going on for some decades – the mortgage system is expected to obtain a strong foothold in Turkey. By evolving saving and investment habits via long-term financial support, the system will offer a floor to increase liquidity in residential investments, which are by nature fixed assets. The mortgage system is expected to have a relatively strong effect on Istanbul's construction industry, which contributes to attracting international construction companies to Istanbul. The increased competition may increase building quality through competition and lead to innovation diffusion through the supply chains. Again, as mentioned before, positive evidence from the more recent inflow of FDI in construction and real estate seems to confirm this trend.

Tourism, events and international branding

The goal to strengthen tourism as part as the regional hub strategy has been explicitly stated in some strategic documents. For instance, Istanbul's Expert Commission Report within the *8th Five-Year Development Plan* (published by the State Planning Organization in 2000), and the *Istanbul 2023 Vision and Strategic Action Plan* (published by the Istanbul Metropolitan Municipality) articulate the municipal level efforts to link the city's urban heritage, culture, tourism and urban developing strategies. According to this vision, the city should increasingly take up its role as a world city within the regional network of cities by concentrating on its service, cultural, historical, financial and managerial command and control functions. Moreover, the *2010 Tourism Vision of Turkey* provides a comprehensive look at the city's tourism policy including concrete projects in particular locations within the city (Box 2.8). From the spatial perspective, this has been reflected in explicit land use and zoning guidelines.

Box 2.7. Restructuring in Dynamic Dubai

The explosive post-1990 growth record of Dubai should be seen in a broader context where two factors stand out. First, since the 1990s, policy makers have been actively working on the strategic diversification of its economy, motivated by the projected depletion of the Dubai oil reserves within two decades. Consequently, considerable targeted government support went into sectors like information technology, finance, tourism and real estate. Second, after the 9/11 attacks, it is estimated that some USD 200 billion of Arab investment funds have been drawn out of the United States and redirected to the Gulf Region.

Dubai has been able to benefit substantially from this re-allocation of portfolios. According to a recent survey on the location of new offices of international law firms, Dubai is one of the top choices, among cities such as Shanghai, Beijing, Taipei and Munich. One of the reasons mentioned is the city's strategic location in relation to the Gulf region. Therefore, especially in relation to firms that move into the region for the first time, Dubai is a logical location choice for firms involved in the larger international energy projects.

Within this broader context, Dubai has been able to show remarkable and fast progress in moving towards a knowledge-intensive economy, which specialises in finance, real estate, IT, business services and tourism. In terms of its financial sector, Dubai is quickly becoming renowned as an international financial capital. Created in September 2004, the Dubai Financial Services Authority (DFSA) is the body that authorises licenses and registers institutions and individuals to operate within the Dubai International Financial Centre (DIFC). The regulatory framework for the sector, for which technical assistance and co-operation has been received from English consultancy firms familiar with the London model, is said to be transparent, market-oriented and reliable. The DIFC caters to the needs of investment banks specialised in asset management, reinsurance, finance and back-office operations by offering extremely liberal conditions such as zero tax on income and profits, complete foreign ownership and no restrictions on foreign exchange or capital repatriation. Likewise, the Dubai International Finance Exchange (DIFX) opened in September 2005 as a regional stock exchange offering trading in dollars. This exchange operates in a free trade area under an internationally recognised regulatory regime, and is not subject to the stock purchase and listing restrictions investors face on the local stock exchange in Dubai. These features, combined with the DIFX's low minimum listing requirement, contributed to the Dubai financial market more than tripling its value in 2005. Most of those companies looking to list shares on the exchange are from the Middle East, but Australian, African and Asian companies are also believed to be considering a DIFX listing.

Source: Based on several sources[9].

Box 2.8. Tourism Vision for Istanbul

The Vision is broken down in four main topic areas representing the different facets of tourism: designing and promoting competitive and sustainable urban destinations; creating and providing quality city tourism through the new "value for effort" approach; using city tourism marketing and promotion to strengthen a city's image as a tourist destination; and managing complex urban systems: industry performance and strategic destination development. Acknowledging the need for emphasis on cultural heritage, the Vision also divides Istanbul into three smaller regions. The first is the Historical Peninsula in the south-east, European part of Istanbul. Home to the Ayasofya, Topkapi Palace and Sultanahmet Mosque, the Vision is to build upon the area's offerings as an open-air museum. The second region is the Beyoğlu-Galata Port, envisioned as a cultural and shopping centre, with Beyoğlu as the centre of movie theatres, cinemas, art display locations, cafes, restaurants and shops with tourism-oriented trademarks and boutique hotels. The Galata Port would contribute an inflow of visitors to the region from the cruise ships that anchor close to Beyoğlu. The project emphasises preserving the city's silhouette and preventing building overcrowding in the region. The third region is the Western Black Sea, to the north of the city along the Black Sea. It is renowned for its natural beauty and as a water source for the city. This part of Istanbul is to be preserved as a natural attraction.

Policy makers would like to privilege the link between history, art and culture, and recreation, fashion and shopping within the city of Istanbul. This is reflected spatially through explicit land use and zoning guidelines: the Historic Peninsula, the banks of the Golden Horn, Beyoğlu-Galata, the two banks of the Strait of Istanbul, and the Prince Islands which are being earmarked for history, culture, art tourism, and the two banks of the Strait of Istanbul, Beyoğlu-Galata, Nişantaşı and Taksim which are reserved for tourism related to entertainment and recreation. Finally, in the Nişantaşı-Levent-Maslak (later Zeytinburnu-Merter) area shopping and fashion tourism is being privileged.

A number of significant recent initiatives aimed at developing cultural amenities to boost tourism needs to be mentioned. The Istanbul Metropolitan Municipality along with the district municipalities are conducting urban renewal and transformation projects.[10] One of the main pillars is rehabilitating the city centre and the historical urban structure. The strategy towards the preservation and protection of cultural heritage is being implemented through a series of renovation, restoration and demolition projects complemented with financial incentives. Moreover, all amenities of Istanbul's historical heritages included in the UNESCO World Heritage List in 1985, (*i.e.*, ancient Hippodrome of Constantine, Topkapı Palace, Yıldız Palace, Süleymaniye Mosque and environs, Zeyrek Mosque (Pantocrator Church) and environs, City Walls, Bozdoğan Aqueduct, and the Golden

Horn), are now under the protection of the Istanbul Metropolitan Municipality. Encouraging these efforts, Istanbul was recently elected the 2010 European Capital of Culture[11] thanks to good collaboration between local administrations and non-governmental organisations. Government officials believe that this opportunity will pave the way to attract 10 million tourists to Istanbul. As a positive direct impact of this nomination the municipality of Istanbul, in co-operation with civil organisations and some entities of the central governments, has already begun to work on several projects to increase the capacities of hotels, museums and other cultural amenities.

The implementation of the Vision suffers however from significant challenges. The projection of 10 million tourists by 2010 seems rather optimistic in light of the relatively flat growth over the last few years, and the fierce competition from other areas in Turkey, such as the coastal Anatolian regions. But more importantly, the city is facing limiting capacity and other significant obstacles. These include many of the general concerns related to the city's overall competitiveness including infrastructure deficiencies, illegal settlement encroachment into recreational and watershed areas surrounding Istanbul, and inner city congestion. There are also major deficiencies, both in terms of policy actions and implementation. First, there is a minimal level of government involvement that would be required to present a broader, long-run strategic perspective for potential national and international investors and visitors to illustrate the positive transformations that are going on in Istanbul. With the exception of the work that is being done by the Ministry of Culture and Tourism, and the Istanbul Culture and Arts Corporation of Istanbul Metropolitan Municipality, it seems that overall city marketing is predominantly left to the private sector and NGOs. Moreover, overlapping responsibilities and cumbersome administrative procedures within the government often blocks the implementation of the strategy and related actions. Finally, the public sector has often been unable to leverage sufficient financial resources required to implement its existing portfolio of heritage projects.

One illustration reflecting some of these deficiencies is the story of Istanbul's bid to become the 2010 European Capital of Cultural. The Istanbul Foundation for Culture and Arts (Istanbul Kültür ve Sanat Vakfı/IKSV), an NGO that stimulates arts and intercultural dialogue through festivals, events and expositions, played an important role in preparing the city's bid. The establishment of the Executive Committee of Istanbul 2010 Cultural Capital of Europe has been approved by the decision of the Council of Ministersat the end of 2005.[12] While the campaign worked as an awareness-raising mechanism amongst local actors, it also reflected a general lack of communication between government and the NGOs, a notable overlap of organisations working on the same theme, both resulting in duplication and waste of national resources aimed at cultural policies. Also, a deficiency in the cultural production infrastructure necessary to compete at the international level was clear, combined with an under-utilisation of the existing production infrastructure. In practice, the city of Istanbul has been relatively passive in marketing itself to the international community, something that could be achieved through a more pro-active media exchange programme. According to the Foundation, cumbersome administrative approval procedures for open-air presentations and shows, as well as camera crews in historical areas, also imply the loss of potential in this area. This situation is only aggravated by the frequent occurrence of conflicting approval procedures among the sub-provinces and central municipalities.

Looking forward, raising the city's tourism stakes requires several areas of action:

1. Image making and tourism development (establishing place identity, transforming ordinary places and eliminating negative images, focusing on symbols); building complementarities between Istanbul and other tourist destinations in Turkey.

2. An integrated strategy that will combine image making, tourism development with crucial components such as building tourism infrastructure (creating tourism districts, ports and riverfronts, space and activity differentiations, convention centres, retail districts, etc.) and other sectoral and urban development objectives.

(1) Image making and tourism development

Pro-active marketing and communication strategies are already being implemented, aimed at attracting a larger number of events, festivals and biennials to the city of Istanbul. In the past, the city of Istanbul has been relatively passive in marketing itself to the international community, something that could be achieved through a more pro-active media exchange programme. Currently this lackluster marketing strategy has been changing with private initiatives (*i.e.*, construction of Formula 1 Istanbul Racing Circuit, increasing the number of private museums such as Istanbul Museum of Modern Arts (Istanbul Modern), Sabancı and Pera Museums, preparation for European Cultural Capital). In this respect, the Istanbul Foundation for Culture and Arts has been able to upgrade and institutionalise events such as the Istanbul International Biennial and the International Istanbul Architecture Biennial. It is also quite active in the organisation of several international music, film and theatre festivals, a policy that is increasingly being followed by the private sector itself, particularly the banks. Istanbul is also trying to promote itself as an important location for international sport events. Since the 1990s, the Turkish National Committee for the Olympic Games and the Prime Ministry General Directorate of Youth has been trying to host the Olympic Games in Istanbul, and have set aside investments for that purpose. Likewise, leveraging its natural scenery, the city is active in promoting itself as a venue for water sports, horse riding, golf and tennis.

A number of interesting initiatives target the market tourism niche of conferences and exhibitions. CNR, a private organisation established in 1985, is actively trying to advance the city of Istanbul in the rapidly changing market for events, fairs and exhibitions. It has established strategic links with international events organisers such as the Hanover Messe and the ITF (International Trade Fairs Groups). In addition, important sectors in the Istanbul economy, such as textile and the fashion industry, automation, machinery and metalworking have increasingly become aware of the need to engage in technological exchange and marketing by means of international fairs and exhibitions. Considering these tendencies, and the bottlenecks on the existing infrastructure capacity for international events, CNR is planning new investments. Also in this arena is the Istanbul Convention and Visitor's Bureau (ICVB), an organisation composed of a series of actors – travel agencies, hotels, convention and exhibition centres, the Turkish Airlines and the Airport Terminal Company, and a series of logistic service suppliers, among others. ICVB is essential for information sharing concerning meetings in the city, most recently through its Istanbul Meetings Planners' Guide, and as a facilitator for bringing international associations and organisations to Istanbul. For example, in relation to city marketing, it has given active support by co-ordinating services such as site inspections, participation in preparatory meetings and familiarisation tours for foreign associations. The organisation is also actively working with the Istanbul Metropolitan Municipality and the Ministry of Culture and Tourism.

Yet, the city of Istanbul will face several challenges in promoting itself as a centre for fair, conference and exhibition tourism. First, some of the private sector players claim that Istanbul will indeed grow in this segment in light of the shift of other activities from Western to Eastern Europe. However, while it may be true that some of the more standardised manufacturing activities will indeed relocate from relative high-cost European centres to cities in Eastern Europe characterised by relatively lower cost structures, it is not clear why the same tendency would apply to high-end activities related to process and product design, marketing and exhibitions. Second, even considering the unlikely hypothesis that this shift will occur, Istanbul will indeed face competition from other Eastern European urban centres that also possess relatively qualified production structures. Finally, in order to face this competition, policy makers in

Turkey should aggressively market and insert some of its strategic sectors into the international network of fairs, conference and exhibitions. There is no indication that the city of Istanbul is actively involved in this kind of work, while the central government has only recently started, within the context of some of the EC-funded support programmes and projects, to connect some SMEs with these international circuits of fairs and exhibitions.

Once Istanbul is committed to developing an international brand image, the city will have to define and test key target markets, identify desired outcomes, find partners and set time frames. Articulating and achieving consensus around an integrated brand for the city will involve defining its essential cultural attributes – liveability, beauty, diversity and history. Some of the key building blocks will be its major signature institutions and built infrastructure, its key physical and spatial attributes (urban parks, green spaces, etc.), and leisure activities specific to Istanbul. Also a new individual brand for Istanbul will demand building up less tangible elements, though equally important contributions such as cultural expression and key related industries, namely Istanbul's fashion, design, architecture, food, restaurant establishments and old historical festivals.

Testing key target markets is necessary to ensure validation and acceptance of, and demand for, the brand and the products that define it. These markets should include both domestic and international targets. At a minimum, the local citizenry will be key to validating the legitimacy of the brand. The next step will be foreign markets, segmented by target class (*e.g.*, academics, students), high-end cultural tourism and industry tourism (*e.g.*, fashion designers). Geographic segmentation should also inform these strategies, differentiating targets by region within Europe, Asia and the Americas and tied to whatever central government strategies have been developed to maximise export opportunities and foreign market penetration for Turkey and Istanbul-based industries. Finally, integrated and differentiated marketing campaigns should be developed and sustained over time to raise awareness in these targeted and segmented markets of the brand and its components and attributes.

To support the city's overarching vision to develop into a regional hub it must define concrete, practical and realistic sectoral and crosscutting outcomes over a specified timeframe, with quantifiable indicators and metrics. Some of the objectives are related to highlighting the city's attributes such as showcasing certain signature cultural institutions, and determining which institutions should be restored. Others are focused on infrastructure improvements like reducing congestion in the Historical Peninsula and other key regions, and making the city more accessible by transit, pedestrian and other transportation methods. Yet a third group would involve expanding the city's offerings by creating more hotel spaces so that visitors can stay longer, creating larger public spaces and opening a greater array of (and possibly more) cultural venues. Finally, Istanbul should make creative use of the possible complementary role that exists with other tourist destinations within Turkey, such as the Anatolian coastal region, Cappadocia and the eastern mountains. In that sense, the city could serve as a main entry gate to several tourist circuits in the country. Consequently, more effort should be put into strategies aimed at capturing Turkish communities living abroad, attracting FDI in order to speed up the modernisation of the hotel and tourist infrastructure and developing specific product market combinations aimed at linking particular assets of the city to (international) target communities. When defining all of these priorities it is also necessary to consider the desired and feasible time frames for achieving the desired outcome – *i.e.*, plans for five years, ten years and that only accomplishable in twenty. Partnering options might present themselves leading to private sector or not-for-profit involvement. Regardless of the means, strategies must be designed for achieving these objectives accompanied by metrics for measuring success.

In terms of tourism development there are a range of novel opportunities for the tourism sector. One lever to increase tourism development would require looking beyond tourist projection figures. A significant surge in Istanbul's tourism revenues could perhaps be obtained if the city were to focus on variables such as the duration of stay and tourist spending patterns. Similar impact might also be derived if the city were to use innovation to attract repeat visitors and cultural events. Another would be to promote "creative cities" where competitive creative industries link with traditional industries, especially for large cities and metropolises, like in Turin, where new offers like chocolate making, aperitifs and a growing Olympic Village are promoted and provided through guided tours, testing, and interactive online platforms. These strategies to commercialise the territorial heritage and the city resources into products, and create new value of old traditions should include safeguards to preserve the quality and the sustainability of the local amenities and attractions. Brand promotion and creating an image is critical for the city's positioning in the highly competitive urban tourism market. The challenge for tourist cities is to search for strong brands that add value by answering to what people want, and what is relevant to them, now and in the future. The new traveller seeks to fit into the community rather than to jump from sight to sight, surrounded by other tourists. The benchmark of success is turning the city from a "place to stay" to a "place to play"; therefore cities need to erode the barrier between residents and tourists to help them interact and enjoy the city together.

As for other metro-regions with world city aspirations, the City of Istanbul should strengthen its role within the network of international relations. Within the context of the strategic vision as elaborated by the Expert Commission Report on Istanbul within the 8th Five-Year Development Plan and the Istanbul 2023 Vision and Strategic Action Plan, the Istanbul Metropolitan Municipality has become much more actively involved in international relations. However to step up its economic promotion efforts it needs to make better use of its existing networks, and establish new international channels. Large cities around the world increasingly perform a crucial role in international relations both by mobilising financial resources and technical co-operation, and attracting productive investments. At present, the bulk of the activities undertaken by the Istanbul Metropolitan Municipality seem to be co-ordinated by the Foreign Relations Directorate of the Department of Human Resources and Education, and focused on the promotion of its cultural and tourism assets. In light of Istanbul's ambitions, and considering the strategic role of cities in the global economy, it is recommended that the position of this directorate within the overall municipal administration be examined to explore the possibility of it taking on a more extensive international relations role.

A number of concrete actions could be taken to strengthen Istanbul's international relations capacity. The goal of municipal international relations would be to promote local economic development, attract foreign investment, technical co-operation and financial resources and, last but not least, to promote the city itself. The creation of a special department or institutional structure for international relations would be in addition to the valuable work done by other agencies, such as the ICVB (Istanbul Convention Visitors Bureau). The creation of such a revised municipal structure would signal to the international community a new momentum in metropolitan policies within the municipal administration of Istanbul. This would symbolise the city's commitment to looking for strategic alliances within the international community, which could then help transform Istanbul into a more liveable and competitive city. The facilitating, mediating and information sharing role of such an institutional structure, also in relation to the political and administrative policy networks within Turkey (State Planning Organization, Investment Promotion Agency, the future regional development agency, provincial bodies, etc.), could prove to be an enormous opportunity for the city of Istanbul. For example, in the short run the metropolitan council is expected to approve a law, which is to ensure that the Istanbul Metropolitan Municipality's investments and services will be increasingly in line with the EU criteria and procedures. This law by itself will imply the need to substantially increase and centralise the information systems on European markets and procedures within the municipality, and creates the potential for a more entrepreneurial and integrated policy for international relations for the city of Istanbul.

(2) Integrated strategy

International evidence suggests that carefully linking strategic urban development and marketing policies facilitates the development of successful differential branding strategies. Several cities and metropolitan regions around the world have turned a crisis or a period of intense productive restructuring into an opportunity to build up a new economic base and socio-economic identity, transforming their previous weak points into competitive strengths. Key elements of such strategies have been the participatory implementation of a series of transformation projects that symbolised the viability of a more liveable future, where several of the threats on sustainable development had been taken away. At the same time, the innovative communication and marketing of these urban development projects have invited local and international stakeholders to be active partners in the launch and implementation of the transformation process towards a more liveable future. Cases such as The Ruhr Valley in Germany clearly demonstrate the power of such differential branding, in which the vulnerability of this city-region, which once symbolised German heavy industrialisation, characterised by such dimensions as poor liveability, environmental degradation and low innovative capacity, was gradually transformed through an ambitious and entrepreneurial strategy based on the environmental revitalisation of the Emscher river located in the valley (Box 2.9). While the Ruhr has used branding for creative crisis management, the city of Istanbul could use the same technique in order to seize opportunities, for example, in moving towards a higher-end economic system".

Greater collaboration among public local authorities is necessary to better integrate a tourism strategy into other objectives for sustainable urban development. For instance, integrating branding strategies into the metropolitan region's and the district authorities' long-term strategic plans, will require collaborating with those agencies governing land-use, transportation and mass transit, and neighbourhood revitalisation. On the Historic Peninsula or in Galata, it will be critical to ensure that spatial planning and land-use objectives for major signature cultural institutions take into account the need to create urban spaces large enough to accommodate the millions of local and foreign visitors annually. The neighbourhood revitalisation objectives capture the need for these spaces and the need for a greater variety of cultural venues for various means of cultural expression (possible through the revitalisation of derelict building stock or the use of inner-city brownfields), and integrate them with such considerations as the location of transit stations, access routes for emergency vehicles and the need for hotel accommodations and affordable housing.

Box 2.9. **Sustainable development after heavy industry?: the role of IBA in reinventing and "re-branding" the Ruhr**

Perhaps one of the most striking examples of differential branding is how the Ruhr Valley reinvented itself in the aftermath of the deep economic crises that hit the region in the 1950s (when coal was replaced by more sustainable and less expensive energy sources), and more particularly in the 1970s, with the sharp competition of Asian NICs in sectors like steel and shipbuilding.

In the 1980s, the future for the Ruhr Valley did not look very bright. While the region was undergoing economic restructuring in its core sectors (steel, coal, metalworking, etc.), the conditions for the elaboration and implementation of a successful economic revitalisation strategy looked indeed quite stark: almost two centuries of heavy industrialisation had ruined the environmental conditions and the liveability of the area.

In 1989 the North-Rhine Westphalia state government and the local leaders of the region (local government officials, entrepreneurs, unions, and academics) created the IBA agency (International Building Exposition for the Emscher River) whose explicit mission was to co-ordinate the socio-economic and environmental revitalisation of the Ruhr. IBA proved to be a flexible and project-oriented broker organisation. Its ten-year mandate was to show the international community that a different and more sustainable Ruhr could be realised with the collaborative efforts of public and private stakeholders. During the 1989-1999 period, IBA was able to implement more than 100 projects aimed at such diverse areas as environmental revitalisation of the Emscher river, alternative sources of energy, eco-tourism, sustainable housing in park areas, technological incubators and urban renovation of deteriorated port areas.

In several aspects, the approach taken by IBA was entrepreneurial in the sense that the organisation did not shy away from the risks that were involved in seeking a new identity and brand for the Ruhr Valley. Clean energy, eco-tourism, quality urban housing projects in park areas were chosen as flagship projects to communicate to the national and international community the German policy makers' promise to transform one of the most polluted areas of the country (and perhaps of Europe) into a more sustainable area. Moreover, it was also remarkable that IBA facilitated the development of a competitive sector of small and medium-sized enterprises – in one of the most polluted areas of post-war Europe – that would go on to produce, market and export environmental equipment and cleanup technology.

Today, although the Ruhr is still facing several challenges in maintaining and creating enough employment, the strategy developed by IBA is considered to be a successful case of differential branding through a careful combination of urban development and communication policies.

Source: Based on Cantz, Hatje (2002), *The Regionmaker. Rhein RuhrCity: The Hidden Metropolis*, NRW Forum Kultur und Wirtschaft, Düsseldorf.

For instance, any eradication of narrow streets and crumbling building stock ought to take into account the need to enhance the vitality of neighbourhoods around existing signature cultural institutions and new cultural venues to make them more attractive to domestic and foreign visitors alike, while fully taking into account the needs of the artistic community and local citizenry that reside in these neighbourhoods. One multi-stakeholder example is the Sultanahmet Local Development Project introduced by the International Competitiveness Research Institute (ICRI/URAK). This local level project has brought together regional tourism sector stakeholders to identify more specific actions to be undertaken. Among these is the organisation of new entertainment alternatives in Sultanahmet, specifically introducing a night life in the region without harming the cultural environment. Other plans to enrich the attractions in the area focus around offering shows of elements of traditional culture and maintaining the visual attractiveness of the area by, for example, maintaining road signs and similar public goods, repairing local public restrooms, etc.

The city could better integrate these cultural strategies with other related sectoral strategies. For instance, Istanbul's fashion and design industry leaders aim to move their industry "up the food chain" to make their labels recognised for their quality and innovative creativity in key high-end international markets. To achieve this objective, one idea being discussed is the promotion of a design district within Istanbul – a fashion neighbourhood like Soho in New York or Noho in Los Angeles that would become known nationally and worldwide for its labels' creativity in design and quality of workmanship. This would require the right mix of incentives and hard work to ensure a critical mass of high-end, export-ready labels. It will, however, be important to include this "neighbourhood" and the labels being produced there as elements of Istanbul's brand and of the strategies aimed at promoting and marketing the brand abroad.

2.2. Coping with congestion and risks

Rapid urbanisation growth and a large influx of domestic and foreign migrants to Istanbul in a relatively short period of time have created huge congestion, proliferation of illegal settlements, and environmental costs in an area at high risk for earthquakes. These issues need to be addressed not only for reasons of sustainability, but also because they infringe upon (or could infringe upon) Istanbul's attractiveness and competitiveness. This section will review current policies in the areas of (1) congestion and transportation; (2) urban development and housing; and (3) environmental and earthquake risks. It appears that much of the structural deficiency is linked with the main challenges facing the overall urban planning system in Istanbul.

Managing congestion and transport

The extent of transport congestion in Istanbul requires bold political measures. Turkish policy makers have recognised that the former Transportations Master Plans (the last one enacted in 1996) have not been implemented, and that the proposed shift in the modal split, away from cars towards the railway system, has not materialised. In fact, with more than 2.5 million motor vehicles, the province of Istanbul concentrates approximately 25% of all cars in the country. The latest comprehensive survey, conducted in 1997, shows private car use represents 33% of total trips and the motorisation rate in Istanbul is the highest in the country. Only prioritising mass transportation can stop this trend. The railway network, both at the national and regional/local scale, remains rather limited. The newly developed systems (tramways, light rail and metro) are too limited and lack sufficient capacity to alleviate metropolitan wide congestion. As a consequence, congestion, particularly on the bridges and on the Karaköy-Beşiktaş and Beşiktaş-Levent-Maslak axis, a high-density services and commercial area, has become a major issue.

A number of positive achievements aimed at reducing congestion in the city deserve to be mentioned.

(1) First, several new projects are in the pipeline or are being discussed to address these concerns. While the investments in the urban rail system between 1983-2004 amounted to a mere 44 km (resulting in a relatively low average construction figure of 2.2 km/year), a series of investments that have been started, or are being tendered, are expected to extend the network to 265 km by 2012 or 2013.[13] One of such investments already underway is the Marmaray[14] project, an undersea rail tunnel across the Strait of Istanbul that will connect the existing rail system with an interchange station and the metro system. Its completion in 2010 is estimated to increase trips by rail from 3.6% to 27.7% and alleviate the current use of vehicles for transporting goods.[15] Total travel time between Gebze and Halkalı (essentially traversing Istanbul) is expected to come down from 185 to 104 minutes through a new upgraded, uninterrupted commuter rail. In addition, the relocation of workshops from the peninsula, a process started in 2005, is also expected to reduce traffic. Finally, the prospect of a third car bridge over the Strait of Istanbul is currently in the discussion phase. The proposal for a second (car) tunnel under the Strait of Istanbul was accepted by the Construction, Development, Transportation and Tourism Commission of the Grand National Assembly of Turkey in 2006. As a consequence, preparations are underway to start construction of the tunnel in 2007 on the basis of a Build, Operate and Transfer (BOT) model. According to the estimates of the Istanbul Metropolitan Municipality, the project is to be completed in 2010, with an annual capacity of 25 million vehicles.

Expanding the railway network will require time and will also be accompanied by the regular delays associated with large projects. In the short run, growth in population and income are likely to further boost the demand for private car mobility in Istanbul. Therefore, in order to cope with extra demand during this transition period, the additional mobility will have to be absorbed by private vehicles, both through investments in new roads, and by strengthening the management for more efficient use of the existing road capacity. Istanbul is implementing measures that take this direction into account. For example, since 2004, 46 new roads and 57 grade-separated intersections, totally 103 infrastructure projects, have been implemented. A total of around YTL 1.1 billion was spent on the construction for these projects, while 72 roads and intersections are still being constructed. The tendering process for 35 out of 54 roads and intersections has also started. In addition, design projects for 66 roads and intersections are on the way, while 23 highway transportation systems are in the planning stage.

(2) Second, the planning process is experiencing a new momentum. In July 2006, the Environmental Order Plan (at the scale of 1/100 000) was finalised and approved by the City Council of Istanbul (see below). Subsequently, the process of elaboration of metropolitan development and master plans (at the scale of 1/25 000) was underway until October 2007 but has not yet been approved by the IMM's City Council. At the same time, the renovation of the Transportation Master Plan is being realised in co-operation with JICA (Japan International Cooperation Agency) and projected to be achieved in 2007. This combination of plans has set the stage for ambitious investments in the urban railway system, aimed at reversing a historical trend of neglect for sustainable land use and transportation policies.

(3) Third, in line with international best practice, Istanbul Metropolitan Municipality has increasingly become aware about the strategic role of the so-called soft policies aimed at *(intelligent) traffic management*, such as road pricing, electronic monitoring of traffic flows and other similar measures. Since early 2006 the city has started to introduce an efficient integrated tariff management system, offering incentives for mass transportation over car use as well as a number of other measures aimed at a more clean transport system (see below). Moreover, in order to stimulate the more efficient use of existing highway capacity, Istanbul will be divided into three main traffic zones, whereby public transportation, parking areas, and road usage will be subject to different tariffs by the year 2012 or 2013 (*i.e.*, at the stage of the consolidation of the public transportation network). A system that makes it more expensive to use cars in the city centre (1st zone) should be put into use. In other words, car users in the 3rd zone are stimulated not to come to the 2nd and 1st zones by their own cars, and to

travel by public transportation by parking their cars at park and ride areas in their own zones, also being stimulated to do so through low parking fees. In practical terms, going to the first zone by car will imply the payment of higher parking and congestion fees (as is the case in Singapore and London).

Although the above policies are steps in the right direction, several challenges will have to be addressed in order to move toward a permanent and sustainable solution for the present distortions in the urban transportation system.

(1) First, the transportation sector remains characterised by a proliferation of actors, operating both formally and informally, among which many are large private companies. A large number of different institutes are involved in transportation in Istanbul (Figure 2.1). This complex and multi-fold system of governance seems to be one of the main obstacles to evolving towards more efficient and transparent planning and management of urban transportation, ultimately resulting in additional high infrastructure provision costs.

- *Officially*: at the central level there are different ministries and administrations involved including TDİ (Turkish Maritime Lines) and TCDD (Turkish State Railways), and the "General Directorate for the Construction of Railways, Ports and Airports" (DLH) linked to the Ministry of Transport. The two main projects managed by these central bodies are the Marmaray project and the third bridge project. At the local level the Istanbul Metropolitan Municipality and its various directorates and departments (see governance chapter) take on the most important role. On the private side, there are several companies that are linked to Metropolitan Municipality (which controls a part of the financial capital), the most important one being the Ulaşım A.Ş. responsible for the railway systems (planning, infrastructure building, equipment supply). The co-ordination between all these official actors is not easy and clear, especially between central and local public authorities. The 2003 UNESCO Advisory Team Report, entitled "Marmaray Rail Tube Tunnel and Gebze-Halkalı surface Metro System" stressed the "lack of co-ordination among the various administrative bodies responsible (for transportation)", and suggested the creation of a "Co-ordination Committee composed of each of the stakeholders"; that is, employers, building companies, the Istanbul Metropolitan Municipality, the Istanbul Archaeological Museum, the Operational Committee, the Board for the Protection N°4 (responsible for Istanbul *intra-muros*), the Board for the Protection N°5 (responsible for the Asiatic part of the metropolitan area), the TCDD (Turkish State Railways), the Ministry of Culture and Tourism and a UNESCO representative.

- At the informal level, the national government often shows a pro-active interest in accompanying, and sometimes influencing private sector decision makers involved in large-scale urban projects. These interaction mechanisms appear to inspire official policy, like the "Project of the 31 road tunnels" announcement, which is meant to trigger concrete action toward alleviating traffic congestion and providing alternatives to the inefficient road network, yet it is not exactly in line with the official priority to increase rail system participation amongst users of other transportation modes.

Figure 2.1. **Governance complexity for transport in Istanbul**

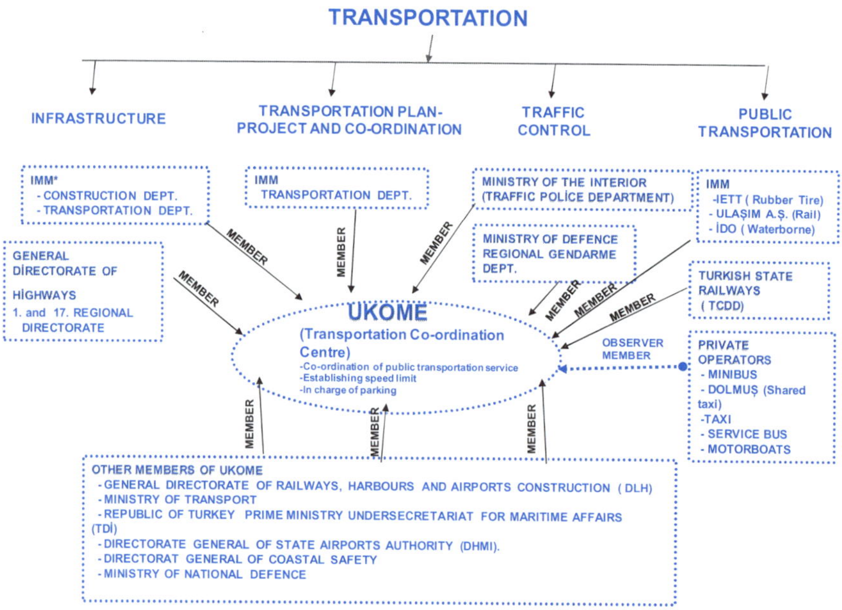

Source: Istanbul Metropolitan Municipality.

(2) Second, as mentioned before, new networks to increase infrastructure capacity require time and investment. The suburban trains connecting the new Marmaray are quite outdated and need to be upgraded to encourage modal shifts. In addition, as seen in the commuting flows, a larger number of trips are made further to the north of the planned Marmaray line, which is relatively far from the centre. Moreover, the

different transportation options and location studies (highway suspension bridge, submerged highway corridor, etc.) should be accompanied with detailed and independent expert studies that specify comparative cost-benefit and impact analysis.

(3) Third, despite the fact that decisive moves towards decentralisation and a more intense participation of the private sector have taken place, additional steps toward increasing efficiency and transparency of decision making in the transportation sector should be taken. Since 2004, a major trend in all Istanbul governance has been a gradual transfer of competences (and property) from central bodies to local authorities. Within the transportation system, this trend is evidenced by the planning of the transfer of rail infrastructure from TCDD (Turkish Republic State Railways) to the Istanbul Metropolitan Municipality within its new sovereignty limits. Moreover, the TDİ's (Turkish Maritime Line) has transferred part of its fleet to İDO (the municipal semi-private maritime transport company). Despite these promising trends the managerial reforms in the transportation sector (tendering procedures, management of the project cycle, etc.) should be broadened and deepened, while its is also recommended that the degree of community participation is increased, also to improve transparency.

Looking forward, a number of actions could be taken to further improve the transport system in Istanbul. They include the following:

- **Streamline and clarify the government structure for transport issues**. Related laws and plans need to be amended because some of the existing laws stipulate various agencies overlap or even conflict, and in some instances do not clearly define or designate the responsible authorities and duties (see governance chapter). Within the municipality, the role of the Transportation Coordination Centre (UKOME) must be clearly reinforced, to encourage close synergy with Ulaşım A.Ş. (the municipal company in charge of the railway systems and the Department of Transportation).

- **Integrating land use planning and transportation planning** would also provide efficient and effective public service provision. Combining land use incentives with transportation and environmental policies will improve traffic flows, reduce trip lengths, and promote a modal shift towards more efficient transport routes and modes. The ongoing new Transportation Master Plan should be formulated in a coherent way with the preparation of a land use plan that will start in 2008, and play a co-ordination role.

- **Further prioritise railway over road network**. This will require improving the existing railway system as well as better connecting the different rail-systems (tram, light rail, metro) with other transportation means.

- **Integrating and improving public transport modes** will maximise the use of public transportation, by enhancing its efficiency and facilitating the modal exchange. The existing transport infrastructure often has hurdles to smooth connection with other rail systems and is not co-ordinated with other transportation modes (*e.g.*, lack of Park and Ride [P&R] spaces). Particularly, sea transportation across the Strait of Istanbul (*e.g.*, vapour, *vapur*) could be better integrated to smooth and proximate connections with other modes (*e.g.*, buses).

- **Enhance traffic demand management (TDM) and provide effective alternatives.** Increasing capacity by construction requires huge costs and time. Soft measures aimed at congestion and pollution reduction, such as congestion charges (road pricing), parking fees, and High-Occupancy Vehicle (HOV)-only lanes, have shown positive results in other countries. For example, allocating one lane on major thoroughfares to public transportation (*i.e.*, buses) and private mass transportation (*e.g.*, buses, minibuses, *dolmuş*) on the Strait of Istanbul bridges and main connecting highways could improve mass transportation flows, stimulating modal shifts to mass transportation. To date introducing "congestion charges" has been successful in London, Stockholm, Singapore, etc. However it would likely be difficult to introduce such measure in Istanbul in the short run as there are currently few alternatives, and as such would only result in increased transportation costs.

- **Improving transparency and communication in the decision-making process for large transport projects**. With almost 60% of the total investment budget of the Istanbul municipality going to transport infrastructure projects, democratic control through public debate and local participation needs to be better ensured. For the moment, the participation process seems to be generally launched from the top after decisions have already been taken. A better communication of the projects in discussion will also avoid unnecessary speculation and strong local resistance that would emerge as reaction against a procedure rather than a project. One possible solution would be to create a consultative body with representatives from the Ministry of Transport, the Istanbul Metropolitan Municipality (including the Department for Environment), the sub-province municipalities, professional chambers, and associations to exchange on a permanent basis views and information on potential and ongoing projects. The above-mentioned "Transportation Coordination Centre" UKOME could have a leading role in the municipality. This would have a positive effect on dispelling rumours of hidden agendas. All the accountability and the reliability of the transportation planning systems will depend on this characteristic. The continuity of the tenders processes could be guaranteed, to prevent project re-tendering related to political fluctuations.

Land use, urban regeneration projects and housing development

Over the last three years urban planning in Istanbul has gone through a rapid and promising process of transformation towards a more open, integrated and decentralised system. First, the scale of planning has shifted towards the regional level. Second, new actors such as the "Istanbul Metropolitan Planning and Urban Design Centre" (IMP), a research centre created to serve the different directorates in the municipalities, has emerged taking on some of the responsibilities for urban and metropolitan planning under the supervision of the Istanbul Metropolitan Municipality. Third, from a methodological standpoint, issues such as environmental and earthquakes risks, and urban transportation, have increasingly been incorporated into the urban planning discourse, while the necessary flexibility has been increased through programmes of "Urban Regeneration".

This positive trend however has not prevented a large and growing gap between planning, and the actual land use and city growth. As mentioned in the section on transportation, and further developed in Chapter 3, planning in Turkey is characterised by a large number of diverse stakeholders with overlapping, and not always clearly defined responsibilities. This pattern is repeated in urban development with central ministries, regional, local and metropolitan bodies, and the private sector, all interacting within a highly complex system. Moreover, authorities quite frequently ignore the plans when introducing special laws and regulations, thereby reducing even further the marginal effectiveness of the system. They tend to generate a large number of plans, often without a clear relationship and hierarchy among them. Over time, this perverse cycle has become embedded in a parallel, highly informal and unregulated circuit of investment, construction and selling of houses and plots, territorially concentrated in the outskirts of metropolitan Istanbul, and driven by interactions between residents, real estate agents, bureaucrats and politicians. As a consequence, it has proven difficult to develop a global and strategic vision of the main priorities for planning the future of the city.

Informal housing, the most challenging land use issue in Istanbul, clearly illustrates this fragmented approach to urban planning. Since the 1960s the so-called *gecekondu,* or squatter settlements, have proliferated becoming the most typical and well-known forms of informal occupation and construction. The populations in these settlements were perceived as a source of cheap labour and a resource during elections for leveraging a large number of votes.[16] In a second stage, with the goal of expanding the real estate markets in the squatter settlements, the *gecekondu* have been consolidated into so-called *Apartkondu,* mainly through the construction of extra floors. This said, the informal nature of land tenure, building codes, standards and zoning laws is extensive, and is not limited to low-income housing, as mentioned in Chapter 1. In the last few decades Istanbul has witnessed a significant increase in these different forms of informal land use development through the construction of skyscrapers and luxury villas along the Strait of Istanbul shores as well as encroachment onto scarce and protected forest areas and water reserves. These trends clearly highlight Istanbul's *"semi-planning"* approach by which the system accommodates projects already in progress, leading to an unsustainable pattern of urban growth.

Illegal or irregular housing has varied negative consequences for development of the economy and of the city in general. First, considering that a large share of a household's wealth corresponds to the value of their housing, the insecurity and legal risks of informal housing reduces the net wealth of families, since an important proportion of their patrimony is at risk. Second, informal housing implies weak or non-existing linkages with the financial sector (considering the lack of appropriate collateral), decreasing the potential leverage of the mortgage system. Consequently, overall welfare is reduced considering the fact that housing is largely financed by families reducing their consumption expenditure or allocating money from family-owned enterprises, facing relatively short payback periods. Third, informal housing reduces the tax base of local governments, thereby lowering its capacity to finance urban services. Moreover, a weak property tax base also tends to have regressive effects, alleviating the more affluent segments from payment. Finally, informal housing development leads to a costly and inefficient "leapfrogging" pattern of infrastructure provision, with additional negative effects on environmental sustainability and earthquake risks.

As yet, the city has not been able to develop a comprehensive, transparent and consistent response to irregular and informal land encroachment and unplanned constructions. Further analysis is required to identify which legal institutions, regulations and procedures must be streamlined in order to make them more efficient, transparent and effective. These efforts are needed to reach transcendental policy objectives such as secure property rights for the population, increasing participation of the financial sector via mortgage loans and satisfactory enforcement of urban development plans to develop Istanbul as an orderly and territorially efficient economy. It is yet unclear which legal procedures are more often circumvented by *gecekondu*, within a possible range of situations such as: (1) formalisation of private contracts regarding property transactions, specifically land or housing units, including inscription of such transactions in public registries; (2) tax issues; (3) compatibility with local zoning and land-use plans, including environmental legislation; (4) compliance with local building standards and codes and safety regulations (electric circuits and other energy installations, structural reliability considering the earthquake characteristics of the region, parking facilities as required for congested areas, etc.), and many more. However, it appears that to a considerable extent the origin of problems is related with local policies, regulations and institutions, to the extent that some sectors of the population prefer to build dwellings in nearby suburban or rural areas around Istanbul, where legal restrictions are considered less severe. Confronted with similar problems, the Mexican authorities have taken important measures to limit the expansion of informal settlements (Box 2.10).

On a positive side, a number of negotiations, mechanisms for financial compensation and initiatives aimed at urban regeneration have been introduced to deal with the issue. However, the negotiation process is characterised by a low level of participation and transparency, and high uncertainty, leading to substantial negative effects on housing investments. In addition, it is not always clear how the gains and losses of relocation and compensation programmes are distributed among stakeholders in the city. For example, it is possible that an illegal construction amnesty may be obsolete in light of new economic opportunities for specific areas where the municipality cancelled many property bills, as was the case in the sub-province of Eyüp. In other cases, the declaration of specific Urban Regeneration Zones has meant that local government started negotiations with inhabitants on the type of construction, forcing them to rebuild their homes according to the new standards of the Regeneration Program. Finally, the socio-economic profile and the lobbying power of inhabitants can have an effect on the outcome of the negotiations process, generally leading to weaker negotiation positions for the more vulnerable segments of the city.

Current urban regeneration policies need to take a more comprehensive approach. These policies intend to address the specific physical conditions of areas, such as the historical peninsula (*Müzekent*), earthquake sensitive sub-provinces (Zeytinburnu), old industrial sub-provinces (Kartal) and the mostly informal suburbs (the case of Küçükçekmece sub-province). There are several indicators that the design of the programme will need further improvements. First, relocation policies for families and small-scale industries, currently a component of urban regeneration within the inner city

Box 2.10. **Fighting informal settlements: the case of Mexico**

Like in Istanbul, illegal land settlements and irregular housing construction in Mexico is not only rooted in poverty, but also linked with inefficient procedures. Incorporating additional peripheral land into urban development has not facilitated the timely delivery of land served with adequate public infrastructure and services at a reasonable cost for the increasing urban population, comprising both new households formed by the natural growth of population, as well as those required by immigrants from other cities or rural areas. Therefore, considering this context, there are incentives for individual low-income households to acquire cheaper land, even if property rights are not well established, land is unsafe (in areas subject to risks of flooding, accidents or other natural or man-provoked disasters) and it lacks basic public services and infrastructure (paved streets, water, electricity, etc.). Moreover, so called "social leaders" sometimes organise collective actions of large numbers of poor families to invade this kind of inadequate area in order to put pressures upon local authorities for subsequent amnesty and regularisation. In other cases, private developers first build large and un-serviced complexes of small houses for middle or low-income families in land acquired illegally and at low prices from communal rural organisations, and in a subsequent phase negotiate changes in urban development plans with local authorities in order to guarantee the provision of urban services and infrastructure to these housing units. In all these cases, large unearned rents are being appropriated by the "social leaders" or the private developers to bribe corrupt officials in certain municipalities or state governments creating a strong incentive for the phenomenon to continue. To overcome these problems, important policy measures have been adopted by Mexican authorities over time: constitutional reforms were implemented in the early 1990s to facilitate social or communal ownership in rural areas that can be transformed into private property, so as to facilitate private investment in rural areas in general, and in peripheral or suburban areas in particular; several projects for the modernisation of public registries of ownership rights have been fostered in the last decade by the federal authorities and several states (including modern technology, training of personnel and procedures to increase transparency and eradicate corruption); improved co-ordination among key public and private actors related with the housing sector through a Presidential Housing Commission; increased efficiency in public institutions offering home financing for workers.

centre and the historical island, should be implemented without disrupting socio-economic ties and community relations, and with sufficient infrastructure to support the newly planned neighbourhoods. Here the newly established urban real estate company will have to develop a holistic and integrated approach to sustainable urban development. Second the Urban Regeneration Program will have to be sensitive to Law No. 5366, approved in June 2005, which authorises local authorities to protect and improve abandoned buildings with the approval of the Council of Ministries. This legal framework permits the expropriation of old buildings in two stages. Municipalities or Provincial Special Administration launch the initial request submitted to the Council of Ministries who votes on creating a special "renewal zone" (*yenileme alanı*). Next, local authorities are given special approval powers over zoning and construction activities.

The Fatih and Beyoğlu sub-provinces represent clear indicators of a general lack of a comprehensive regulatory and financial framework that integrates urban regeneration, housing and urban development objectives, and protects low-income dwellers. These two sub-provinces are the first to operate within the provisions of the law, having designated the neighbourhoods of Neslişah and Hatice Sultan as renewal zones. Within the limits of these zones, 571 owners and 391 tenants have been invited to participate in the programme, aimed at protecting historical buildings and improving urban design patterns in the areas. Under the current negotiations framework, tenants without property bills have been simply invited to leave the neighbourhood without financial compensation, while the 571 owner-occupied dwellers have received a lump-sum compensation of YTL 500/m^2 (around USD 350/m^2). Although the municipality of Fatih declared itself open to alternative proposals, the negotiations framework is too restrictive (only open to owner-occupied dwellers) and complex to allow for effective civil society participation as the inhabitants lack the necessary know-how, financial resources and time to contribute. Another deficiency is that the historical and community networks of some local groups are ignored by the authorities, forcing individuals and families to leave the historical peninsula. These intangible costs of breaking up community networks are not calculated by the local authorities, and are also not followed-up by programmes aimed at financial compensation for the more vulnerable neighbourhood segments. Notwithstanding the UNESCO warnings regarding the consequences of urbanisation on cultural heritage in the historic peninsula, large construction projects are foreseen in the so-called protection programmes of cultural heritage.

Istanbul could look to other metropolitan areas for inspiration in creating a comprehensive strategy for upgrading and formalising informal settlements. Governments all over the world have been losing financial resources; both through infrastructure provision in unplanned areas, and in expensive relocation programmes for moving families from high-risk areas. Beyond the cost factor, governments have also failed to tap financial and entrepreneurial resources that circulate within these informal economies. Indeed, improving and mainstreaming programmes aimed at upgrading and regulating squatter settlements would create a more solid basis for local economic development strategies and social capital in these areas, inserting them into the wider socio-economic and urban fabric of the city. Mass production of low-income housing and specific mortgage programmes, like those implemented recently in other parts of Turkey, will be necessary but insufficient responses. The example from Rio de Janeiro (Brazil) suggests that a metropolitan city can reap beneficial results by using an integrated approach towards upgrading and regulating squatter areas (Box 2.11). The spatial and temporal integration of the economic, social and physical dimensions of upgrading in specific slum areas increases the effectiveness of sectoral programmes as compared to a scenario where each of these activities would have been implemented in a scattered manner, over different periods, and in separate neighbourhoods. Indeed, evaluations undertaken by agencies such as the Inter-American Development Bank on integrated upgrading strategies have shown a more sustainable increase in the living conditions of lower income families previously living in slum areas.

Box 2.11. A successful approach to integration between squatter settlements and the urban fabric: the Integrated Slum Upgrading Program "Favela Bairro" in Rio de Janeiro, Brazil

In Rio de Janeiro, almost 20% of the population, some 1 000 000 inhabitants are living in *favelas* (squatter settlements). These slum areas arose when liberated slaves immigrated to the urban centres at the end of the 19th century. In addition, and as a consequence of the "urban reform" movements, low-quality squatter tenement housing, located in the old CBD, was relocated to the outskirts of the city in the beginning of the 20th century. The Brazilian industrialisation model also contributed to the growth of slums areas. It is estimated that the slum population increased 11 times as fast as the non-slum population in the last decade, leading to extremely high-density figures in these areas (in the range of approximately 980 persons/hectare).

In 1996 the municipality of Rio de Janeiro in partnership with the Inter-American Development Bank (IADB) launched the Favela-Bairro project seeking to transform squatter settlements into community neighbourhoods. With a budget of USD 300 million for stage one, the aim was to improve the living conditions of the inhabitants of 54 slums and eight irregular settlements, reaching a target group of approximately 220 000 people. While 60% of the financing came from the IADB, the local government and its partners contributed 40% of the financial resources. In its second phase, another USD 300 million loan was awarded under the same conditions to reach another 52 slums and 17 irregular settlements bringing the accumulated total to approximately 420 000 persons, almost half of the population living in squatter settlements.

Box 2.11. A successful approach of integration between squatter settlements and the urban fabric: the Integrated Slum Upgrading Program "Favela Bairro" in Rio de Janeiro, Brazil (*cont.*)

The innovative character of the programme has been its multi-sectoral and holistic approach towards slum upgrading, recognising the need to link physical investments in basic sanitation, access roads, electricity and community centres to complementary dimensions of community participation, education, employment and income generation. In effect, the programme has been operating along the following dimensions:

- Infrastructure: implementation and maintenance of basic infrastructure (water supply, electricity, green areas, drainage and flood protection, solid waste, etc.);
- Regularisation of land tenure;
- Land and road planning: optimisation of internal land use, and circulation and improvement/implementation of access roads;
- Education: education on the community processes and procedures (how to use the new equipment, environmental awareness, notions of citizenship, etc.);
- Urban planning: implementation of community infrastructure (squares, small commerce, community centres, etc.);
- Social programmes: creating kindergartens and child-care facilities, reducing school absenteeism; and
- Income and employment programmes: creating co-operatives, designing several schemes aimed at micro-credit, providing vocational training in partnership with community organisations and the private sector, etc.

Nowadays, the programme is considered one of the successful examples of integrated upgrading of urban Brazilian squatters, and is starting to serve as a reference for other Brazilian cities.

Source: Brakarz, J., M. Greene, and E. Rojos (2002), *Cidades para Todos. A experiência recente com programas de melhoramentos de bairros* (*Cities for All: Recent Experiences with Neighborhood Improvement*), Washington, DC.

The city of Istanbul should urgently set up mechanisms to avoid increased gentrification and social exclusion from real estate market operations. Successful local economic development strategies tend to result in pressures on land and real estate prices, with negative effects on the more vulnerable segments of the city. Moreover, the more recent data on FDI indicate that Istanbul has recovered from its earlier financial crises, and that the real estate markets are again becoming increasingly attractive for international investors. While this by itself is important evidence of the vibrancy of the city, the other side of the coin is that increasing pressure on the local real estate markets can be expected in the coming period. To combat the increasing threat of gentrification and social exclusion through real estate markets, the city of Istanbul should increase its managerial and institutional capacity to capture more of the real estate property value increases resulting from public investments in infrastructure and zoning changes. This capacity will be fundamental in gaining leverage over market actors, and to cross-subsidise and include the more vulnerable segments of the city. The new mortgage system[17] and the mass housing projects for low-income target groups represent only one (rather limited) response to this complex challenge. In addition, both the specific urban transformation projects (ports, hotels, office towers), and the relocation and removal of substandard and squatter housing, should be carefully evaluated and inserted into a city-wide urban development plan. For example, detailed and participatory appraisal of project scenarios may surface signs that relocation will be a more costly operation (in terms of infrastructure and hidden transportation costs from the new locations, disruption of intangible economic community networks in existing locations, etc.) compared to integrating low-income communities into the socio-economic fabric of the city. In that respect, it is recommended that the newly established public real estate company be required to operate under a transparent and decentralised system of project formulation, implementation and monitoring.

Urban planning in Istanbul addresses the concentration of population issue in a limited way. The vision for spatial development throughout Istanbul is expressed both in the Environmental Order Plan and the 2023 Strategic Plan, both of which are being elaborated by the Municipality. The first was formerly drawn by the Ministry of Environment and Forestry but then devolved to the Municipality whilst the second has been elaborated under the responsibility of the Istanbul Metropolitan Municipality. The last Environmental Order Plan elaborated in July 2006 aims to transform Istanbul into a financial centre and delocalise industrial activities outside the city centre. More concretely, the metropolitan area has been divided in eight sub-zones with several "activities centres". This polycentric structure should be supported by a transportation system as well as major housing and infrastructure development projects. This vision clearly targets a more even pattern of urban development with the objective to relieve the pressure on the centre by creating new centres of attraction in the city outskirts. Overall, existing actions (such as the decision to build a third bridge on the Strait of Istanbul more to the southern part of the metropolitan areas) and those that are provided in the strategic and environmental plans aim to develop a more polycentric metropolitan city. The main concern to better control the oversize growth of Istanbul is not appropriately addressed.

Environmental issues and earthquake risks

Moving towards more sustainable urban development is probably one of the most important challenges for Istanbul. Generally speaking, sustainable development and environmental considerations have only recently been taken into account in Istanbul. Until recently, protection of the environment was limited essentially to policy on water (cleaning up rivers and stretches of water) and on waste management. The efforts made by the Municipality of Istanbul with regard to water management deserve special mention, however, since they have been quite remarkable (Box 2.12). For some time, a wider concept of the environment has begun to be adopted, one which includes air quality. The main cause of air pollution is said to be from the use of coal (or brown coal) for heating and, to a lesser extent, from unregulated industrialisation. Often, environmentalist arguments are used by those opposing major building projects (universities, professional bodies, notably the association of architects, and other local associations).[18] Conversely the traumatic effect of the 1999 earthquake probably played a catalytic role in raising awareness of the unsustainable pattern of Istanbul's rapid development. This section will address environmental issues in three related specific areas: (1) the environmental impact of uncontrolled urban development; (2) the environmental risks due to natural disasters and the over-use of the Strait of Istanbul; and (3) the environmental impact of transport pollution.

(1) Uncontrolled urban development

Illegal settlement proliferation has exacerbated environmental risks in Istanbul. The example of the Ömerli watershed clearly illustrates the dramatic consequences of haphazard land use developments. Its surrounding areas have been facing exponential population growth from 36 860 in 1985 to 257 204 in 1997. Likewise, between 1985 and 1990, the average population growth around the watershed exceeded the average rate for Istanbul as a whole (26.8% *versus* 5.7%, respectively). The newly created *gecekondu* city, with an estimated population of around 170 000 to 350 000 inhabitants, is a direct consequence of these developments. The area represents substantial threats in terms of health, environmental and earthquake risks. In general, inhabitants are suspect of the basic sanitation in the Ömerli area, a direct indicator being that in general the people in Istanbul do not drink from the tap, but buy their water.

Box 2.12. Water management in Istanbul

In the early 1990s significant improvements in water management and infrastructure investments have been the key initiatives conducted by the Istanbul municipality to overcome severe water shortages triggered by the rapid population surge. As mentioned in Chapter 1, in the early 1990s Istanbul experienced severe water shortages as in-migration (14.6% annual growth in 1980-85) had surpassed the projected water demand. Then huge investments (USD 3.6 billion in 1994-2004) were made to improve and expand water and wastewater systems (Altinbilek, 2006). Several large-scale transmission projects were started. For example, seven hydraulic barrages were built between 1994 and 2000 to meet the exponentially growing water demand. With new investment the water reserve capacity increased from 590 million m^3 per year (1994 figure) to 1 170 million m^3 per year (2005 figure), and the capacity of water refining facilities increased from 1 million m^3 per day (1994 figure) to 3.6 million m^3 per day (2005 figure). Between 1994 and 2005, the length of the water transmission network multiplied by two. Moreover, water quality has improved recently by sharp increases in wastewater treatment (95% in 2004) and new treatment plants. A survey in 2004 shows that 35% of the customers drink tap water, which is an increase from 10% in 2000. The unaccounted for water rate has been reduced from 50 to 34%.

Nowadays Istanbul has enough drinkable water resources, thanks to pro-active water management backed by successful infrastructure investments. Since 1981, water and wastewater management have been under the authority of the Istanbul Water and Sewerage Administration (ISKI), an independent metropolitan agency with 9 000 staff and an annual operating budget of USD 1.65 billion in 2007. ISKI has the right to set water and sewage tariffs with no external approval. In 2004, ISKI formulated the Water Master Plan to address the long-term scope until 2040 for population estimates, water requirements, water resources, water purification and sewerage work, and the recycling potential of treated wastewater. It includes new large-scale water supplies projects, including new pipelines for transporting water from the Asian side to the European side, to meet projected demand until 2040. With the increase in ISKI's competencies evidenced in the 2004 legislation, the ability of ISKI to fight against invasion of water reserves by informal settlements has significantly improved. Since a large portion (97%) of water supply of Istanbul is from surface sources, Istanbul has designated water protection zones to preserve watersheds from increasing pressure of population growth. For instance, a new satellite system permits ISKI to immediately detect new informal structures in the preserved watersheds area, and after detection of such informal housing ISKI destructs all of them in a very decisive way. In 1994, ISKI performed the Golden Horn Environmental Rehabilitation Project, the world's largest estuary cleaning operation dedicated to the decontamination of the Marmara Sea beaches and the surrounding areas that totalled a cost of USD 653 million. This project was awarded First Prize in the 2002 Metropolis Award.

Source: Altınbilek, D. (2006), "Water Management in Istanbul", *Water Resources Development*, Vol. 22, No. 2, 241–253.

Again the current pattern of relatively fragmented, parallel and "semi-planned" urban development does not lend itself to addressing sustainability concerns. For instance, planning for sustainable development in the Ömerli watershed has resulted in a dispute, due to lack of horizontal and vertical co-ordination between the bodies involved, and in the presence of overlapping responsibilities. The Ministry of Environment and Forestry, the Ministry of Finance, the Ministry of Public Works and Settlement, the Ministry of Health, and the ISKI (the metropolitan water and sewerage administration of the Istanbul Metropolitan Municipality), are all, to some extent, involved in the sustainability of the Ömerli watershed whilst the State Planning Organization approves public investment projects. However, this has been challenging due to the serious overlap in watershed-related planning responsibilities amongst the local, provincial and national actors. This complex and multi-faceted environment is further aggravated by local elections and party dynamics that frequently trigger *ad hoc* amnesty procedures and relaxation of density restrictions around watersheds. The dynamics of electoral disputes and party politics, and the informal negotiations of occasional conflicts between technical staff and politicians have proven to be at least as important as the formal regulatory and institutional framework, charged with providing guidelines for the overall land use patterns in the watersheds around Istanbul.

(2) Earthquake disasters and risks

Earthquakes pose a significant environmental threat, seen in the 1999 Marmara earthquake with its epicentre very close to the city which evidenced the need for safer building stocks. The private sector (particularly SMEs) and individuals tend to ignore unforeseen losses and pay less attention to the structural soundness of their property. Although more large companies and individuals have bought insurance since the Marmara Earthquake, most SMEs and people still have no insurance and have hardly improved their assets, mainly driven by lack of financing. The best solution for substantially decreasing casualties caused by possible earthquakes is to have seismic resistant buildings. A sizeable proportion of current construction activities are not in compliance with the formal regulatory framework. The huge stock of *gecekondu* housing, built illegally without regard for land use permits or building standards, represents a potential time bomb of damage and loss of lives. It is a great challenge to convince the private sector and individuals of the value of safer buildings and involve them in joint disaster reduction – requiring them to rebuild or reinforce the majority of the existing building stock according to anti-seismic building code standards. Newly introduced stricter regulation and punishment for informal housing will improve the situation. Furthermore, as another big earthquake is predicted to occur in the near future, preventive measures for reducing congestion could also contribute to mitigating the potential damage. Considering the high concentration of urban functions in Istanbul some measures should be taken to reduce concentration of population, firms, industry and activities in the metropolitan area.

A number of studies have been produced to assess and provide recommendations for a comprehensive earthquake prevention strategy, but with no clear implementation mechanism.[19] This series of studies provided a quantitative analysis of the possible casualties and damage to Istanbul, and served as a wake-up call for policy makers to take action. Based on these studies, the Istanbul Metropolitan Municipality commissioned an extensive study on means for substantially decreasing casualties and damage from possible earthquakes. At the request of the Istanbul Metropolitan Municipality academics from the four major leading universities of Turkey (Boğaziçi, Istanbul Technical, Middle East Technical and Yıldız Technical Universities) were mobilised to address a wide range of issues and formed a consortium to produce the Istanbul Earthquake Master Plan (IEMP/IDMP). The overall purpose of IEMP is to enhance safety and total quality of life in the city of Istanbul by:

- Reducing infrastructural deficiencies
- Gradually eliminating the unauthorised housing stock
- Integrating city management processes
- Protecting the natural and historical assets
- Reclaiming urban quality and identity
- Stimulating the participation of the local communities in the management of the city
- Providing comprehensive rehabilitation of high-risk areas
- Retrofitting or removing buildings according to local plans

A 1 300-page study highlighting the critical issues facing Istanbul is complemented with a group of independent international experts commissioned by the Istanbul Metropolitan Municipality, tasked to review and provide additional advice and opinions on the study. The IEMP itself created a comprehensive meta-analysis of a compilation of studies covering a broad range of topics describing in detail the analytical frameworks and their findings. Nevertheless, the above-mentioned study did not result in a kind of manual for policy implementation for substantially decreasing potential future earthquake damage. The absence of a comprehensive executive summary targeted at policy makers reduced the effectiveness of the lengthy, highly technical study.

The impasse surrounding the Istanbul Earthquake Master Plan (IEMP/IDMP) is once again symbolic of the level of semi-planning in Istanbul. Although the political will and the expertise are present, a critical link with implementation is missing. More specifically, there is no detailed roadmap for implementation that indicates priorities and mechanisms to convince policy makers and citizens of the real economic value and opportunity costs of risk reduction. The IEMP is a wealth of precious ideas for Istanbul's disaster reduction that need only be transformed into policy, eliminating the need to "re-invent the wheel" with another brainstorming for disaster reduction. Rather the challenges are how the IEMP can incorporate into the main priorities streamlining, priority setting within realistic timelines, structural orientation, and evaluation of the costs and financial implications of each of the proposals as well as mechanisms for conflict negotiation and consensus building among stakeholders on the main priorities. The draft bill on addressing urban area needs for transformation, development, and investment, which is currently pending in Turkish parliament, is expected to address and clarify these issues. On the basis of these missing parameters, the document needs to be "translated" into a more structured agenda for policy makers.

It should be noted, however, that some progress in this area is being made. Individual elements of IEMP/IDMP are being adopted and implemented, like the recent publication of a wide variety of reference material aimed at raising public awareness of earthquakes. Law enforcement on illegal occupation through *gecekondu* is also being intensified. Furthermore, expert seminars on the risks of earthquakes, and how to address local opinion leaders, are being organised. Out of the wealth of ideas contained within IEMP some practical activities have also been started. For example, in partnership with foreign donors, major projects such as the seismic reinforcements of the bridges of the Strait of Istanbul are to be implemented. The Zeytinburnu Project, implemented in Istanbul's built-up area, and aimed at urban renewal and seismic safety, is also showing progress. Another example is the Istanbul Metropolitan Municipality Disaster Coordination Center (AKOM). In 2001 the Istanbul Metropolitan Municipality established this emergency operations centre in the outskirts of Istanbul, so that in the event of an emergency, key emergency responders could find one another. Additionally, cargo containers storing emergency response tools such as shovels, saws, buckets, generators, first aid kits, etc., were painted orange and placed in small parks and along roadside strips. These are evidence that Istanbul authorities are aware and planning for possible future earthquakes. While this shows some progress, though the majority of the proposals contained in the IEMP/IDMP are still awaiting implementation.

More generally, disaster management requires streamlined governance and wider co-operation with the private sector and individuals. The governor is responsible for emergency command, though overall disaster management is the mayor's responsibility. Closer collaboration between these two actors would bring efficient and effective outcomes. In other nations with two tier local governments, such as Japan, the municipal mayor is responsible for taking the lead in the event of a disaster. If the severity of the incident is too great, the mandate will pass on to a higher level such as the prefecture governor then Minister of Disaster Management and Prime Minister. This is also the case for the Strait of Istanbul, which requires closer collaboration of all maritime affairs actors including the Ministry of Transport, the Directorat General of Coastal Safety, the Governor of Istanbul, research centres as well as international co-operation. As is often the case, disasters have triggered severe macroeconomic and structural policy changes, and offered opportunities to accelerate and reinforce reforms. Since congestion of population, firms, industry and centric functions is vulnerable to disasters, an epicentral earthquake in close proximity to a densely populated urban area will cause serious damage not only on physical structures but also to economic and social structures. In other countries policy reforms after urban earthquake disasters have placed a focus on disaster management, particularly on the precaution and preparedness stages (Box 2.13).

(3) Transport, pollution and environment

Public authorities, and especially local ones, are beginning to include environmental considerations to a greater extent into their transport policies. A number of initiatives aimed at reducing traffic congestion and by the same token pollution, are worthy of mention since they demonstrate that environmental concerns are beginning to be included in transport policies in practice and are no longer merely a stated intention. They include the following:

- **Regulating heavy goods vehicles in transit and measures to direct automobile traffic to the second bridge.** For some years, heavy goods vehicles in transit have no longer, without special authorisation, been able to use the first bridge over the Strait of Istanbul, one of these most centrally located bridges. The reasons for this are twofold: the need to make traffic in the centre more fluid, and the desire to limit exhaust pollution (or more accurately, to move it elsewhere). Another measure taken has been to remove the cash payment booths on the first bridge – effective as of the beginning of April 2006 – in an effort to discourage private car drivers from using this bridge. Already, there has been a significant decrease in traffic.

Box 2.13. Lessons from urban earthquake disasters in other countries

The Great Hanshin-Awaji Earthquake in Japan

Kobe, a Japanese city with a population of 1.5 million, endured a great earthquake with its active fault line directly beneath the city at dawn on 17 January 1995. The quake claimed 6 433 lives and ruined 250 000 buildings (105 000 completely collapsed and 144 000 partially collapse). Almost 80% of the victims died in the collapse of old dilapidated wooden houses and in the massive fires that followed the quake. Lifeline services were interrupted, particularly sewage and gas systems, all of which were only restored after long delays. Elevated expressways collapsed, and railroads and ports suffered great damage as well.

The Great Hanshin-Awaji Earthquake caused JPY 10 trillion (over USD 100 billion) in damage, which was 2.5% of Japan's GDP at the time, equivalent to the Hyogo prefectural budget for six years. This case was significantly beyond the capability of even the prefectural government to bear, although initially local governments had primary management responsibility. One of the most serious problems is delay of first response due to lack of information. The pre-established damage reporting system, which had worked in other disasters, did not function well. Initially the central government was not able to collect enough information and co-ordinate the necessary immediate action because local government command was paralysed due to damage at its headquarters in addition to interruption of telecommunications and even satellite system.

Another important issue which drew great attention was that it was in fact the buildings dating back before the reinforced seismic building code of 1981 that caused a large majority of deaths. The general public was only made aware seven years after the earthquake. The announcement ultimately leads to various efforts for retrofitting and reinforcement of existing buildings.

After the earthquake, the central government drastically revised and created disaster-related laws, including emergency response procedures, fiscal protocols, reconstruction, and precaution/preparedness measures to accelerate the reinforcement and retrofitting of existing buildings. The government also used this opportunity to invest in disaster prevention resources such as a seismic observation facility, information and communication systems. Extensive review of the building safety of public infrastructure and buildings, and reviews of safety standards were conducted. The Japanese government drastically revised the Basic Law on Disaster Prevention (1961) and the Basic Plan for Disaster Prevention* (formulated in 1963 and partially amended in 1971) to respond to the present socio-economic conditions, and to clarify the responsibilities at each level of government. The Special Measures Law on Earthquake Disaster Prevention was also enacted, which stipulates a five-year plan for urgent earthquake prevention works and its special financial measures as well as the creation of earthquake research units.

Box 2.13. **Lessons from urban earthquake disasters in other countries** (*cont.*)

Within the central government, the Minister for Disaster Management has recently introduced a nationwide support system for disaster emergency response through a co-ordinated organisational effort (Police, Self Defence Forces, hospitals, etc.). Prefecture and Municipal levels have also contributed by establishing the Local Disaster Prevention Council and preparing local disaster plans. Although the local government is responsible for taking necessary action within its jurisdictional areas in the event of an emergency, based on the scale of disaster and damage level, prefecture and central governments also assist municipalities in various ways. The Great Hanshin Earthquake also made citizens aware of disaster issues and even compelled them to get involved in voluntary activities. Evacuation drills have been more actively conducted at the community level, in schools and throughout the business sector, as well as large-scale co-ordinated exercises.

Since this time Japan has been confronted with a number of disasters including earthquakes, typhoons and floods, with each event contributing to the review and improvement of the disaster management system.

The Northridge earthquake in the United States

The Northridge earthquake occurred at dawn on 17 January 1994 in Los Angeles, California. Fifty-seven people were killed, more than 9 000 were seriously injured, approximately 100 000 homes and businesses were damaged, and more than 20 000 people were displaced from their homes. The earthquake caused economic losses estimated at USD 49.3 billion (USD 41.8 billion in direct economic loss and USD 7.5 billion in indirect economic loss) (Petak, 2000). Damage extended across an area of approximately 900 km^2, with severe damage concentrated in the residential and commercial buildings, and lifelines in the epicentre region. In addition, major freeways including the Santa Monica Freeway (Interstate Highway 10) suffered serious damage including the collapse of numerous bridges.

This damage has shown that the existing building safety standards were unable to withstand such a big earthquake. Above all, the earthquake highlighted the vulnerability of apartment complexes built over parking garages. After the earthquake, building regulations have been modified to create more earthquake resistant buildings and infrastructure. In an effort to strengthen disaster preparedness, an earthquake research centre was established, and a wide collaborative research and information network was developed.

The local government, namely the City of Los Angeles and the State Government of California, took a number of practical measures while the Federal Emergency Management Agency (FEMA) also contributed to by providing personnel and financial support for the recovery. One example of this was the City of Los Angeles red-tagging damaged buildings unsafe to enter, yellow-tagging limited entry buildings and designating 17 "Ghost towns" with

Box 2.13. Lessons from urban earthquake disasters in other countries (*cont.*)

concentrations of red- and yellow-tagged multi-family structures in one or more adjacent city blocks as prioritised recovery areas. The extensive public investment in these areas induced private investment.

The Northridge earthquake transformed the city's risk management strategy including making the insurance system and catastrophe modelling far more effective than before. Claims in Northridge totalled USD 15.3 billion (over 60% were from personal line exposure), far beyond initial expectations. In 1996 the California legislature created the California Earthquake Authority (CEA) as a privately funded, publicly managed organisation for offering standardised, limited, residential earthquake insurance coverage.

* At the national level, the Central Disaster Prevention Council, including the Prime Minister as a chairman and members of government agencies and institutions, holds the main responsibility for disaster management. The Council formulates the "Basic Plan for Disaster Prevention" which defines the basic guidelines for establishing a disaster reduction organisation, and promoting disaster prevention programmes and rescue and relief operations, including scientific and technical research work.

Source: Data for the Japanese case came from the Cabinet Office's 2002 Annual Official Report on Disaster Prevention, June 2002 (Japan) as well as other several sources[20]. Data and information from the US case came from Petak, William (2000) "The Northridge Earthquake USA and its Economic and Social Impacts." EuroConference on Global Change and Catastrophe Risk Management, IIASA, Laxenburg, Austria, Risk Management Solutions (RMS) (2004) The Northridge, California Earthquake -RMS10-year Retrospective-, RMS. *www.rms.com/publications/northridgeeq_retro.pdf* as well as other sources.[21]

- **Preferential pricing policies and incentives in "public" collective transport.** In order to encourage the use of boats, seen as more environment-friendly, the municipal authorities have introduced lower fares (at certain times)[22] and accelerated the integration of maritime traffic into the single pricing system (giving the right, within a timeframe of an hour and a half, to use several modes of public transport successively with a single ticket).[23] The municipality does this primarily through its intermediary IDO,[24] the semi-private company set up by the Mayor's office, which since March 2006 has administered all public marine vessels. But these campaigns and initiatives have not yet resulted in any considerable or permanent increase in the share of maritime transport in the total of intra-urban travel (a share which has fallen sharply since 1980), in spite of the introduction of two new passenger/car ferries (in July 2004) and the introduction of new lines like the Pendik-Yalova (since 8 July 2004). The introduction of a "magnetic ticket" (or "intelligent ticket" – *Akbil*) has been an important step in encouraging the use of public transport, beyond maritime transport alone, rather than private cars. While not enough time has yet passed to assess the impact of this new system, it would appear that some types of behaviour have changed.

- **Banning private collective transport within the historical peninsula.** The historical peninsula, approximately 1 500 hectares, is the symbolic, geometric and historical heart of Istanbul. In spite of the measures taken since 2004, it retains a functional and economic centrality beyond tourism alone. Limited by its Byzantine walls, this peninsula is structurally clogged. The major "works" of the 1930s (Boulevard Atatürk), then the 1950s (creation of roads between the walls and Aksaray, *Vatan and Millet Boulevards*) began the process of automobile penetration, which was completed in spectacular fashion by the opening up of the roads along the shoreline. Saturation point has now been reached. Before taking measures against private cars, the local authorities turned their attention to independent lorry drivers and small private collective transport operations (*dolmuş* – shared taxis or minibus). But in Galata and Karaköy, the bans issued have not been observed, anymore than the shopkeepers and craftsmen have moved out of the area in spite of the incentives introduced more than 20 years ago. Moreover, under the "Istanbul: Museum City" project launched in May 2004, the peninsula is first and foremost to serve tourism (as well as residential) functions. To this end, an attempt was made on moving activities generating nuisance and traffic out of the peninsula – various workshops and businesses causing a nuisance were moved to areas far out from the centre (such as Ikitelli and Tuzla) – and a strict traffic plan is in the process of being adopted.

- **Introducing "Green" buses** that run on gas and pollute less than buses that run on diesel. At the same time, an effort is being made to renew the bus fleet, to improve comfort, ensure access for handicapped persons, and meet environmental considerations. Thus, dozens of buses have recently been introduced, replacing part of the obsolete (public) fleet.

- **The involvement of IDO in roll-on/roll-off freight and passenger transport.** With the aim of reducing intra-urban heavy goods traffic, the Istanbul Metropolitan Municipality announced that by the end of the year 2006, regular roll-on/roll-off lines would run between Ambarlı (west periphery of Greater Istanbul) and Bandirma (on the south bank of the Marmara Sea, near Bursa). Two vessels, each with a capacity of 250 lorries, should help to reduce intra-urban traffic.

These initiatives remain, however, somewhat uncoordinated, given the absence of a more comprehensive crosscutting environmental policy. This problem is linked in part to the current institutional set-up:

- The Metropolitan Municipality of Istanbul has a "Directorate for the Protection and Improvement of the Environment" whose budget and responsibilities are fairly limited. For some years, this Directorate has published data on the state of air pollution at regular intervals.[25] However, "the environment" remains first and foremost the quality of surface water. Consequently, it is the municipally-managed ISKI (Istanbul Water and Sewerage Administration) – a large organisation in terms of its budget, staff and powers – which in practice has a quasi monopoly over municipal policy on the environment.
- The municipal authorities have also just added an additional body, specialised in environmental engineering, a private law company[26] whose goal is to help Istanbul comply with European standards, in particular in the sphere of the environment, while working to improve the quality of life. So far, however, it has launched few initiatives and has a low profile, indeed almost no profile at all in the field of the environment.
- At the provincial level, the Provincial Special Administration (also has a "Directorate for the Environment and Forests" which acts through a foundation ("The Istanbul Foundation for Environmental Protection"), created in 1991. This Foundation receives part of its income from the tax on exhaust emissions ("*Egzos Emisyon Pulu*").
- As for local neighbourhood authorities, they launched largely symbolic initiatives such as the organisation of awareness campaigns (especially during "Environment Week") or events (such as the "Day Without Cars") aimed at promoting alternative non-polluting modes of transport.

The assessment of the existing institutional arrangements with regard to the environment clearly demonstrates that environmental considerations have not been integrated across the board and collaboration has been limited), particularly with regard to transport policy. In other words, the crosscutting nature of environmental policy, which should concern all branches of municipal activity, does not yet seem to have been recognised or acted upon. Moreover, the absence of an independent agency capable of producing reliable data on the environment is also a problem. The "Chamber of Environmental Engineers" (ÇMO), created recently reflects the emergence of an occupation, as yet little recognised, that could represent independent partners to the movement. It can make proposals and criticisms, in particular with regard to transport policy, but for the moment remains sidelined.

2.3. Istanbul in Turkey: the challenge of regional development policies

Regional disparities in Turkey and overflow of population into Istanbul are the two sides of the same coin. As mentioned in Chapter 1, Turkey displays the largest disparities among OECD countries. While a slow convergence process seems to be detected, it would take decades to bridge the income per capita gap among regions. Meanwhile, Istanbul has registered dramatic demographic growth much of which comes from other regions in Turkey. The resulting over-concentration in Istanbul has reached its sustainable limit, necessitating a national strategy for managing future growth. Experiences of containment policies in OECD countries (Paris in the 1960s, Tokyo from 1959-2002, London from 1965-1979 and Seoul from the 1970s to present) have provided mixed outcomes. There is little reliable data showing whether constraints on the growth of the major region actually displaced economic activities to other domestic regions, in attempts to offset the loss in the major region with higher growth elsewhere in the country (OECD, 2006a). OECD studies have demonstrated that regional development policies are needed to tackle regional disparities by focusing on strengthening the competitive advantages of regions (OECD, 2005d).

Past regional development policies in Turkey have reinforced the polarisation effects on a few cities. Traditionally, public investment policies in Turkey have been centrally managed and based on a sectoral approach. Until the 1960s, priority was given to national industrial development with no real regard for addressing regional disparities. To the extent that there was a regional focus the emphasis was on physical development planning. Even if these regional plans aimed to level off over-urbanisation and relocate industries towards outskirts with physical development plans, they ended up encouraging the agglomeration of industry and services in a few cities in western Turkey, only further reinforcing regional disparities.

When an explicit objective to address regional disparities was introduced, it was not supported with appropriate policy tools and institutional co-ordination. Since the 1960s the five-year National Development Plans have had a regional development component aimed at reducing regional disparities. The main focus of regional development policies was on encouraging private investment through incentives in less developed regions, mainly in industrial sectors, and, through large public infrastructure investment, intended to make lagging regions more attractive. The plans have also provided support for "Priority Regions for Development", "Organised Industrial Zones", "Small Industry Estates", and rural development projects. There has, however, been a consistent tension in the plans between two main goals, *i.e.*, "maximising national income" on the one hand and, "reducing inter-regional disparities" on the other. The plans have also not been fully implemented often because either rapid change in the scope of the investment agenda or because inadequate resources were allocated to them, and because of inefficient mechanisms of co-operation amongst institutions.

The introduction of further reforms was not sufficient for addressing the issue. Although there were substantial developments in focus and emphasis within the centralised planning framework, attempts to reduce regional disparities were not a success. Reform included a series of changes to the planning approach in the 1980s away from a plan driven by import substitution toward a focus on the development of an outward-looking export based economy. Although the plans did contribute to mobilising local potential they were unsuccessful at reducing regional disparities. The reasons for this include: insufficient selection criteria for the identification of priority regions resulting in a large number of such regions, and then the subsequent difficulty in determining provincial development priorities and the misallocation of public investments in lagging regions (resulting for example in unused airports).

A new approach to regional policy has been emerging in recent years. Policy makers are aware that the failure to reduce regional disparities in Turkey will imply a continuous drain on Istanbul's resources and infrastructure, and ever increasing flows of informal migration into the city. Therefore, they tend to agree on focussing on the following action lines to address regional disparities: promoting other regional poles of growth and their integration within internal markets, and creating more integrated development policies, to better mobilise local resources and actors by supporting them through the appropriate governance, models and institutional structures. This new approach, once implemented, will move regional policy of Turkey closer to the approaches in other OECD countries. The prospect of EU accession has been a catalyst for this new policy direction.

A number of concrete actions have been taken in this direction. For instance, the Preliminary 2004-2006 National Development Plan already focussed on the promotion of human and institutional capacity, competitive small and medium-sized enterprises and rural local economies in less developed regions to reduce disparities in income, employment and socio-economic infrastructure. The 9th National Development Plan for 2007-2013 adopted on 28 June 2006,[27] emphasises the inter-regional income differentials in Turkey, and between Turkey's regions and EU regions, and includes plans to overcome inter-regional migration problem and provide higher-quality urbanisation. The plan also alludes to developing regional cities to strengthen the competitiveness of other regions and counterbalance the weight of Istanbul. Moreover, a new spatial division of Turkey into 26 NUTS 2 regions has been developed as well (Box 2.14). Turkey has enacted the legal framework for creating Development Agencies (DAs), which are institutions established in NUTS 2 regions, designed to enhance co-operation amongst public and private actors in order to promote regional development (see Chapter 3). As of September 2006, two DAs have been established, one in Izmir (the third biggest city in Turkey) and the other in Adana and Mersin (medium-sized cities). In the State Planning Organization, co-ordination and control entities are being established (the EU Regional Department Programmes and the Monitoring and Evaluation Department).

Box 2.14. **NUTS 2 regions in Turkey**

Turkey's administrative hierarchy from 1925 onwards has consisted of provinces, counties, towns and villages. In the 1950s the country was further divided into seven geographical regions, each one encompassing about ten provinces. There are, however, no governance institutions at the level of the seven 1950s regions.

A new tier designated in 2002 groups the 81 provinces into 26 NUTS 2 clusters. The regulation has also coined provinces as NUTS 3 level, and designated the new 15 adjacent NUTS 2 groups as NUTS 1 level. The reason for the recent stipulation is that the seven geographical regions are not appropriate for regional policy purposes due to their sheer size and the provinces are too small for developing a coherent and efficient regional policy. The recent regulation was also laid down to ensure harmonisation with the EU region definition and to achieve both more efficient implementation and analysis of regional development policies.

The NUTS 2 regions are relatively homogenous regions in terms of size (spatial coverage), but include considerable variation with respect to GDP per head and population. Istanbul, for instance, has the highest population amounting to 14.7% of total population. None of the NUTS 2 regions lie above 60% of the average EU 25 income level. The poorest region has a GDP per capita of 11.5% of the EU 25 average, and in the wealthiest region GDP per capita is 52% of the EU 25 average. The province of Istanbul is a region at all NUTS levels.

Conclusion: towards the implementation of a coherent and comprehensive strategy

There are several positive initiatives ongoing aimed at stimulating a more competitive Istanbul. Policy makers in Turkey have shown increasing awareness of the fact that a competitive and liveable Istanbul requires initiatives aimed at both strengthening existing and attracting new enterprises to the city. Significant efforts in both these areas have yielded positive results for segments such as pharmaceutics, logistics and textile sectors. In the textile industry for instance, the Istanbul Textile and Clothing Export Union (ITKIB), a semi-public organisation located in the Under-Secretariat of the Prime Ministry for Foreign Trade, has managed to improve mechanisms for information sharing, and co-operation among small and medium-sized enterprises and facilitate penetration into export markets. The organisation is presently involved in an EU financed project aimed at building a co-operative network of SMEs that movies moving towards a more design and fashion intensive production complex that is able to compete in international markets. Likewise, in the context of the EU pre-accession phase, the Turkish government has negotiated a similar support from the EU for the elaboration and implementation of a broad based and integrated policy framework for cluster development and support. These are promising initiatives that should be followed up quickly. The implementation of Technoparks, and the increased priority on National Science and Technology Development Policy initiatives have been positive marks of an increased awareness of policy makers of Turkey on the role of learning and innovation systems in the global economy. These efforts could be complemented by specific strategies to tap all the potential of FDI in technology transfer, for instance, through such approaches as learning by doing and using. More specifically, in segments such as logistics and finance, where the inflows of FDI have indeed been impressive in recent years, there is a need for a strategic framework to make the best of their potential. The government has also made some initial steps toward establishing a national level industrial and technological development policy, with positive spin-off for sectors such as logistics and textile. Within the new regulatory framework several areas are relevant to urban and metropolitan competitiveness, namely attracting Foreign Direct Investment, deepening and broadening of financial liberalisation (with positive spin-off on the Istanbul Security Exchange, ISE), and creating a positive environment for innovation. In addition, as mentioned before, KOSGEB Turkey is setting up an enabling framework to support small and medium-sized enterprises implement strategies aimed at their managerial and technological modernisation. Finally, Development Agencies are the new regulatory framework for regional development policies, showing a certain commitment to a more participatory mode of governance.

Public policies are needed to accompany the adjustment process and foster the potential of specific niches. The economic basis of Istanbul is complex and relatively diversified. The restructuring process is moving in the direction of a command and control profile for the Istanbul economy within the national and international context (based on its financial, logistical and producer service hubs). The city of Istanbul has the potential to be home to a major part of these advanced services – such as finance, insurance, real estate, legal and accounting services, investment banking, pension and holding companies, etc. – within its so-called polycentric metropolitan area. Despite the fact that sectors such as car manufacturing have relocated outside the city (to Bursa, etc.), these advanced services will increasingly remain clustered in the city of Istanbul. Consequently, within the Balkan-Caucuses area, and with the right public policies in place, this bolsters Istanbul's potential for assuming the role of a regional hub in advanced producer services. Moreover, the presence of large industrial complexes that both offer potential and challenges cannot be underestimated. The adjustment process in these segments should not be left to the market alone, but rather be accompanied by specific public policies. The textile and clothing sector is a paradigmatic example. The potential of niches in design and fashion must also be viewed with its challenges as specific business segments that operate according to informal work practices, outdated managerial and technological production processes and counterproductive cost based competitive strategies. In practice, dealing with the multi-faceted structure of the textile sector will require a comprehensive policy framework that is able to simultaneously create a Textile Cluster Agency or a Fashion Institute, and transform the practices of informal businesses into economic units that are capable of generating decent and sustainable jobs.

A pro-active strategy is however needed to foster economic growth and address challenges in a more coherent way. There is a need for an active, territorial strategy to respond to the main limitations and potentialities of the city, and to give clear signals to the national and international community of Istanbul's new, differential brand. In the absence of a broader strategy, the city's historical, cultural and natural attractions, together with its geographical location, are likely to be under-utilised. Likewise, Istanbul has a legacy of disorganised land use, squatter settlements, environmental deterioration and earthquake risk. Failure to develop a policy agenda that deals with these challenges will only intensify its social and infrastructure bottlenecks, and may eventually affect the city's sustainability and competitiveness in the medium run. An active territorial strategy must not only be ambitious, but will require a multi-sectoral, integrated and a holistic perspective to urban development planning and implementation. In what follows, we will illustrate these issues with some examples.

A more flexible and multi-sectoral approach to urban development would facilitate this task. The relatively centralised, sector oriented and technocrat model of urban development planning will be increasingly limited in light of the increasing complexity and internationalisation of Istanbul. As mentioned before, the approach to planning in Turkey is characterised by a prevalence of sectoral analysis that gives priority to technical expert knowledge, *versus* information obtained through community based planning mechanisms. This model will increasingly face its limits in light of the global transformations that are taking place, which require faster, more participatory and dynamic sources of information collection, processing and analysis. As mentioned in Chapter 1, there is a lack of data on important dimensions of Istanbul (informal sector, housing and urban development patterns, recent trends in productive restructuring, etc.), which, by itself, render difficult a consistent city planning process. In addition, the classic expert driven planning model is also contradictory to the policy ambitions of the city of Istanbul as a global gateway city, which implies a more open ended and participatory model of policy elaboration and implementation. A more flexible approach to urban development planning would also imply overcoming the false idea of an intrinsic dichotomy between the environment *versus* the economy, the social *versus* the economic, the formal *versus* the informal, the legal *versus* the illegal, and, last but not least, centralisation *versus* decentralisation. Like many metropolitan areas, Istanbul will face the challenge to abandon some of these false dichotomies in order to advance in its transformation towards a more liveable and competitive city.

The international market branding strategy should be made more explicit through use of a participatory strategic planning approach. The ongoing initiatives towards the modernisation of Istanbul need to be broadened, strengthened and integrated into an entrepreneurial and comprehensive branding strategy that will give the right signals to the local, national and international community about the future trajectory of the city. In that sense, the creation of design clusters in the textile sector, the installation of FDI one-stop shops, the dissemination of Technoparks, the transformation of the Istanbul Stock Exchange into a regional financial hub, the modernisation of the logistics sector, and the revitalisation of historical and cultural tourism should all represent different dimensions of the city's determination to move out of its low-cost, high competitive market niches towards a virtuous trajectory based on differentiation, generation of local wealth, innovation, value-add and entrepreneurial spirit. In that respect, policy makers and stakeholders involved in the future of the city need to strengthen and integrate their varied previous initiatives, and communicate and market them in the international community. Elements of this new Istanbul brand have already been suggested by policy makers. For example, several of the more strategically oriented policy documents express the need to move towards a highly liveable, open and multi-cultural gateway city, which, through its successful economic performance based on knowledge intensive activities, tourism and business services, will also progressively succeed by including the more vulnerable segments of society. Nevertheless, as also suggested by international evidence on urban and regional revitalisation, ambitious views on urban restructuring should be elaborated, implemented and tested through broad based and participatory strategic planning. This will also help to correct and complement more technical views on "the new brand", and augment the leverage of individual urban transformation programmes. The latter can be understood in light of the fact that local stakeholders, once they feel they "own" part of the process, will more easily invest and buy into the strategic project of building a better future for the city of Istanbul.

The new institutions for regional and metropolitan economic development planning could be better utilised as active motors of change. For example, the Development Agencies should be utilised as experimental learning platforms for establishing participatory networks. In light of the limited experience accumulated – at least up at present – with this type of approach, it is recommended to start working with specific projects, and to allow private and public stakeholders to go through an incremental process of learning by doing. In that respect, the role of NGOs like the Istanbul Foundation for Culture and Arts (IKSV) and that of the History Foundation of Turkey (*Tarih Vakfi*) and Human Settlements Association (*İnsan Yerleşimleri Derneği*) in successfully mobilising the city in its campaign to become the European Cultural Capital can be taken as a good example. This local mobilisation of public and private actors, however troublesome and contentious it might have been in its initial stages, may also have stimulated social capital growth, and reinforced the positive momentum of the city itself. Therefore, experimental participatory and voluntary schemes of inter-municipal co-operation are needed to stimulate complementary bottom-up planning models. There is ample international evidence of the potential of such an informal learning by doing approach in the context of fragmented institutional municipal structures (see chapter on governance).

Horizontal and vertical information sharing among local, provincial and central governments needs to be improved. Perhaps as a result of the rather rapid transformations that are going on in the society of Turkey, there is a surprising lack of information sharing across projects and policies, which leads to negative effects on competitiveness. In the future, information sharing on the details of programmes and policies is likely to improve the quality of policies aimed at competitiveness.

Looking forward, Istanbul's historical, locational and geographical advantages should be transformed into dynamic competitive assets by means of an explicit economic strategy for the metropolitan area. The cornerstones of this economic strategy could be built on three basic pillars, *i.e.*, the creation of information systems in order to strengthen economic policy making, participatory governance and, finally, the potential positive inter-dependencies between metropolitan and national policy making.

- First, and as mentioned earlier, a dynamic and updated information base on such strategic dimensions as informal housing and urban development patterns, the socio-economic profile of households, metropolitan labour markets and productive restructuring, is missing. Consequently, there is a significant weakness in the basis for economic policy making. An explicit strategy that would both tackle the absolute lack of reliable and updated information, and strengthen the linkages between these information systems and the process of strategy formulation, would be highly beneficial for the quality of economic policy making in Istanbul.
- Second, the degree of participation in the planning cycle should be increased. In fact, planning involves both processes (negotiating conflicts, building incremental consensus, etc.) and products (the actual planning documents and frameworks that guide the development process). In that sense, one particularly promising application of a more participatory model of governance is in the possible linkages of physical and master planning, on one hand, and the local economic development strategies, on the other hand. For example, more technically oriented discussions on the impact of several land use scenarios could then be complemented by visions of opinion leaders from academia, private sector and NGOs.
- Third, both the city of Istanbul and other regions in Turkey could reap substantial benefits from more careful management of the inter-dependencies between the metropolitan economy of Istanbul, the national macroeconomic scenario, and the development potential of other regions in Turkey. The level of the exchange rate, for example, implies specific gains and losses between the more service oriented city of Istanbul (in favour of higher exchange rates) and export oriented manufacturing regions (that benefit from lower exchange rates). In order to avoid specific confrontational scenarios between Istanbul and the export oriented regions, the local service sector in Istanbul should be

keen on developing active strategies aimed at increasing its productivity levels. Another example of positive inter-dependencies is related to the exploration of complementary niches in (international) tourism between Istanbul (gateway city) and other regions such as the Anatolian coastal region.

Finally, although the fundamentals of the overall structural macroeconomic reforms triggered by the central government are going in the right direction, both Turkey and the City of Istanbul should nevertheless be prepared to deal with the eventual adverse economic shocks. In that respect, as has been documented by Öniş and Rubin (2003), the poor were relatively more affected by the 1994/2001 crises, leading to a loss in social capital, increasing poverty rates and the rise in parallel planning circuits and rent seeking mechanisms (once more crowding out the more vulnerable segments of Turkish society). Therefore, the social dimensions of the policy reforms that have been set in motion should be explored, and inserted as an intrinsic element within the overall policy approach. Some examples of this emerging social policy agenda have been mentioned in this report, and should be mainstreamed in order to cushion eventual macroeconomic shocks (reducing the tendencies towards an informalisation of the economy, upscale and mainstream inclusive housing and urban development policies, streamline educational policies, etc.).

Notes

1. First created in 1995 under the name of "Technology Monitoring and Evaluation Board": TİDEB, the name was later changed to TEYDEB "Technology and Innovation Funding Programs Directorate".

2. Technology Development Foundation of Turkey (TTGV) (Türkiye Teknolojiyi Güçlendirme Vakfi/TTGV) is a foundation established by 26 private sector companies, six public institutions, 10 umbrella organisations and 14 individuals. TTGV is established in accordance with the international loan agreement signed between the Republic of Turkey and the World Bank. TTGV is subject to all regulations on the foundations of the Republic of Turkey.

3. This techno-city is located in Maslak, a new business centre hosting Istanbul's financial cluster (with many large banks' headquarters located in this district).

4. Rent rate is EUR 6 per m^2.

5. According to the data from the Under-Secretariat of the Treasury, between 2000 and 2005, 7 493 foreign firms have invested in Turkey. The breakdown of these companies by mode of establishment was: company establishment (5 775), branch office establishments (216) and participation in national firms (1 502). In other words, in terms of the number of firms, some 20% of the FDI could be characterised as investment into joint ventures.

6. The European charter for small and medium-sized enterprises is aimed at strengthening the role of the European economy within the global system on the basis of viable and competitive SME.

7. Container capacity is measured in 20-foot equivalent units (TEU).

8. The amendment in the legislation to allow private port activities has had significant influence on the emergence of private ports into the Ambarlı port complex. Recently Marport, a joint venture formed by the Arkas subsidiary, Limar and MSC took over Armaport, the second largest container terminal in the Ambarlı port complex. Over the coming few years, Marport is planning to expand and upgrade Armaport, through an enlargement of container terminal area and the acquisition of modern

equipment. The main private investment strategy in the Ambarlı port complex has focused on terminal development, enlargement or modernisation to attract global operators. This trend may also be coupled with strategies to create logistics facilities.

9. December 2005, "Shanghai and Dubai Top Office Openings Survey", *International Financial Law Review*, London, p. 1; April 2006, "Dubai Exchange Set for Listings Surge", *International Financial Law Review*, London, p. 1; KPMG (September 2005), "Dubai International Financial Centre Issues New Laws", *International Tax Review*, London, p. 1; Lee, Eric (Spring 2005), "Dynamic Dubai", *Harvard International Review*, Vol. 27, Issue 1, Cambridge, pp. 12-13 (2 pp.); October 2002, "UK Firms Advise on Creation of Dubai Financial Hub", *International Financial Law Review*, Vol. 21, Issue 10, London, p. 7; Parsa, Ali, Ramin Keivani, Loo Lee Sim, Seow Eng Ong, Bassam Younis (2002), "Emerging Global Cities: Comparison of Singapore and the Cities of the United Arab Emirates", *Journal of Real Estate Portfolio Management*, Vol. 8, Issue 4, Boston, pp. 95-101 (7 pp.); Al Maktoum, Sheikh Mohammed Bin Rashid (Jan 2001), "Dubai: Regional Hub for the New Economy", *The OECD Observer*, OECD, Issue 224, Paris, p. 7 (1 p.); October 2000, "E-commerce Brings OECD to Dubai", *The OECD Observer*, OECD, Issue 223, Paris, p. 6 (1 p.); Andersen, Arthur (December 2000/January 2001), "Dubai Makes a Bid for E-business", *International Tax Review*, Vol. 12, Issue 1, London, pp. 47-49.

10. The projects aiming at protecting the historical urban fabric are the "Zeytinburnu Pilot Project", the "Küçükçekmece Sub-province Olympic Village and Environs Urban Transformation Project", and the "Fatih Sub-province Urban Transformation Planning Project", the "Istanbul Historical Peninsula Fener and Balat Districts Rehabilitation Project".

11. The European Capital of Culture is a city designated by the European Union for a period of one year during which it is given a chance to showcase its cultural life and cultural development. A number of European cities have used the City of Culture year to completely transform their cultural base and, in doing so, the way in which they are viewed internationally.

12. The bill (No. 5706) that states that Istanbul is ready to be European Capital of Culture 2010 was approved in Parliament on 2 November 2007. This law decrees the establishment of an Agency for a European Capital of Cultural which is composed of three committees (co-ordinating, executive and advisory boards) as well as a wide range of stakeholders, including the following: a Secretariat General, representatives from the Ministry of Finance, Ministry of Culture and Tourism, the Ministry of Foreign Affairs, the Governorship of Istanbul, Istanbul Metropolitan Municipality, Prime Ministry Secretariat General

for EU Affaires, RTÜK (Radio and Television Supreme Council), General Directorate of Historical Foundations, professional institutions, such as the Istanbul Chamber of Architects, and NGOs like the Istanbul Chamber of Commerce (ITO), Istanbul Chamber of Industry, TÜRSAB (The Association of Turkish Travel Agencies), academics and experts.

13. Projects under construction include the Kadıköy-Kartal metro line (21.7 km), the Levent-Hacıosman (8 km), the Taksim-Yenikapı metro line (5.2 km), the Aksaray-Yenikapı LRT metro line (700 m), the Otogar-Bağcılar LRT line (5.4 km), the Bağcılar-İkitelli metro line (15.9 km), and the Topkapı-Sultançiftliği tram line (15.5 km.) totalling 72.5 km of new lines. Projects currently being tendered total 44 km including the Bakırköy-Beylikdüzü high capacity LRT (25 km) and the Üsküdar-Çekmeköy high capacity LRT (19 km).

14. The project includes a 13.6 km crossing with four new underground stations and the upgrade of 63 km of suburban train lines in order to create a 76.3 km long high-capacity line between Gebze and Halkalı. It has been constructed by earthquake-resistant engineering against magnitude 7.5 level earthquakes. It is scheduled for completion by 2010.

15. The current Strait of Istanbul crossing consists of 46% automobiles, 28% bus, 19% sea, and 7% company and school buses (Haluk Gerçek).

16. The concept of *gecekondu* can sometimes be misleading. Sometimes, the figures provided include only the first generation of illegal constructions. However, in other cases, statistics on *gecekondu* include luxurious villas and illegal buildings (*kaçak yapı* in Turkish).

17. The new Mortgage Law came into effect in March 2007.

18. Such as that in Arnavutköy, one of the neighbourhoods which might be chosen for a third road bridge over the Strait of Istanbul.

19. First, the comprehensive earthquake damage assessment and seismic micro-zonation done by the Japanese International Cooperation Agency (JICA) at the request of the Istanbul Metropolitan Municipality in March 2002, laid the foundation for a series of counter measures aimed at reducing earthquake risks. In addition, an earthquake risk assessment report for the Istanbul Metropolitan Area was conducted by Boğazici University (famous for its Kandilli Observatory, which monitors seismic activities throughout Turkey) with the support of the American Red Cross. The Boğazici University, with the support of Munich-Re Group, also implemented earthquake risk assessment for industrial facilities. The World Bank also introduced the Marmara Earthquake Emergency Reconstruction (MEER) project, which included both soft measures (*e.g.*, efficient disaster insurance schemes, modifications to related laws, developing risk-based municipal master plans) and hard measures

(*e.g.*, construction of permanent housing, repair of existing housing stock and health-care facilities, rebuilding and repair of infrastructure and lifelines). The Turkish Improvement of Natural Hazard Insurance and Disaster Funding Strategy Project was implemented under a joint project between the Under-Secretariat of Turkish Treasury and the World Bank.

20. Other sources include: the Cabinet Office of the Japanese government's website *www.bousai.go.jp/index.html* (Japanese); Hyogo Research Center for Quake Restoration (2005), *Lessons from the Great Hanshin Earthquake*, translation of selections from *Daishinnsai Hyaku no Kyokun* (*100 Lessons from the Great Hanshin Earthquake*), Creates-Kamogawa Publishers, written by over 50 scholars, citizens and activists who have been involved in the post-disaster reconstruction process after the great earthquake, *www.shinsai.or.jp/hrc-e/publish/lessons_ghe/*; Chang, Stephanie E. and Nobuoto Nojima (1999), "Measuring Post-Disaster Transportation System Performance: The 1995 Kobe Earthquake in Comparative Perspective", *Transportation Research*, *www.cive.gifu-u.ac.jp/~nojima/pdf/2000_transportation_a.pdf;* Nishikawa, Satoru (2006), "Progress of Disaster Administration Management in Japan", presentation material, JICA Seminar, June 2006, Istanbul; Shrestha, Bijaya (2001), "Disaster Reduction and Response Preparedness in Japan: A Hyogo Approach", second Tampere Conference on *Disaster Communications*, Tampere, Finland, 28-30 May 2001, *www.reliefweb.int/telecoms/conference/cdc2001/bks.doc.*

21. Other sources include: Cooper, James, *et al.* (1994), "The Northridge Earthquake: Progress Made, Lessons Learned in Seismic-Resistant Bridge Design", *www.findarticles.com/p/articles/mi_m3724/is_n1_v58/ai_16112780/pg_2;* Johnson, Laurie A. (2000), "Kobe and Northridge Reconstruction – A Look at Outcomes of Varying Public and Private Housing Reconstruction Financing Models", presented at the Euro-Conference on *Global Change and Catastrophe Risk Management: Earthquake Risks in Europe*, International Institute for Applied Systems Analysis (IIASA), Laxenburg, Austria, 8 July 2000, *www.iiasa.ac.at/Research/RMS/july2000/Papers/johnson_housing0401.pdf*; Loukaitou-Sideris, Anastasia and M. Kamel Kamel (2004), "Residential Recovery from the Northridge Earthquake: An Evaluation of Federal Assistance Programs", *www.ucop.edu/cprc/eq%20recovery.pdf*; OECD (2004), *Large-scale Disasters*, OECD Publications, Paris.

22. Between 1 and 31 December 2005, the price of the "intelligent ticket" was reduced by 50% between 10 a.m. and 4 p.m.

23. With the launch in early February 2006 of the single (90-minute) ticket to include boats, passenger use of boats increased considerably (+24% in one month). According to the Chairman and Managing Director of IDO, the losses incurred by the introduction of this single ticket (YTL 500 000)

have been more than offset by the gains (externalities at last taken into account) in the sphere of the environment. This assumes, although it remains to be proved, that the increase in passenger use is due to car drivers who have stopped using their cars. IDO recorded something to the order of a 2.5 increase in revenue in 2005 over 2004 (*i.e.*, a total of USD 185 million); cf. 19 January 2006, *Forum Diplomatik*, p. 3.

24. İstanbul Deniz Otobüsleri, IDO (Istanbul Seabuses and Fast Ferries, Inc.)

25. In addition to eight fixed measurement sites, it has, since 1995, had two vehicles at its disposal, one on the Asian bank and the other on the European bank, responsible for taking measurements at regular intervals.

26. Industrial and Commercial Company of Istanbul for Gas and Fuel Supply (IGATAŞ), *www.igatas.com.tr*. Among the tasks the company has set itself are: "environmental harmony", "compliance with the Kyoto Protocol" (which Turkey signed officially on 24 May 2004) and the "search for alternative energy sources". This new body also has other tasks which have little to do with the environment ("promoting employment and social harmony", etc.).

27. The reason for the one-year gap is to adapt to the EU's new fiscal period and implies that 2006 will not be covered by a National Plan.

Chapter 3

Governance for a Sustainable Mega-city

Introduction

Istanbul faces some difficult issues that make governance of the mega-city region especially challenging:

- *Dealing with rapid population growth.* As noted in previous chapters, Istanbul has witnessed the largest and the fastest population growth among OECD metropolitan regions. Since World War II the population has increased ten-fold, with a major inflow of migrants from the poor agricultural regions of Turkey in the 1980s and early 1990s. This migration continues and the city is projected to grow substantially over the next 20 years. This presents major problems for service delivery and a strain on the capacity of city region governance.
- *Fostering international competitiveness.* Like other OECD metropolitan areas, Istanbul needs to adapt its existing strategic framework into a clear and comprehensive vision for future development to achieve its aim of becoming a more competitive and liveable city in the global economy, and in particular to reach its goal of becoming a regional hub in the Euro-Asia region and a centre of innovation and knowledge in Turkey. Since opening to the international economy, and thanks to the implementation of a broad range of reforms, Turkey has seen impressive economic growth. That said, much remains to be done to face increasing competition from low cost, labour intensive emerging economies in Asia, in terms of increasing productivity, upgrading to more advanced technology-based activities and incorporating the large informal sector into the economy.
- *Coping with social polarisation.* Within its strategy to foster its international competitiveness, Istanbul has to cope with social polarisation between those who benefit from the new economy and the

many who are left outside. This challenge is common in many metropolitan areas transitioning towards a knowledge-based economy; however, in Istanbul this trend is exacerbated by the mega-city's increasing migration. Early waves of migrants were able to find land on which to live and over time their dwellings have become incorporated into the urban system, with the help of political patronage. However, with the focus on world city competition politicians are now inclined to utilise any remaining land for world city functions, making life more difficult for recent immigrants (Keyder, 2005). In this context of increasing polarisation, major governance issues include maintaining social stability and developing opportunities for public participation.

- *Addressing environmental concerns*. As most large OECD mega-urban regions, Istanbul is a major island of wealth and growth but the scale of industry growth, resource usage, and goods and capital flows are having a serious impact on the global environment with enormous land consumption, air pollution, and water management. This context demands a more integrated city development strategy, linking housing and urban development, environmental preservation and local economic development within a broader objective to build a more competitive and liveable city.

- *Natural crisis*. In addition to these challenges typical to mega-cities aspiring to world city status, Istanbul has experienced natural crises in recent years. There was the major water shortage of 1994 and the serious earthquake of 1999 in Turkey, raising speculation that Istanbul could be hit worse in the future. These events demonstrated the importance of having efficient, co-ordinated governance systems.

The changes needed to address these challenges are often systemic and not easily remedied through short-term measures. Instead, they require a robust system of governance and a clear long-term development framework. The system of governance in Istanbul has undergone a major process of transformation that has contributed to improving management and planning in the region. Istanbul has greatly benefited from the decentralisation process in Turkey, with new actors emerging at the local and metropolitan levels. New legislation has been passed and the necessary processes for implementation are continuing through secondary legislation, preparation of regulations and guidance for local administrations. Still further efforts are needed to improve the principle of subsidiarity, enhance local capacity and resource management, and further engage civil society in local governance. Improvement in the overall planning system is also needed to address crucial issues related to transport and congestion, urban development and housing, environment and earthquake risks. New institutional tools are currently being developed to address urban planning and to foster regional development. They will be addressed in this chapter along with the above mentioned governance issues.

3.1. The institutional and fiscal challenges

The institutional framework in Turkey and Istanbul

Turkey is a unitary state. The sub-national government level in Turkey consists of three tiers. It includes 81 provinces (Provincial special administration), 3 225 municipalities and 35 000 villages. Alongside this structure is the provincial administration, an arm of the central government, at the province, sub-province and township level (there are no townships in Istanbul).

- **Provinces** operate as field branches for the central administration and are also described as the provincial special administrations. These local administrations are established to carry out tasks in the places within and beyond municipal boundaries, within their respective provinces. Once a province is established as the agent of the central government, a provincial special administration is also automatically established as a local authority. The governor is the highest authority of the administration and is appointed by the Council of Ministers and approved by the President. Almost every ministry has a field organisation at the province level and some such as education, security, agriculture, tourism, sport, social services, have more than one. The governor has dual functions as an agent of central government and the head of the provincial special government, responsible for the operations and surveillance of all field organisations.
- **Municipalities** are established in settlements that have more than 5 000 inhabitants and in provincial and sub-province centres regardless of their population. The basic duties of municipalities include cleaning, public transportation, water supply and sanitation, public works (local road construction and maintenance) and public safety. Under the 2004 reforms they also have some educational responsibilities. There are currently about 3 225 municipalities including: metropolitan municipalities, metropolitan sub-province municipalities, metropolitan first level municipalities and non-metropolitan municipalities. Originally, a metropolitan municipality is a municipality that has more than one sub-province or first level municipality within its boundaries. In 1984 the first three metropolitan municipalities were set up (Istanbul, Ankara and Izmir). More were established in the following years and the

number of metropolitan municipalities rose to 15 in 1993 and 16 in 2001. The mayor is the head of the municipality and is directly elected in elections held every five years. The July 2004 law redefined a metropolitan municipality as an area that has more than 750 000 inhabitants in the city and surrounding settlements, and that meets a few more technical criteria.

- **Villages** are settlements with populations of less than 5 000 inhabitants.

Istanbul is the main metropolis of Turkey – as indicated by its economic and cultural importance, population size, and attractiveness to migrants. It carries considerable political weight in national politics, with more than 10% of the deputies sitting in Parliament. In administrative terms "Istanbul" can mean a number of things – it can be the province or the metropolitan municipality. After recent reforms the boundaries of the province and metropolitan municipality of Istanbul currently coincide. Istanbul is a province, as well as a Provincial Special Administration, which, as indicated above, means that it is an arm of the central government. The contours of Istanbul province were recently reviewed (in 1995, and again at the end of 1996), with the promotion of a former precinct (Yalova, on the southern coast of the Gulf of Izmit) to the rank of province. The "Istanbul Metropolitan Municipality" was established in 1984. However the administrative limits of the Istanbul Metropolitan Municipality were modified in July 2004: the territory of competence was enlarged from 1 830.92 km^2 to 5 343.01km^2, covering the whole province. The Istanbul Metropolitan Municipality can be considered the main beneficiary of this legislative change. The competences of public management are now concentrated at the level of the metropolitan municipality, according to the law of July 2004, strengthening its competency, parallel to the geographical reconfiguration. Until July 2004, only 35% of the Istanbul province – 183 092 hectares – were under the control of the municipality but the extension in area has widened its authority to include peripheral urbanised areas.

The Metropolitan Municipality of Istanbul has many lower tier local authorities within its boundaries (Figure 3.1). Almost all of the metropolitan municipalities in Turkey constitute the core of a metropolitan area, with surrounding authorities retaining their own responsibilities. The situation is different for Istanbul: the Metropolitan Municipality has jurisdiction over the whole area, but with 73 lower level authorities within its area. These lower tier authorities are made up of 32 sub-province municipalities and 41 first level municipalities.

Figure 3.1. **Institutional framework in Istanbul Metropolitan Area**

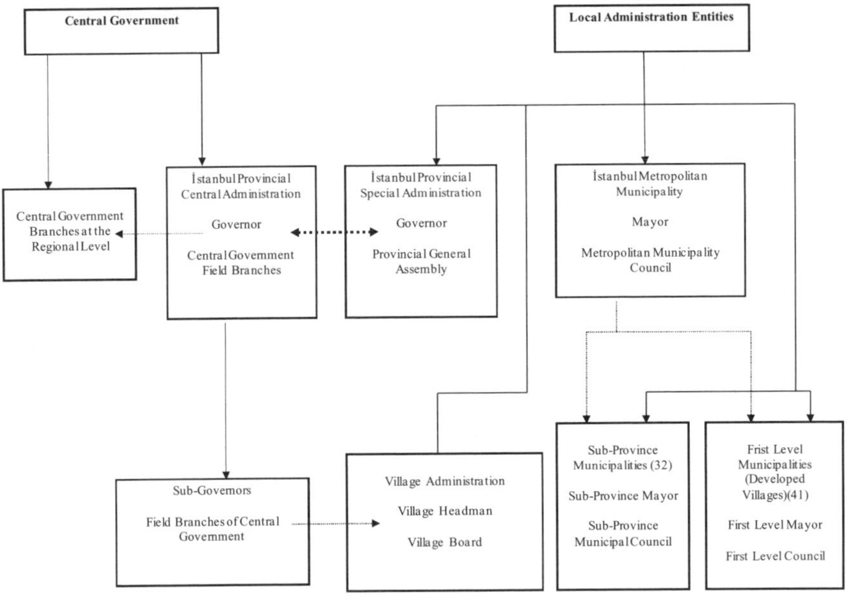

The Istanbul Metropolitan Municipal Council is the decision-making body and contains representation from the lower tier authorities. It is made up of the Metropolitan Mayor, 73 mayors from the 32 sub-province municipalities and 41 first level municipalities, and a further 274 council members from these same authorities, for an overall total of 348 members. These additional members from the lower tier authorities make up one-fifth of the total council membership and are selected based on who had the highest number of votes. The Istanbul Metropolitan Municipal Council convenes for five days in the second week of every month. The Metropolitan Council has the power to discuss and approve some decisions of lower tier authorities in addition to its own duties, for example to ensure consistency in budgets or integrity of services.

Istanbul can also refer to an urbanised functional region that exceeds the limits of the metropolitan municipality and of the province, but not represented by any administrative or institutional body. The July 2004 law was an attempt to adjust administrative boundaries to match the functional area that had extended well beyond the 1984 boundary. However, as mentioned in Chapter 1, industrial areas like Çorlu (in Tekirdağ) and Gebze (in Kocaeli) are part of the Istanbul labour market area as defined by commuting flows but not included in the definition of the metro-region. The surrounding provinces of Kocaeli and Tekirdağ could be considered as part of a functional metropolitan area defined by production and consumption links, while other surrounding provinces (Bursa, Sakarya, Yalova) still maintain strong economic linkages within a larger Polycentric Greater Istanbul. These different definitions have important implications in terms of planning, and require co-ordination mechanisms at different scales.

The allocation of responsibilities within Istanbul

A number of recent laws have affected the responsibilities of the different levels of government in the Istanbul region.

1. The most recent laws regarding the assignment of duties to the ***Provincial Special Administration*** were passed in 2005. These duties are associated with health, agriculture, industry and commerce, civil works and housing, soil preservation, the prevention of soil erosion, culture, art, tourism, social services and social aid, child-care centres, the provision of land for the construction of school buildings for primary and secondary education, and the construction, maintenance, and repair of these buildings. This law also tasks the Provincial Governor with ensuring co-ordination of services on a provincial scale across other local governments and agencies. Further duties relate to economic matters such as approving a budget, deciding on investment partnerships, and the purchase and sale of fixed property. The Provincial Special Administration prepares a Strategic Plan and Performance Plan that is used as a basis for the budget. Provincial local governments outside Istanbul also prepare strategic plans. All provinces in Turkey also have Environmental Order Plans (1/100.000 scale) that are prepared by either the metropolitan municipalities or the provincial special administrations pursuant the respective act. In Istanbul this plan is prepared and approved by the Metropolitan Municipality.[1]

2. The duties of the ***Istanbul Metropolitan Municipality*** cover a wide range of urban services that are considered most effective when conducted at this level. This was recently formalised in legislation that called for local authorities to undertake all duties not specifically under the central government's authority.[2] The law allows these duties, originally assigned to the Metropolitan Municipality, to be delegated to lower level authorities or performed in conjunction with them. According to the law, the Metropolitan Municipality prepares a strategic plan, annual goals and investment programmes as a basis for their budget. The lower-level authorities provide comments that the Metropolitan Municipality incorporates as it prepares the Master Plan for the whole area, and approves the lower level plans prepared by each

sub-province or first level municipalities. These lower level plans, or implementation plans, should conform to the Master Plan and if an authority does not prepare one within a year of the approval of the Master Plan, the municipality can prepare the lower level plan.

3. The duties of the lower level authorities, ***sub-province and first level municipalities***, are defined by law as those not assigned to the Metropolitan Authorities. They cover the more detailed responsibilities, such as regulatory procedures, and collecting solid waste; inspecting for health hazards and public safety; building car parks and recreation areas; building and maintaining secondary and local urban roads; building and maintaining facilities for health, education, and culture; protecting cultural, natural and historical assets; offering social and cultural services for the elderly, women, children and disabled; providing burial services; and offering training for skills and trades.

This review of the duties of each level of government reveals an overlap of responsibilities, as well as scope for special arrangements between the Metropolitan Municipality and certain lower level authorities. Such an overlap is not in itself necessarily a problem, if the specific role of each level is clearly set out – *e.g.*, higher levels responsible for planning and lower levels for implementation. However notwithstanding this, there does seem to be an opportunity to clarify the arrangements in some areas. Some agencies have been set up to attempt to improve co-ordination across Istanbul, such as the Infrastructure Coordination Centre (AYKOME) and the Transport Coordination Centre (UKOME), but as will be developed below, the challenges of transport and infrastructure development require further co-ordination.

The organisation of local government finance

Sub-national revenues in Turkey are relatively limited, but municipal revenues have grown substantially over the last decades. The share of sub-national government revenue was 4.76% of GDP in 2000; this is a relatively low share when compared with other OECD countries. Over the last decades, there has however been considerable revenue growth amongst municipalities, the most substantial sub-national government tier. In 20 years the municipal revenues almost tripled (Figure 3.2). In 2000 their revenues amounted to 4.41% of GDP. Although the revenues of provinces also grew fast, their revenues are still quite low (0.29% of GDP in 2000).

Figure 3.2. **Local government revenues as percentage of GDP (1980-2000)**

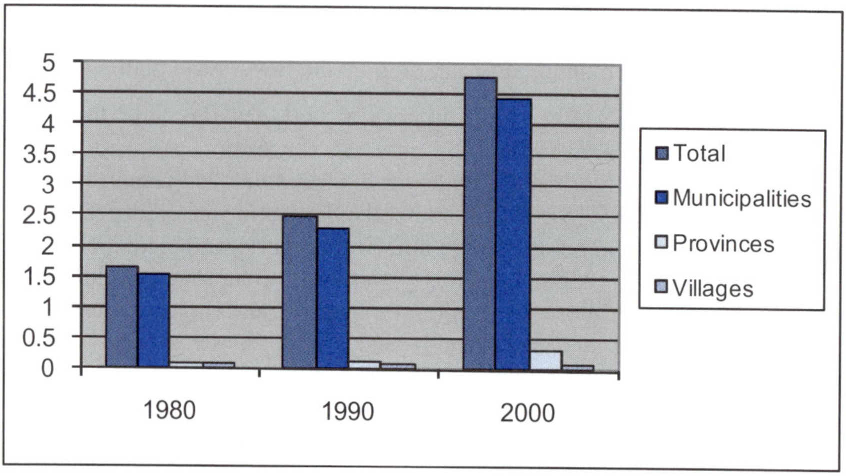

Source: Güner, Ayse (2003), "Financial Viability of Local Governments in Turkey", conference paper, Istanbul.

The most important source of finance for local government comes from the allocation of central tax revenues (revenue share). Both provinces and municipalities rely for a large part on revenue sharing. Under the current revenue sharing scheme a certain percentage of the central tax revenues are distributed to sub-national governments, based on criteria of population, with approximately 85% of the *provincial* revenues attributable to this tax revenue share. In addition, provinces have their own revenue sources (taxes, duties and fees) and receive conditional grants from the central government. Almost 50% of *municipal* revenues come from revenue sharing (Figure 3.3). Approximately 10% of municipal revenue comes from local taxes. The most important local tax is the property tax, but a lot of other local taxes exist. Fees are of minor importance, although a diversity of fees exists. Almost 40% of municipal revenues consist of non-tax revenues, such as revenues from borrowing.

Revenue sharing is especially important for metropolitan municipalities such as Istanbul. Currently the revenue share is 1.12% for provinces and 6% for municipalities. The metropolitan municipalities generally get a revenue share that is commensurate to the general tax revenues they generate within their boundaries. The share of generated tax revenues that metropolitan municipalities can keep is 5%. All metropolitan municipalities keep 75% of this share; the other 25% is transferred to a fund for metropolitan municipalities. The aim of this fund is to support the disadvantaged municipalities, done by allocating the 25% based on population. Since rich metropolitan municipalities such as Istanbul have tax revenues per capita

Figure 3.3. **Composition of municipal revenues (2002)**

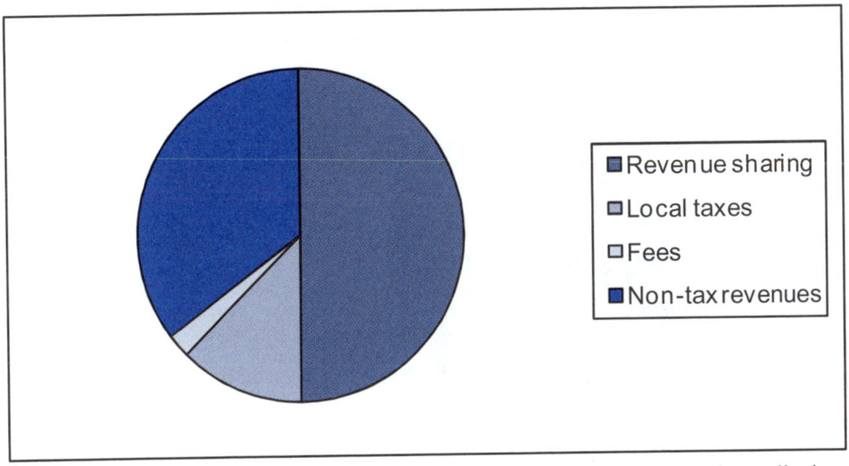

Source: Kerimoglu *et al.* (2005), Fiscal decentralization: a new approach to alleviate poverty and regional disparities, UNDP, Tesev, Istanbul.

that can be up to six times higher than those of some metropolitan municipalities, allocating a part on the basis of the population criterion is equalising. Still, Istanbul receives a large share of the tax sharing system and the tax share is the most substantial part of its budget, almost 70% (Figure 3.4). The tax revenue share is far more important for the budget of the Istanbul Metropolitan Municipality than it is for other metropolitan municipalities.

Local taxation in Turkey does not provide substantial sub-national revenues and is extremely restricted. There are quite a variety of locally collected taxes in Turkey. Municipalities collect taxes on property, solid waste, advertisements, entertainment, communication, electricity and gas consumption, and fire insurance. However from an international perspective, the amount of locally collected tax revenues is relatively low (Figure 3.5). Of course, this relatively low share of sub-national tax revenues mirrors the relatively low share of sub-national expenditures: many services are centrally provided. Municipalities do not have the freedom to set the rates or bases of their local taxes. The sub-national taxes are collected locally and the revenues from them are completely determined by the local tax base (in contrast to the tax revenue share system). The most important local tax is the property tax, like in many OECD countries. The centrally set rate, for metropolitan municipalities is 0.2% and 0.1% for other municipalities. The central government also issues rules on how the property value has to be determined.

Figure 3.4. **Revenues on the budget of Istanbul Metropolitan Municipality (2004)**

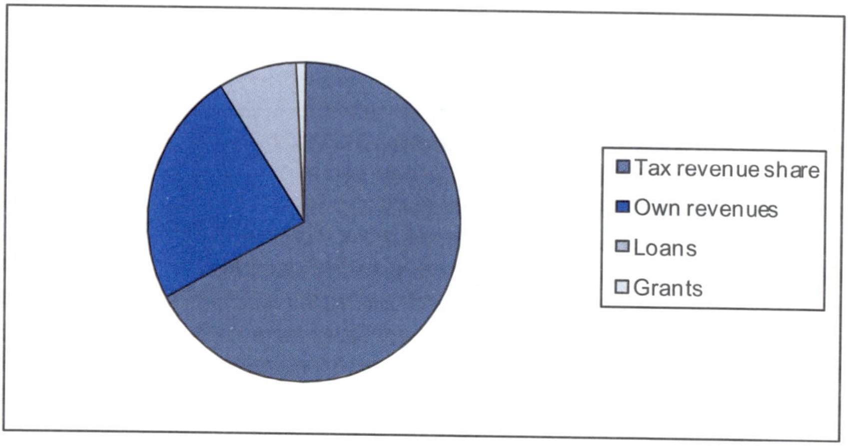

Source: Data provided by the Budget and Finance Directorate Istanbul Metropolitan Municipality.

Figure 3.5. **Sub-national tax revenues as a share of total tax revenues (2005)**

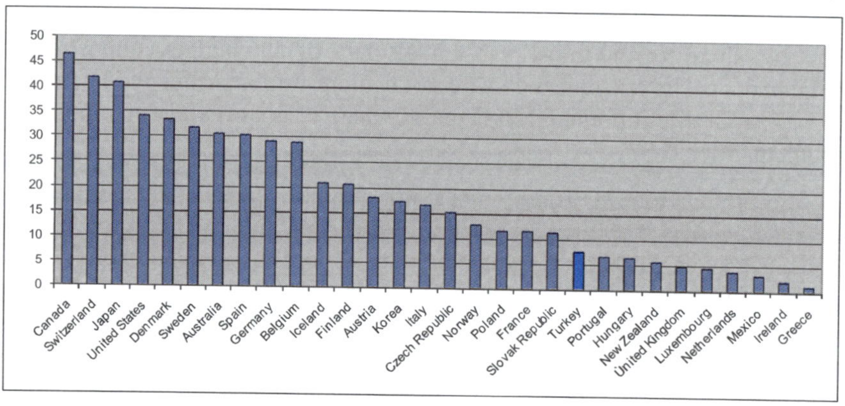

Source: OECD Revenue Statistics Database 2007.

Municipalities in Turkey are allowed to borrow from one another, which creates a substantial source of revenues. Borrowing is allowed only for financing projects with an investment programme. The Provinces Bank provides the credit after it has approved the repayment plan and reviewed the numerous rules for determining the amount that can be borrowed.[3] Municipalities can also borrow money from abroad from foreign and international institutions. Issuing bonds is another tool for financing projects. While many municipalities are carrying debts, it does not seem that there are any problems in the Istanbul area. A relatively large part of Istanbul Metropolitan Municipality revenues come from borrowing: 8% in 2004, and up to 15% in 1994. The new municipal law has introduced the concept of debt stock. The central government has imposed several precautions and restrictions to public institutions to ensure budgetary discipline. The municipality has been using the services of three international rating firms (S&P, Fitch, Moody's) for external audits since 1999. The foreign debt repayment performance has been rated BB- by those firms that periodically brief international investors.

Fees, user charges and grants play a marginal role in the municipal finance of Turkey. Fees bring in a small share of sub-national revenues in Turkey, as compared to other OECD member countries. Although municipal councils can determine tariffs for the user charges, many charges do not have a maximum fee that is indexed, which results in collection costs often exceeding the revenue of the charge. User charges are collected for sewerage, water, and road construction and improvement. Like in many OECD countries with relatively small sub-national tax revenue shares, local politicians may have an incentive to rely on central government rather than local revenue sources, as a way of avoiding the tax-related political risks. Grants, mostly conditional, make up a significant share of the revenues of the provincial special administrations. However, grants play a relatively small role in municipal finance in Turkey. Most are unconditional grants, usually given by the Ministry of Finance; conditional grants come from other ministries.

A number of issues arise from these financial arrangements:

(1) Transparency

The revenue sharing system is in theory predictable and stable: sub-national governments know in advance how much they will receive in revenues. The allocation is simple, as it is based solely on population size, and is transparent. The system is easy to administer since it requires a minimum of data, elementary calculations and a minimum of expert manpower. However, it de-links taxation and spending, thereby weakening taxpayer accountability.

For several municipalities, revenue sharing is less transparent and predictable due to the system of debt reduction. The Provinces Bank pays the revenue share transfer to municipalities and provinces on a monthly basis. The Ministry of Finance transfers the origin-based revenue share to metropolitan municipalities. The Provinces Bank has information on the debt positions of sub-national governments and can withhold part of the transfer to municipalities by applying a deduction if they consider that debt repayments by the sub-national government unit have stagnated and to make sure that the basic debt repayment principles are respected. Previously this debt deduction could amount to the whole transfer originally destined to the municipality. Recently this deduction has been capped at a maximum of 40% of the transfer. The deduction is supposed to be applied objectively to all sub-national governments that refuse to pay back their debts. Since 2007 the Provinces Bank is operating as a bank, limiting local government access only to information related to its own tax contribution. This differs from many other OECD member countries in that there is no real local countervailing power to monitor and guarantee that debt reduction is applied similarly in like cases. Although the Provinces Bank is independent, it falls under the responsibility of the Ministry of Public Works and Settlement, opening the possibility of influence.

(2) Suitability to Istanbul's needs

Some of the elements of the local finance system in Turkey raise some challenges for Istanbul. Although Istanbul, as a metropolitan municipality, can set a property tax rate that is twice as high as in non-metropolitan municipalities, the property tax presents several challenges in Istanbul. First, due to illegal dwellings, a pervasive issue in Istanbul (and Ankara), is the municipality cannot tax a large portion of the population to which it provides services. Second, since the tax base is revaluated every four years on the basis of increases in construction costs, not market values, the revaluation likely omits the scarcity (and thus higher value) of property in Istanbul. Third, the revenue sharing system is based on population statistics carried out every 10 years, with the last survey done in 2000. In the meantime yearly projections are made, though clearly with margins of error. Since the population growth in Istanbul is very rapid, this mechanism causes considerable revenue losses.[4]

As compared to other regions in Turkey, the system is quite generous to Istanbul. The origin-based tax share for metropolitan municipalities works to the advantage of Istanbul. Most companies have their headquarters in Istanbul, which means that their consolidated budgets are taxed in Istanbul rather than in all of the cities in Turkey where they might have operations. This means that Istanbul Metropolitan Municipality gets a relatively large amount of money of the tax revenue system, compared with other metropolitan municipalities. Moreover, lower level municipalities (sub-provinces and first level municipalities) in Istanbul have to transfer 35% of their tax share to the Istanbul Metropolitan Municipality; this is to finance services that the metropolitan municipality is providing to lower level municipalities. Of the remaining 65%, 10% has to be transferred to the

Istanbul Metropolitan Municipality for transportation investments. Lower level municipalities in the Istanbul metropolitan area are concerned that they have to transfer too many funds and do not have enough left for their own needs; this is compounded by their perceived increased responsibility for tasks that fall under the responsibility of the metropolitan municipality.

(3) Local autonomy

Istanbul has limited fiscal autonomy: it cannot raise tax rates beyond the rather strict upper levels determined by law by the central government. This makes it more difficult to be responsive to the preferences of citizens and firms. Municipalities in Turkey have no flexibility to collect level revenues: the revenue share is fixed, local tax rates are subject to strict upper and lower limits, fee rates and user charges are fixed and outdated, and borrowing is subject to central government control. The consequence is that municipalities are bending the rules to get more revenues, for example via the valuation of property. Municipalities in Turkey do not uniformly do the valuation of property. Since municipalities cannot influence their rates, they have an incentive to value their tax base too high when they have financial problems, which can lead to valuation in property that can be difficult to justify when compared to those in other parts of the country. A major rationale for decentralisation and local public service provision is that it allows for adjustments and adaptation of local preferences of citizens and firms – and thus leads to more efficiency. The very limited local fiscal autonomy forms an important obstacle for the benefits of decentralisation to materialise.

(4) Inter-municipal equalisation

The fiscal system of Turkey does not currently provide for inter-regional equalisation as the revenue sharing is neither based on any estimate of local expenditure needs, nor on the reduction of sub-national fiscal disparities. There are however some arguments to justify this situation. As the local tax base is limited, there is not the need to equalise for differences in this respect. Until now the services run by municipalities have not been subject to large differences in costs or needs. However this will change with increasing decentralisation and as services that do vary between municipalities, such as educational facilities or social services, are taken on by municipalities. One of the major arguments to support greater equalisation in the system relates to regional disparities. There are huge differences in wealth and employment opportunities between the regions of Turkey, resulting in the major internal migration into Istanbul, so any equalisation system to reduce regional disparities could help to alleviate this pressure. An equalisation system based on a regional need formula would provide a framework for the operation of the Regional Development Agencies. Within this framework, financial equalisation should be based on objective criteria.

Normally, an equalisation scheme should lead to an allocation less favourable to Istanbul, though current proposals favour Istanbul even more. Recent reforms promise decentralisation of many tasks to provinces and metropolitan municipalities, among which are certain social services and education tasks. There are large discrepancies in the indicators that determine the costs of these services. Istanbul is one of the wealthiest municipalities, on the upper tail of other social indicators (employment, poverty, etc.), but less so on education indicators. Evidently, with an allocation of the revenue sharing that takes differences in social-economic indicators into account, Istanbul would receive a smaller part than it receives now (Neyaptı, 2005). Yet, the new draft law on Provincial Special Administration and Municipal Revenues outlines criteria for allocating the tax revenue share. In this proposal population will determine 75% of the allocation, and the other 25% will be based on performance and the level of affluence. It should be made clear that the equalisation mechanism will have to reduce financial disparities between sub-national governments in line with practices in many OECD member countries.

The decentralisation process in Turkey and its impact on Istanbul

Turkey remains one of the most centralised countries in the OECD (Figure 3.6). Central government has a major role in local issues through the powers of central ministries and its provincial administrations. Sub-central governments perform only 9.5% of total primary public spending (OECD, 2004c). Municipalities used to be subject to the approval of the Minister of the Interior for their budgets, and the Minister had several sanctions. Procedures have changed with the new Local Authorities Law that increased municipal autonomy for submitting budgets without central government intervention.

Central government still retains substantial control over sub-national governments. The Ministry of the Interior employs around 170 inspectors and 125 controllers to supervise the administrative tasks of local governments and perform sub-national unit audits every three years. If intervention is required, in cases of complaints, problems or disobedience, the government can decide to start a court case against the local government. This could result in mayoral suspension (with an opportunity for appeal) and in a series of court cases that can take longer than a year to resolve.[5] Despite the amount of central control, the availability of data on the performance of

Figure 3.6. **Sub-national expenditures as share of total government expenditures (2004)**

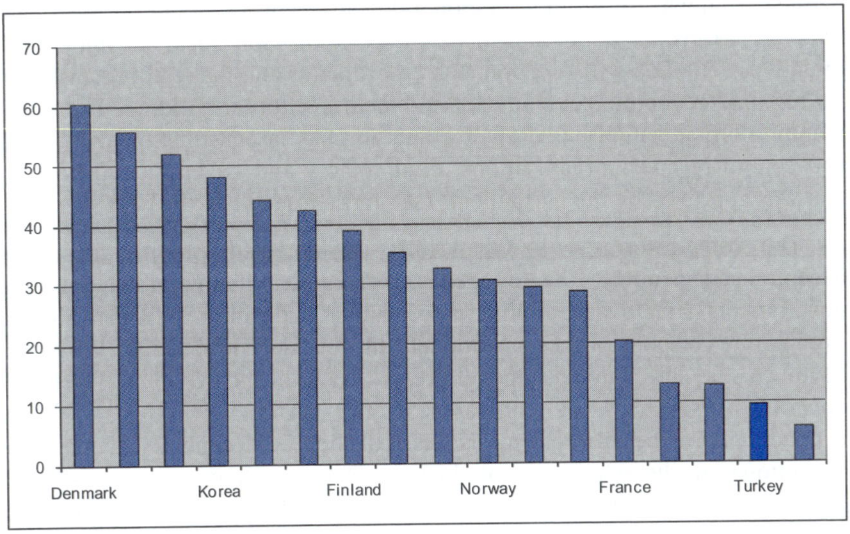

Source: OECD National Accounts Database 2007. Data for Turkey date from 2000.

sub-national governments is a concern. The combination of strong centralised characteristics and small municipalities (62.5% of municipalities have fewer than 5 000 inhabitants) is most likely affecting the efficiency of the public administration, the speed of administrative processes, initiatives at the local level, and flexibility. Local governments have little control over their resources, have weak relatively local institutional capacity compared to that of the centre and are subject to many central regulations. However, the local government's dependence on the central government has diminished significantly over the last two years with new laws regulating the transfer of authority to the local governments. This process is favourably affected by the fact that local administrators eventually find their way to central government posts and Parliament.

Decentralisation of public administration has been considered a key government priority in Turkey since the early 2000s, along with acceleration of the EU accession process. The Public Administration Framework Law of 2004 aimed to give a major push to substantive decentralisation. In addition to this framework law, three other laws were adopted to create new mechanisms to transfer major spending powers: Provincial Special

Administration Law; Metropolitan Municipalities Law; and Municipalities Law. Development Agencies (DAs) are also planned in the 26 newly defined "regions", to promote regional development focussing on local and regional assets, and to enhance co-operation for local development initiatives. The DA will function as a co-ordinator and the lead organisation for regional economic development and local institution-building. The State Planning Organization has drafted a law on DAs in consultation with local and central business organisations, civil society and governmental bodies, that was approved by the parliament[6] (see further details in the next section).

The 2004 reforms will, when fully implemented, provide for more decentralised spending. The key idea is to strengthen the role of sub-national governments and to decentralise more public expenditures. When all the expenditure responsibilities mentioned in the decentralisation laws are devolved, the sub-national expenditures will amount to 20-25% of general government revenues, as compared to the current 9.5%. Most of the expenditures of the different ministries will then be decentralised, with the exceptions of the Ministries of Justice, Defence, Interior, Finance and Education. In addition, local governments, essentially municipalities, will be granted new powers such as the management of urban planning, municipal budgets will not need the approval of the Governor (the provincial representative of the central government) and there will be more flexibility on personnel management.

Laws on decentralisation have been enacted or are under discussion but changes will take a while to implement. Although expenditure responsibilities are devolved in theory by means of the four laws mentioned above, in practice this will only take place when central budgets (and the corresponding personnel) are devolved. This is part of the law on municipal revenues and several sectoral laws which will likely be implemented in steps over several years. The selection of the areas to be devolved is subject to political dynamism that is at the moment difficult to predict – rural development was recently devolved, and culture and tourism are currently under discussion. There is no explicit programme plan that is being followed for devolving expenditure responsibilities. In addition, the Public Administration Framework Law has not been accepted.

Local public capacity needs to be enhanced as a corollary to decentralisation. It is acknowledged that some progress has been made in the recruitment procedures for the Turkish civil service, at the central and local levels (OECD/SIGMA, 2006).[7] The problem is rather to attract competent white-collar staff into local civil service. Currently, it seems that factors like rather low salary levels (compared to skilled positions in the private sector), and the centrally determined wage system that restricts municipalities from adjusting the salary to local circumstances may have a disincentive effect to entering the local civil service in Turkey. Many OECD member countries are confronted with similar problems, and have had to increase wages for local civil servants. The problem is also to train civil servants, so that they have improved managerial skills, both for human resources and budget. In the context of decentralisation, the question of staff transfers across levels of government is important as well: to strengthen local capacity, some civil servants working for the central level could be redeployed at the local level.

Continuous training of local civil servants should be encouraged, and with particular focus on key managerial skills. Training and education is needed to prepare staff for the new tasks and responsibilities (including education in foreign languages and EU regulations). Istanbul has started this effort, as seminars and courses are held regularly for vocational training within the Istanbul Metropolitan Municipality, and also in order to increase the level of the performance of municipal employees at every unit and level. Efforts should also be made with local politicians accustomed to their role deferring to the centre, to support them in exercising their new powers. Like other OECD member countries, Turkey might like to consider establishing a national organisation that is oriented towards developing local capacity. Such an organisation could be geared to the needs of government at the city and local levels. Box 3.1 provides an example of how another country, namely the United Kingdom, has created agencies to address this issue of local capacity building. A national agency in Turkey could also benefit from establishing links with these agencies in other countries to exchange ideas. Strengthening local capacity also requires that financial resources be devolved in parallel to match the resources to the new responsibilities.

Regulations on sub-national staff might be reviewed to improve institutional capacity. The municipal limit on the number of staff and total for personnel expenses, in the medium term, are not to exceed 30% (for metropolitan municipalities) or 40% (for other municipalities) of the budget of that municipality. For the time being, municipalities have time to adjust to these percentages, but it is unclear for how long. These measures might be understandable within the light of the over-employment that is reported to have taken place in several municipalities. A maximum percentage of 30 or 40% however seems quite rigid, especially when the vision for the future is to devolve many labour intensive sectors to the municipalities.

Box. 3.1. Improving skills and capacity in local government: the example of the Improvement and Development Agency (IDeA), England and Wales

The IDeA is an organisation run by local government for the benefit of its local government membership. As central government has certain controls and monitoring powers over local governments there are benefits in keeping the IDeA independent of central government. The IDeA has a Board of Directors with five members appointed by local governments (through the Local Government Association) and one representative each for regional employers, central government, academia, private sector, trade unions, and regulatory bodies. The IDeA is set up as a company wholly owned by the Local Government Association (this is an association of all local governments in England and Wales).

The IDeA supports the self-sustaining improvement and development within local government by: connecting ideas and expertise; focusing on best practice and forward thinking; delivering a flexible range of tools and services; carrying risk on behalf of local governments through innovative initiatives. The focus is on four areas: improving the quality of leadership; strengthening corporate capacity; improving service delivery in education, children and adult social care services; helping councils build sustainable communities.

The approach of the IDeA is oriented at developing self-improvement in local government. Amongst its activities are councillor and officer peer reviews, developing and disseminating best practice, conducting courses on leadership for senior officers and politicians, long-term support for 'weak' councils, coaching and mentoring programmes, advice on specific services, and guidance on working in partnership with business, communities and other stakeholders.

The IDeA is funded largely through a top slice from the Rate Support Grant (RSG). This is the grant that central government allocates from national taxes for local government. Another major source of income is from central government grants that are allocated to the IDeA for training related to new government initiatives.

Source: www.idea-knowledge.gov.uk.

3.2. Ensuring a better management for urban development

Even more than other types of metropolitan areas, the path and the extent of urbanisation in a mega-city like Istanbul require sound urban management, efficient planning and well operating local institutions. In particular in a centralised country like Turkey, complex inter-governmental relationships can limit the effectiveness of policies undertaken by different levels of governments. Policies may be duplicative or unintentionally interfere with each other, retarding rather than stimulating urban development. Horizontal co-ordination and more systematic integration of spatial planning, transport infrastructure, and socio-economic development is also particularly challenging for Istanbul. As mentioned in Chapter 2, the development of mega-urbanisation has gone ahead of urban planning and the provision of public facilities. Especially outside the core city, the informal and illegal housing areas built by the migrants themselves have led to an extensive settlement structure, with serious consequences on transport and land use, and thus for the environment and public health. The ability of the main local actors to face these challenges will depend highly on their internal organisation and capacity, as well as on how well they can foster public confidence, trust and civic participation for an efficient urban development process.

Streamlining institutional governance and inter-governmental relationships

The current complex and fragmented governance structure gives rise to conflicts among the different actors operating in the Istanbul metro-region. Chapter 2 provided several examples of a fragmented governance system including in transport, which involves a large number of different bodies from all levels of government and from the private sector. There are also several areas where unclear delineation of responsibilities and co-ordination problems among the different public authorities create conflicts that are sources of inefficiency. For instance:

(1) Some conflicts may arise due to the strong involvement of the central government and the provincial authorities over local affairs and overlapping responsibilities. Despite both being considered local government entities, the province and the metropolitan municipality operate as parallel bodies covering the same areas, with the former acting more as an operating branch of the central government at the local level. Although the members of the provincial general assembly are elected by the people, the assembly cannot always exercise its full decision-making prerogative because some decisions of the Assembly are subjected to the approval of the provincial governor who is appointed by the Council of Ministers. Sub-province municipalities are also under the control of the provincial administration, which controls *a posteriori* the legality of the initiatives undertaken by the sub-province municipalities, notably how "public work contracts" are assigned, and the way the public lands are used. This control

exercised by the central level is based on different laws that assigned precise topics to municipal assemblies (Law 5393/18) and organised the ways sub-provincial and first level municipal assemblies decisions had to be implemented (Laws 5593 and 5216).

(2) Different ministries also intervene in several policy areas, especially infrastructure and land use development, sometimes in contradiction with municipal interests and urban plans. According to the current law, some of the major infrastructure projects in Istanbul are under the control of national government. Controversy has been raised over the central governments control over real estate properties that were transferred to the metropolitan municipality with the 2004 July law. For the metropolitan municipality, the land properties portfolio was seen as a means to ensure new incomes for the municipality. There are however some exceptions. For example, the provisional article of the Law No. 5234 of September 2004 reinforces the competences of the Ministry of Public Works and Settlement and gathers all real estate properties within the area used as "Haydarpaşa Port" and places them under the responsibility of the Treasury of the State under the Turkish State Railroads (TCDD).[8] In addition, sub-province municipalities have seen a reduction in their powers as they are no longer able to set clauses of suspension, publicity and claims for annulment against the Ministry of Public Works and Settlement, who is now entitled "to act by itself", without consulting the municipalities. Some ministries, like the Ministry of Public Works and Settlement, the Ministry of Transport, and the Ministry of Tourism and Culture, often pursue projects that contradict the urban planning of the metropolitan municipality. The case of a huge building being erected in a no-building zone near the Strait of Istanbul, the Süzer Plaza (known as Gökkafes), could be quoted here. In the middle of the 1990s the limits of two contiguous municipalities were redrawn by the central power to enable the construction of this building and the Ministry of Culture and Tourism was able to approve the realisation of the building against the wishes of the metropolitan municipality and contrary to all the local urban planning documents. There is still a pending judicial case concerning this now famous building.

(3) Due to the predominant sector-based approach of central government, there are sometimes conflicts between the central authorities themselves. For example, the national "Council for the Protection of Cultural and Natural Heritage" is in conflict with the Ministry of Culture and Tourism, about a site on the Strait of Istanbul, listed by the first as a protected area, and allocated by the second for tourism development. Heritage protection is especially prone to these sorts of conflicts. For instance, there have been some disagreements between the Higher Council for the Protection of Cultural Monuments,[9] dependent on the Ministry of

Culture and Tourism, and the metropolitan municipality. At the provincial level the Governor has supervisory powers over the central government agencies in the province and tries to ensure co-operation and co-ordination among them. Central ministries have province directors that report to the Governor – there are 44 in the Istanbul Province and 88 central government administrative agencies. However, since the agencies' authority often extends beyond the provincial boundary they sometimes bypass the Governor and liaise directly with their respective superior ministry or organisation.

(4) On some issues, metropolitan and second tier local authorities also have overlapping responsibilities and conflicting relationships. Tasks that in most OECD countries are devolved to lower level government, such as sewerage system management, street cleaning etc, are in the hands of the Istanbul Metropolitan Municipality. This is remarkable, especially since the size of the sub-province municipalities (most have at least 200 000 inhabitants) far exceeds the average size of a municipality in the OECD countries (approximately 15 000 inhabitants). The result is an accountability problem: citizens complain to their sub-province municipalities, but these bodies do not have the influence or resources to improve the services. Sub-province municipalities in Istanbul have to transfer 35% of their tax share to the Istanbul Metropolitan Municipality to finance services that the metropolitan municipality is providing to sub-province municipalities. Of the remaining 65%, 10% is transferred to the Istanbul Metropolitan Municipality for transportation investments. Disquiet over the responsibilities is also linked to finances as some sub-province municipalities complain that they transfer so much they are unable to cover the costs of their own needs. They remark that Istanbul Metropolitan Municipality sometimes does not meet its commitments, for example with main road maintenance, so that the sub-province municipality – under pressure from its own population – takes the responsibility upon themselves. The sub-province and first-level municipalities' decisions concerning redevelopment are subject to the approval of the metropolitan government, a process than can take a lot of time. The powers that give the metropolitan municipality the ability to become involved in the lower level plans has been said to constrain the planning authority of the sub-province and first level municipalities. This situation is also typical to large metro-areas in Korea and Japan that are represented by a large metropolitan government (OECD, 2005g and OECD, 2005h).

Two main areas could be targeted to streamline the institutional governance framework and inter-governmental relationships:

- *Better redefinition of individual competencies among the different institutional actors.* The on-going process of decentralisation requires the clear allocation of powers, tasks, responsibilities and resources amongst levels of government operating within the same geographical area, as well as effective instruments of co-operation. In particular, the decentralisation process should go hand in hand with a better understanding and implementation of the principle of subsidiarity. In some areas, like environment and water issues, municipalities should be more involved and get further responsibilities, along with other levels of governments (*e.g.*, in the case of water management, along with the provincial operating agency ISKI and the central body the General Directorate of State Hydraulic Works [DSI]). The role and competencies of the current Provincial Special Administration needs to be better assessed in light of what should be its main objectives and how it can be used to avoid duplication with the Metropolitan Municipality's competencies.

- *Improving collaboration between municipalities, in particular between Istanbul Metropolitan Municipalities and sub-province municipalities.* All cities have the need to establish co-ordination between local authorities in their area. Cities such as Istanbul with a metropolitan authority are at an advantage as this can form a valuable vehicle for horizontal co-ordination. However, very large cities have an added problem as the number of authorities requiring co-ordination can get very numerous. In Istanbul there are 73 lower tier authorities. The Metropolitan Municipality's council draws from all these authorities providing a useful arena for co-ordination, though its large membership can make co-ordination somewhat cumbersome and regular dialogue with each lower tier authority difficult. In this situation the dominant political party is likely to become an important vehicle for co-ordination but this lends itself to political bias. The 2005 Law on the Unions of Local Administrations, which establishes a legal framework for developing efficient collaboration between municipalities, should be fully utilised. In London a debate is taking place because the Mayor believes that having 33 lower tier authorities places too much of a burden on him to undertake dialogue with them all and he favours amalgamation into five or six bigger authorities. Although these authorities would have great resources as a result, each would have a population of about a million, which typically translates into less involvement of local citizens. A response to this would be a third tier of elected urban neighbourhoods – an idea which is being explored by the British national government.

Establishing a consistent strategic planning framework

The urban planning process in Istanbul has undergone tremendous positive changes. The recent expansion of the Metropolitan boundary to coincide with the province presents an opportunity to formulate a good strategic framework that covers a reasonably large area and improves the possibility for co-ordination between the Municipality and the Provincial Special Administration. Moreover, the planning responsibilities have been transferred to the Istanbul Metropolitan Municipality since 2004, including the competence for drawing and monitoring the Environmental Order Plan which was under the responsibility of the Ministry of Environment and Forestry as well as the Strategic Plan and the Metropolitan Area Plan. Progressively, the scale of planning accounts for the functional evolution of the metropolitan area as the regional development scheme produced by the Metropolitan Municipality now covers a wider geographical area, more precisely that of the Old Marmara region. New concepts have been introduced in the planning exercise such as urban regeneration ideology, and earthquake and tourism and environmental and transport issues are progressively taken into account. Finally, a wider range of actors are being involved in planning, and new methods such as the necessary flexibility and time phasing have been introduced.

The planning process in Istanbul is however facing severe implementation issues. First, the multiplications of plans, partly due to the multiplication of actors, is leading to a diluted global vision and focus on the principal priorities (Figure 3.7). Within the Istanbul Metropolitan Municipality, there are different directorates in charge of planning, which often leads to increased transaction costs and fragmentation in the decision-making process.[10] As noted in Chapter 2, this is particularly apparent in transport and land use planning. Second, in terms of physical planning, the strategy functions are divided between the Metropolitan Municipality and the lower level municipalities – the former focussing on the broader master plan while the lower level produces implementation plans that conform to the master plan. This highlights the urgent need to ensure a clear hierarchy among all these plans; too many plans kill the planning. Third, another issue in the planning process is related to the common practice of local authorities to depart from the plans, which leads to making the plans inefficient or obsolete. The multiplication of special laws and regulations also tends to reduce the value of these plans. Istanbul would benefit from a less iterative planning process and in particular a clearer implementation programme.

Figure 3.7. **Different types of plans in the Istanbul Metropolitan Area**

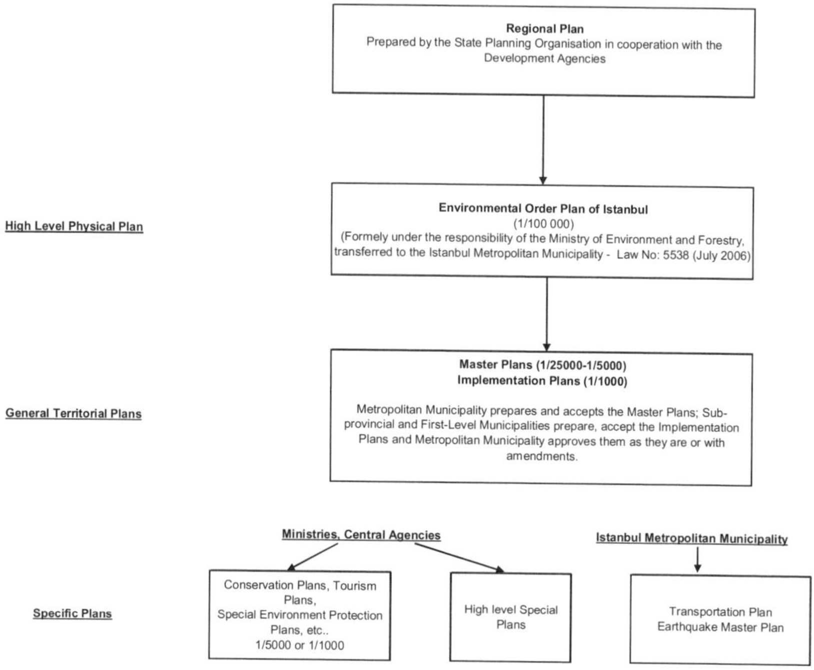

There has been a lack of a clear strategic plan for the Istanbul Metropolitan Municipality that carries public support and legal authority. A Master plan was prepared in 1995 that targeted the year 2010. This sought to achieve a balance between the development of the city as a world metropolis and the enhancement of its historical and commercial centre. It aimed to preserve the natural forestry and water catchments areas through a spatial strategy along the East/West axis. However there have been problems in implementation as many urban developments were not in conformity with the plan. The plan is intended to provide the basis for lower tier plans but many have not followed the strategic plan – administrative complexity has been a problem.

The authority of the plan has also been often affected because it was ignored when some organisations wanted to carry out their short-term development projects. The example of the "Levent–Maslak" axis that has been developed as the new financial and central business district neighbourhood is an illustration of how powerful organisations or people having an interest in a project can override the plan policies. The main instigator for this was the Ministry of Culture and Tourism who has the authority to undertake projects under the "Tourism Encouragement" Law (No. 2634). However the definition of legitimate tourism projects includes hotels and high-rise office developments. The project went against the 1995 plan, and further encroachment is now expected at the north end of the axis into the protected forest area – again against the plans. As the development has not been embedded in a plan, there is some concern that the impact on the surrounding neighbourhood has not been adequately addressed. The need for the development to be provided with transport means that the transport provision will be responded to in an *ad hoc* way rather than as part of a comprehensive long-term transport plan.

The plan must be given stronger legitimacy with more projects developed within the framework of the plan. If Istanbul does not tighten down on compliance it will continue to develop in an *ad hoc* manner that will not improve the efficiency of the city, or its image as a world city. Long- term plans are needed to deal with issues such as homeless children, underground urban infrastructure, long-term environment investment, educational support programmes and security matters. Many OECD cities and metropolitan areas have developed plans that provide a strong long-term strategic framework. This is welcomed by investors as they need to ensure that their involvement in development has a secure future, and can be supported by the infrastructure they need. Although the detailed mechanisms vary due to differences in legal and administrative traditions there are some common principles across countries (Newman and Thornley, 1996). The plans formulated at different levels are created so that they are in conformity with each other. They are also given some kind of legal or statutory strength, with a transparent formal amendment process for any proposal that is deemed to go against the plan.

Plans should not be just traditional land use master plans but also incorporate all policies, for example economic policy, environmental policy, cultural policy. As previously stated, decision-making criteria seem to be essentially driven by short-term views and financial returns – mainly tourism and real estate. Issues such as homeless children, underground urban infrastructure, environment investment, educational support programmes, security matters, which all require long-term plans are forced to take second rank. The decisions regarding transport infrastructures of great magnitude (bridges, expressways) – which largely determine the forms of urbanization – seem to also be directed by land properties and real estate perspectives. As already mentioned in Chapter 2, it is essential to ensure a better integration between land use planning and transport planning, or between land use and the plan for earthquakes. It is also crucial to ensure a statutory conformity between plans at different levels.

More generally, there seems to be a lack of connection between discussions about the future economic vision for the city and the more detailed, closed process of urban development. In other metropolitan areas, policies are prepared by agencies specialised in integrating them into the comprehensive strategic metropolitan plan, such as regional development agencies. The formulation of these plans includes full public participation at both early and adoption stages. Istanbul would benefit if it strengthened its planning system, giving it greater legitimacy and broadening the scope of the strategic level plan. There is no one formula for doing this and local circumstances need to be taken into account. Johannesburg could be an instructive example as the city is facing challenges similar to Istanbul in its attempt to become a regional-level world city while also addressing the poverty of a significant proportion of the city population. London has a similar population size to Istanbul and faces many similar issue of co-ordination across its different agencies involved in strategic planning (Box 3.2). In the case of Istanbul, establishing clear linkages between urban planning and the future development agency (see next section) will be crucial in this respect.

Box. 3.2. **Examples of strategic planning approaches: Johannesburg and London**

There are many different possible ways of tackling the strategic planning approach according to local circumstances, as illustrated by the examples of Johannesburg and London. The common aims are to produce a robust strategic framework that can enable co-ordination to occur across policies, across short and long-term objectives, and between governmental levels. These two examples illustrate the wide-ranging scope of these strategic plans.

Johannesburg is a city undergoing a major transition. It is striving to become Africa's leading world city, while also addressing the severe poverty afflicting a large number of its inhabitants. In 1997 the city faced a major financial crisis when it was unable to pay for the supply of electricity. In this context the city decided to prepare a strategic plan to cope with its problems and chart a way forward. In contrast to previous ad-hoc approaches the new plan provided the vision and proposed a comprehensive prescription for a more permanent 'state of health' for municipal government in Johannesburg (City of Johannesburg Council, 2001).

The planning process involved two plans – iGoli2002 and iGoli2010.

Box. 3.2. Examples of strategic planning approaches: Johannesburg and London (*cont.*)

The first of these was a three-year plan oriented towards getting the institutional structures right and a sound financial system with more cost effective service delivery. It involved the creation of a single municipal authority for the city. A comprehensive review was then undertaken of all service functions to find their most effective form of organisation, some new authorities were set up, some functions privatised, some maintained in-house. This comprehensive review approach enabled them to address the fragmentation and duplication, and improve accountability.

IGoli2010 is a long-term plan to transform the city into "a globally competitive world-class African city" (City of Johannesburg Council, 2001). In order to achieve this, the plan seeks to balance between enhancing its basic service delivery and achieving economic growth and competitiveness. City functions need to be given 10-year targets and are required to formulate a plan of delivery, while the economic advantages of the city need to be developed. The first step was procuring and recording reliable data and information. Studies were carried out to determine the scale of poverty, future service needs, and economic opportunities. Business and financial services, and trade were the fastest growing sectors while manufacturing was still important. The six key strategic priorities of the city were identified as: economic development and job creation; service delivery excellence; customer care; safety and security; inner-city development; dealing with the HIV/AIDS crisis. Goals and targets were set up for each priority and the iGoli2010 plan is expected to inform all the actions, including financial plans, of the authority and other agencies. This will provide a fully integrated long-term strategic approach.

There was no strategic plan for the metropolitan area of ***London*** after the Greater London Council was abolished in 1986. Brief strategic priorities for the city were set out by central government and local plans were prepared by each of the 33 lower level local authorities. Various agencies had to be set up to co-ordinate services that operated throughout the metropolis. However, it was generally felt that decisions were fragmented and that attempts at co-ordination unsatisfactory. There was also no overall vision for the future of London, a critical missing piece, especially for business, for the city to compete satisfactorily in the increasingly competitive environment of globalisation.

When the Labour Party won the national election in 1997 it decided to remedy the problems of London government and establish a new strategic planning approach. The Greater London Authority Act of 1999 set out the planning requirements of the new metropolitan authority. This required the Mayor to formulate eight new strategies for the city: The Spatial Development Plan; The Economic Development Strategy; The Transport Strategy; Bio-diversity Strategy; Noise Strategy; Air Quality Strategy; Municipal Waste Management Strategy; Cultural Strategy. The aim of these strategies was to enable London to meet its goals of strengthening its position as a world city while also creating a sustainable environment.

Box. 3.2. **Examples of strategic planning approaches: Johannesburg and London** (*cont.*)

The eight strategies are expected to be in conformity with each other and the Spatial Development Plan is intended to play a co-ordinating function as it draws together the spatial aspects of all the other strategies. The Spatial Development Plan – renamed the London Plan by the Mayor – has to go through a process of statutory public consultation including an Examination in Public. The other strategies do not have to go through this same formal process but their policies are incorporated in the London Plan. For example, the London Development Agency (LDA) produces the Economic Development Plan, partially by integrating the policies of the RDAs (regional development agencies) into the overall strategic planning process. It helps that the Mayor is ultimately responsible for the LDA.

In addition to those strategies set out in the legislation, the Mayor has voluntarily formulated other strategies such as the Energy Strategy, Housing Strategy, and Children's Strategy. The law also requires the Mayor to take account of three "cross cutting themes" in all his policy work. These are: the health of Londoners, equality of opportunity, and sustainable development. The London Plan is now undergoing revision and a major new theme is the impact of climate change on London.

These strategies are aimed at producing a comprehensive and integrated policy approach across the Metropolitan area. The lower level local authorities produce more detailed plans and these must conform to the London Plan, a policy that is strictly enforced. The boroughs have the opportunity to express their views during the preparation of the strategic plans and at the Examination in Public. The interaction between the London-wide (GLA) strategies and those of the broader functional region are less well developed. This broader region does not have a clear integrated plan for its own area – strategic policies for the area surrounding London are developed in a more piecemeal way including those of two further RDAs, and the policies of central government (including the Thames Gateway Strategy for the area from London downriver to the coast).

Source: The London Plan, GLA (2004), *www.london.gov.uk* and Johannesburg City Council (2001), "Johannesburg – An African City in Change" Zebra Press, Cape Town.

The recently formulated Environmental Order Plan for Istanbul does not yet address these concerns appropriately. The Istanbul Metropolitan Planning and Urban Design Centre (IMP) prepared this plan under the auspices of the Istanbul Metropolitan Municipality.[11] This plan was presented to the public in an attempt to make it a comprehensive plan, and academics were included in the process and worked on various aspects of the plan. A consultation process was conducted involving organised groups, particularly from the business sector. However, four professional chambers (Chambers of Architects, Urban Planners, Environmental Engineering and Civil Engineering) have filed lawsuits with the Council of State regarding the procedures and content associated with this plan and the trails are currently underway. The plan was produced within a year and a half year and this limited the opportunities for participation and debate. The Mayor presented the plan to the Metropolitan Municipal Council in July 2006 and it was approved.

It should also be mentioned that – in line with international best practices - Turkey is experimenting with more flexible multi-stakeholder agreements aimed at incorporating more collective action and policy networks into the broader planning framework. For example, in order to guide land use in Istanbul toward more polycentric and balanced spatial development, a protocol was signed at the end of 2006 that involved the Ministry of Environment and Forestry, the THRACE provinces (Edirne, Kirklareli and Tekirdag), the THRACE Development Union and the Metropolitan Municipality of Istanbul. The objective of this protocol is to discuss, develop and implement the planning process in a collective and co-ordinated manner. With the aid of the new enabling regulatory framework in the development agencies, technical staff and resources will be made available to trigger this promising planning innovation. Initial contacts with the Union of the Municipalities of the Marmara Region and its straits (chaired by the Mayor of Istanbul) suggest that other provinces within the Marmara region could also be involved in this initiative.

Civil society participation, collective interests and transparency

A number of positive trends towards greater transparency in urban decision making and the involvement of the public must be highlighted. The new concept of civil society in Turkey,[12] has witnessed an important development after the Habitat-II summit held in Istanbul in June 1996, which provoked the emergence of numerous associations. Actually, the 1999 earthquake caused a shock within the civil society, particularly in urban areas like Istanbul, provoking a boost in civil society participation in governance. As a result, numerous associations have appeared, steadily claiming their right to be involved in the management of local affairs. The population has realised the crucial necessity to participate in the politics of prevention and post-crisis management. Now, the local associations, the Metropolitan Municipality, the provincial administration, the sub-province municipalities and the first-level municipalities are involved in common projects in order to make inhabitants aware of the encountered risks. The Turkish state has recently taken some initiatives to increase transparency in decision making and encourage participation. Some of these have occurred as part of the EU accession process and some in response to the potential of the Internet. In 2003 a Law on Access to Information was passed to increase transparency and openness in public institutions and professional organisations and the 2004 Laws on Municipalities included the official involvement of civil society in local policy making.

In Istanbul, there are several examples of greater public and civil society organisation involvement in urban development. For instance, the Istanbul Foundation for Culture and Arts initiated a campaign for nominating Istanbul as European City of Culture in 2010 but struggled to gain official recognition from government institutions. Over time this changed and a wide range of government and civil society interests contributed to the bid. A new structure has been put in place to prepare for the event with half government and half civil society involvement. Other foundations, habitually linked to industrial groups, play a crucial role in the cultural life of the city. There are some sectors, such as tourism, where stronger ties have developed with civil society representatives. For example, the Istanbul Tourism Platform,[13] which brings together representatives from unions, sector representatives, entertainment associations, local communities, academics etc., meets on a monthly basis and works on projects to improve tourism within Istanbul. The organisation structures for the forthcoming development agencies (see below) also places importance on dialogue and the involvement of a wide range of representative organisations. At the local level, the number of civic associations has steadily increased, especially at the neighbourhood level and in the promotion of environmental issues. Some sub-province municipalities, like Beyoğlu with its "Local/Civil Co-operation Centre", have set up independent bodies devoted to encouraging and promoting greater co-operation with the citizens.

Notwithstanding these positive signs, the participatory culture remains relatively weak. Increasing public participation is a task that all OECD cities find difficult but Istanbul faces some particular challenges. Until now civil society has not generally been involved in decision making prior to the decision. A structural inconsistency can be found in the fact that institutions are not open to professional chambers and other competent organisations, like the "Chamber of City Planners and the Chamber of Architects". There are also different kinds of organisations with different relationships to the public authorities. There are organisations closely linked to the public authorities or to large private companies like foundations (namely the social and charitable foundations created by the province) or associations, and they appear to be dependent on the political authorities. There are then the professional bodies organised in Chambers, like the Chambers of Architects, the Chambers of City-Planners, the Turkish Medical Association (TTB) or the Turkish Bar Association (TBB) with their own special legal statute. These actors, now deeply involved in the local debates, are still trying to be more systematically involved in decision making and particularly in the elaboration and monitoring of urban projects. This activity dates back to 1980s, with organised opposition to the municipal programme of demolition in Beyoğlu-Tarlabaşı, and to the opening of a high-intensity traffic avenue through an old neighbourhood known for the number of historical buildings. There are also more independent and non-professional associations that are demanding more involvement. The Local Initiative of the Arnavutköy neighbourhood is a good example of this phenomenon. It was set up in 1998 by some residents of this neighbourhood (located along the Strait of Istanbul, on the European side) to protest against the project of a third car bridge on the Strait of Istanbul. Similarly, the mobilisations to oppose some projects or some buildings can be quoted (like the Parkotel in Gümüşsuyu or the Gökkafes/Süzer Plaza skyscraper in Dolmabahçe, both located in Beyoğlu). Some of the more active associations are operating on environmental issues, sometimes using links with international associations that give them relative independence to develop their strategies (*e.g.*, threatening interruption of international traffic on the Strait of Istanbul, water pollution, air pollution, car traffic, lack of green areas).

In many metropolitan areas throughout the world, corruption at the local level hinders public confidence and thus the efficiency of urban development. In Turkey, EU regulations have recently become a huge motivation for the country to strengthen its attempts to tackle corruption – the current government even made anti-corruption one of its manifesto themes. However according to a recent EU assessment (European Commission, 2006), the momentum for reform is slowing down and many of the measures taken, *e.g.*, the 2003 Law on Access to Public Information, are not strong enough to deal with the issue of lack of transparency.[14] It is unlikely to be solved by punitive measures and requires reforms throughout the system of governance. This "operating context" within which decisions are made can either limit or encourage corrupt practices. The whole governmental system therefore needs to be considered from this perspective; therefore increasing transparency and public involvement are necessary but not sufficient. At the local level, Seoul provides an interesting approach to involving the public in controlling corruption (Box 3.3).

Box 3.3. Encouraging citizen participation in controlling corruption: the example of the Seoul Metropolitan Government

Seoul has gone to admirable lengths to encourage direct public participation in controlling corruption. For example, there are simple-to-use mechanisms for residents and non-profit organisations to request audits of agencies in the event that a breach of law or other harm to the public interest is suspected. The city has also made excellent use of Korea's very high rate of Internet dissemination to craft an online system for handling civic affairs called OPEN (Online Procedures Enhancement for Civil Applications). This project originated with the 1998 announcement of an "all-out war on corruption". OPEN is applied to 70 different areas of civic administration that are at high risk of misconduct, including taxation, sanitation and construction. By accessing the city's Internet website, residents can monitor the progress of their applications and other business with the city. The system discloses the department in charge, the supervisor, contact information, details of the job, the handling process, and related laws and regulations.

Seoul's administration has bolstered the incentives to report suspected cases of corruption by offering financial inducements to residents. These inducements are comprehensive in scope, in that they apply at the city and the gu levels (districts) as well as within the local public enterprises that the city has established or invests in. The potential reward for a substantiated report of corruption varies from KRW 100 000 to KRW 1 million. At the end of 2003, there were 22 rewards given totalling KRW 5.6 million.

The city has also encouraged direct citizen representation in the decision-making process through various oversight committees. By May 2004, there were 43 committees in Seoul with a total of 1,249 members. The committees are set up and operate according to laws and ordinances, and carry out inquiries, reviews and resolutions. Of the membership, 1,096 members (87.8% of the total) were from civic groups, whereas only 153 members (12.2%) were city officials. Over 30% of the committee members are required to be women in order to increase female participation in social affairs. This figure is scheduled to increase to 40% by 2007.

The use of committees needs to be accompanied with clear standards and guidelines for the committee members – especially the representatives from civil society – to facilitate their ability to identify problems in the area they are overseeing. An example is seen in the United Kingdom. The half-million appointees who serve as non-executive "governors" on monitoring bodies have often been too reactive and willing to be led by the executives. The problem was that UK governors' oversight functions cover a vast administrative terrain that includes the National Health Services, housing association boards, police authorities and schools. An inquiry into the performance of the monitoring bodies concluded in 2003 that there was a "failure of governance" because the skills and commitment of the governors were "being wasted". The inquiry's recommendations were incorporated into "Good Governance Standard for Public Services" established by the Independent Commission of Good Governance in January 2005. As it expands its own citizen oversight mechanisms, Seoul would do well to learn from the pitfalls other systems have encountered and their subsequent reforms.

Source: OECD (2005), *OECD Territorial Reviews: Seoul, Korea*, OECD Publications, Paris.

A potential area of corruption, that has attracted reform, is the process for tendering contracts. One aspect of this is the role of the public companies and the way they interact with the municipalities. Mostly created in the late 1980s these companies have become more and more important since the middle of the 1990s. Since the beginning of the 2000s, the sub-province municipalities have also created their own public companies. A main issue linked with the duality of municipality and public companies results in two parallel and often competing structures (*e.g.*, in transport management). However with a new 2003 law on invitation to tender, companies linked to the Metropolitan Municipality are beginning to lose their monopolies. Now the Metropolitan Municipality's requests for proposal have to be conducted in a more open manner. For example, at the end of 2003, Kültür A.S., the municipal company in charge of cultural policy lost its right to manage the "CRR Konser Salonu", one of the most famous places for cultural events. The company that offered the lowest bid won the tender against the municipal company that had been managing this place for more than ten years. However although improvements can be seen, the tendering laws need to be more universally and strongly applied.

Planning can also create opportunities for corruption. Everywhere, urban development projects can create large profits and planning decisions on zoning can potentially release major benefits for actors. Notwithstanding the existence of laws requiring politicians and public servants to reveal their assets, the OECD/EU Assessment, at least in 2005, calls for improvement in this area (OECD/SIGMA, 2005). In particular, rather than relying on punitive measures for specific cases, more systematic measures can be taken. One is to develop a culture of public interest that guides the actions of politicians and bureaucrats. A second is a vigilant and independent press and public debate, although their ability to monitor is dependent on the degree of transparency in the decision-making process. A third approach is to remove all the factors that make corruption easier – such as complexity in the decision-making structures, difficulties in establishing accountability, overlap or ambiguity in the laws and regulations, and too much flexibility in the planning system. A key element in such reforms is the strengthening of the planning system so there is less room for individual influence. Likewise the excessive use of amnesties in construction undermines the status of the plans and regulations. There should be clarity in the planning framework, both legally and in terms of who is responsible for preparing the plans. As mentioned above, there should be statutory conformity between plans at different levels. When plans are formulated they should go through a procedure of public involvement to try and achieve consensus. Once adopted, the plans should have legal weight, and any changes to the plan should need to go through a similar public process.

While political authorities have perfectly understood the necessity to refer to civil society in their discourse, this has been more a source of ideas or a useful marketing tool, and less a real input into decision making. However, as all OECD metropolitan regions experience, more meaningful participation is not an easy process to establish. There are dangers involved, for example in raising expectations for public influence beyond practical possibilities, and hence generating alienation. Trying to involve people in a *fait accompli* could also create a backlash. Alternatively a participation exercise may only attract the involvement of a particular section of society, say the more educated, reducing the value of the results as an expression of the whole society. Nevertheless increasing public involvement and improving the relationship of trust between citizens and government is essential. This will improve the efficiency of decision making, utilising the experience and knowledge of local people and minimising lengthy processes of conflict. It will also create a more stable society that is essential for investment and economic growth. Some lessons from the past experience for improving participation in other cities include:

- Disseminating information broadly to encourage diverse participation;
- Beginning early in the decision-making process when alternatives are still under consideration;
- Utilising different methods of involvement, from focus groups to public meetings or the Internet;
- Recognising different methods may be needed for people with different levels of education;
- Tapping into people's existing networks where possible.

In this respect public participation at the lowest level of government – the neighbourhood (*mahalle*) – could be further developed. It might be possible to delegate some decision-making functions for very local issues, *e.g.*, street cleaning, traffic controls, or environmental improvements, to this level and give citizens some decision-making powers as these are often issues that attract a lot of public concern. There are a number of cities that are moving towards more neighbourhood level democracy. Lessons might be learned from these examples in Busan and Porto Alegre, although such initiatives need to be particularly moulded to local circumstances (Box 3.4).

Box 3.4. **Neighbourhood level participation: The examples of Busan and Porto Alegre**

Neighbourhood participation has to evolve from the particular local circumstances. It is often useful to start with small initiatives, taking advantage of *ad hoc* opportunities, and gradually building these up into a more comprehensive system. The following examples in Busan and Porto Alegre illustrate this. The second example also shows that allowing a degree of local involvement in financial allocation can be one that creates a lot of local involvement.

Busan's Local Autonomy Centres:

In 1998, Korea launched an administrative restructuring which made local government office space available for other uses. "Local autonomy centres" were set up in these spaces to give the local community a place to meet. The centres aim to promote community involvement among the population, and become the closest level of local democracy to the people.

In 2002, the city of Busan set up over 200 of these centres with supervisory committees of about 20 people drawn from civil society. Locally elected officials also sit on the committees in an advisory capacity. The centres primarily offer cultural programmes but some have also been involved in civic education and alleviating social problems. So far these centres have been rather limited in their impact but they do have the potential to play a more important local democratic role. They could be given more resources by local government and if the committee members were elected it would generate more public interest. They could also vary their programmes more to the specific needs of each area.

Participatory budgeting in Porto Alegre:

The participatory budgeting process in Porto Alegre, Brazil, is one of the best know examples of successful collaboration between civil society and the state. It was initiated by the Workers Party city government in 1989 but became so popular that it later became independent of any political party and has been adopted by other major Brazilian cities. When the Workers Party took control they set up 16 open assemblies across the city in which citizens could express their demands for financial investment. In many ways the participatory budget is a small initiative with small objectives – bringing ordinary people into the discussion of how to distribute basic investment among their neighbourhood. However the impact of this involvement goes beyond this as it is an educative process and breeds a new culture of involvement. Significant transformation has taken place across the city in the way that civil society participates and organised civil society has expanded.

Source: OECD (2005), *OECD Territorial Reviews: Busan, Korea*, OECD Publications, Paris and Albers, R. (1998), "Learning Democratic Practice and Distributing Government Resources Through Popular Participation in Porto Alegre, Brazil" in M. Douglas and J. Friedmann (eds.), *Cities for Citizens: Planning and the Rise of Civil Society in a Global Age*, John Wiley and Sons, Chichester, pp.39-66.

More transparent mechanisms in the decision-making process could be introduced at the metropolitan government. It was already mentioned that in order to improve public participation in transport planning and projects, and to minimise the impact of hidden agendas and costly opposition, the current "Transportation Coordination Centre" UKOME could have a leading role in a newly established permanent consultative body that would gather representatives across levels of government, professional chambers, and associations to regularly exchange views and information on potential and ongoing projects. Such mechanisms could also be extended to urban projects that are of general interest.

3.3. Promoting a regional growth strategy

The persistence of large territorial disparities and the process of reforms launched by the opening of EU accession negotiations raise the issue of developing a new regional policy approach in Turkey. In this respect, the first task is to promote a sound legal and institutional framework, as well as adequate administrative capacity, to ensure the effective planning and implementation of regional policy. The implementation of a multi-level governance system – characterised by a clear definition of responsibilities amongst different levels of government and new mechanisms of co-operation amongst institutions – is acknowledged as the biggest challenge for Turkey with respect to the development of a regional growth strategy.

One of the most important initiatives currently underway in the field of regional development, is the establishment of regional development agencies. In February 2006 the law took effect that sets out the principles and procedures regarding the establishment and duties of development agencies (DAs). According to the law, development agencies will be gradually set up in NUTS 2 regions, one of which is to be Istanbul. In July 2006, two pilot DAs were established by government decrees TR31 (Izmir) and TR62 (Adana, Mersin) in NUTS 2 regions. As of February 2007, General Secretaries of both DAs have been appointed and the expert staff has been selected for recruitment. The DAs are expected to play a key role in bringing in more operational effectiveness and efficiency in regional development polices, with an emphasis on the role economic competitiveness. They are a support to bolster city and regional capacity to compete more effectively in the global economy. The agencies will be formed in a gradual manner under the oversight of the Council of Ministers. The State Planning Organization will be responsible for co-ordinating the agencies at the national level by providing assistance and guidance on planning, programming and project designing, and by monitoring the implementation of plans and programmes. In Istanbul the DA will cover the geographical area of the province and the Istanbul Metropolitan Municipality.

The DAs have a number of broad objectives as they combine the functions of an investment promotion agency with that of regional development with both economic and social aims. Their stated objectives are: to accelerate regional development, to promote sustainability and reduce intra- and inter-regional development disparities, all by enhancing the co-operation amongst public, private sectors and NGOs, and ensuring the efficient allocation of resources. They will not be involved in detailed implementation but rather will focus on providing support to the planning studies of local authorities, on promoting the investment opportunities of the region, on encouraging co-operation and carrying out analyses to identify resources and opportunities of the region. The DAs will also promote activities related to bilateral or multi-lateral international programmes and contribute to the development of projects in the region within the context of these programmes. As a single port of call for investors, they will help with the necessary permit and licence procedures. They will also stimulate the creation of a menu of business development support services aimed at small and medium sized enterprises (such as information, consultancy, research, training and the streamlining of permitting and licensing procedures).

The DAs will be set up as corporate bodies subject to private law, in an attempt to create a new kind of organisational structure that is more dynamic and flexible to facilitate swift decision making. They will also take a participatory approach to encourage dialogue and include the private sector viewpoint. The Istanbul DA's organisational structure will follow a relatively standardised model characterised by the presence of the following four bodies:

- The *Administrative Board* is the central decision-making body of the DA. In Istanbul, it will be comprised of the Provincial Governor (Chairman of the Board), the Chairman of the Provincial Council, the Istanbul Metropolitan Mayor, the Chairman of the Chamber of Industry, the Chairman of the Chamber of Commerce and three representatives of the private sector and/or NGOs elected by the Development Council.
- The *Development Council* will act as an advisory body to guide the DA. The membership of the Development Council, which will be limited to 100 members, is intended to represent the range of interests in the region and will be drawn from the private sector, NGOs, universities, public institutions, and local governments. The Development Council will appoint its own chairman and select the three representatives of NGOs/private sector to sit on the Administrative Board.

- The *General Secretariat* is the executive body reporting to the Administrative Board and designed to provide operational strength and capacity to the DA. It will have access to dedicated funds, and carry out a number of functions. Composed of a staff of approximately 50, it will provide technical assistance for the planning studies of local authorities, assess project proposals from the private sector, NGOs and local administrations, make suggestions to the Administrative Board for providing financial support, and evaluate and monitor the supported projects and activities. This body will also prepare an annual working programme and budget, and set up programmes in areas such as promotion and marketing, and information technology.
- *Investment Support Offices* will exist within the secretariat for providing guidance on procedures for investors.

The Development Council will make comments on the work of the Secretariat and the Administrative Board will make the decisions. The funds for the RDA will come from the allocation of funds from other bodies, and supplemented by donations and aid. They will get 0.05% of the general budget tax income, 1% of the provincial special administration income, 1% of the municipality incomes, 1% of the incomes of the Chambers of Commerce and Industry, and any funds acquired from the European Union.

Although little progress has been made in implementing the Development Agency (DA) in Istanbul, it looks like an interesting and necessary addition to the region's institutional structures. The Development Agency is expected to be a key player in developing a more participatory and multi-layered system of governance. The Istanbul DA's plan to involve a broad range of representative organisations into a dialogue is a welcome and necessary approach, particularly toward creating a climate of transparency and participation. The private sector is well represented in this process and it may be worth considering whether, to meet the social objectives of the Development Agency, more efforts need to be made to ensure a full range of social interests are included. Moreover, the fact that the DAs will be subject to private law provisions will ensure fast decision making, and flexibility in staff employment, budgeting and project financing.

Yet, the current DAs project is not without criticism. A number of issues could be considered. For instance, the most innovative aspect of DAs is expected to be the promotion of co-operation mechanisms amongst public institutions (central and local), private actors and NGOs. In this context, it will therefore be important to strengthen the tools for managing negotiations and conflicts amongst actors and, at the same time, to ensure that the Development Agency does not intervene as a new structure overlapping current institutional functions. Moreover, the hybrid nature of the new entity (a hybrid public/private body) – while ensuring fast decision making and flexibility – could create some management difficulties in the long run: *i.e.*, as the Agency is not subject to the provisions regulating Public Procurement Law (Law No. 2886 and Law No. 4734), the management of EU funds could not be provided. The DAs themselves do not fall under the application of the Public Procurement Legislation and the Law for Public Finance Management and Control, which is a questionable fact. However, the beneficiaries of the funds, as possible procuring entities, are subject to the procurement rules and procedures (SIGMA, 2006).

One particular issue to monitor will be how the Development Agencies fit into the existing structure and network. Regional development agencies have been established throughout Europe and have similar objectives of regional promotion and development. However the detailed operation of an agency varies because it has to be embedded into a country's existing institutional and political landscape. Setting up a regional development agency in a federally oriented country such as Germany is very different from doing so in a centrally oriented country with no tradition of regional government, such as the United Kingdom. The UK example also shows how the regional development agencies may need to adapt to the different circumstances of different regions within a country, from those with a very strong regional identity such as Scotland, to areas where it is difficult to identify a regional entity at all, to the special needs of the large metropolis of London. In considering this variety, one of the key questions is how the regional development agency interacts with the other governments of the region and their democratic processes.

The current model of the DA in Istanbul shares some similarities with the existing Istanbul Economic and Cultural Collaboration Council (ECCC), commonly called Istanbul Council. The ECCC was created in 2000 and gathers the official institutions of the province, municipalities, professional chambers and representatives of associations. Its key objectives are: (1) the co-ordination of official institutions, local authorities, professional organisations and civil society representatives in the province of Istanbul; (2) a solidarity platform and co-ordination function; (3) economic, social and cultural development, investment and problem solving programmes (planning and monitoring) at the local level; (4) resolution of the structural problems of the region, and of all the consequences they may have. Although the Istanbul Council has no comparable legal provision, like the text of Law on the DA, the objectives are comparable. In addition to some details like the number of representatives on the Council, or the presence of the same actors with slight differences in the configuration, the important points are the reference to co-ordination at the regional level and the presence of the Governor, as chief of the executive body. Of course, this council exists only for Istanbul and has no legal character at the national scale, as there are not equivalent institutions in other regions.

In the Istanbul case, it is important to establish a clear relationship between the decision-making processes of the DA and those of the Province and Istanbul Metropolitan Authority. In the 2005 Provincial Administration Law and 2005 Metropolitan Municipalities Law it states that a high level spatial strategy at the province level should be prepared. However the laws do not clearly articulate the relationship between the Istanbul Metropolitan Municipality and the Province. This lack of clarity makes it fundamental to strengthen co-operation tools between the DA and local institutional actors in the preparation of regional strategies and plans.

The implementation of new regional policies also demands a change in governance at the central level. The first task is to strengthen the collaboration between sectoral and regional directorates within the State Planning Organization (SPO) – which plays a prominent role in planning regional policy at a national level – as well as promoting the efficient exchange of information and better horizontal co-operation amongst central administrations (*i.e.*, via the establishment of an inter-ministerial committee).[15] Developing knowledge and information is crucial for a good implementation process. In Italy, the implementation of the new governance system for regional policy hinges on the exchange of reliable, timely and meaningful, quantitative information. Within such a system, general policy targets and the "rules of the game" are set by upper level government through technical and political consultation with the lower levels, and the specification and implementation of these targets (and the allocation of rewards and sanctions) require diagnostic monitoring through partnership networks (Barca, Brezzi, Terribile and Utili, 2004). In this respect, the development and diffusion of economic, social and environmental statistics and indicators at the territorial level, coupled with the establishment of standardised methodologies and common approaches for evaluating and monitoring public investments (at the central and local levels), is a necessary prerequisite for the effective planning and implementation of regional development programmes and projects. In this respect, establishing a monitoring and evaluation system in DAs similar to the existing one for EU regional development programmes monitored by the Monitoring and Evaluation Department of SPO is encouraging.

Finally, it will also be important to develop, notably at the municipal level, the administrative capacity for the evaluation, implementation and monitoring of programmes and projects. For example, in Italy the establishment of technical units, both at central and regional levels, for the evaluation and monitoring of public investments – coupled with sanction and reward mechanisms in the regional allocation of funds – was a fundamental instrument for strengthening the capacity of regional administrations to screen and select interventions and monitor their implementation. In Turkey, it will be important to define in the short-term a system of incentives for administrations (central and local) to ensure the quality and homogeneity of the evaluation and monitoring of public investments. Developing sets of key performance indicators, standardising methodologies, and creating common approaches for evaluating and monitoring public investments will play a key role.

Conclusion: Istanbul governance is a local and a national challenge

Istanbul is undergoing a major transformation of its legal and institutional framework. Many new laws have been passed in recent years that are pointing towards a new administrative and financial context; however the implementation of many of these laws has been slow. The current need is to identify the blockages to progress and create the conditions that will allow the transformation to have a concrete effect. The blockages are not limited to a few elements within the system, but rather are of a more systematic nature and occur at many points across the spectrum of governance. Such difficulties need to be simultaneously addressed at many levels. At a broad level there is the need for a cultural change and improved education over the way that urban decisions are made. There are new institutional arrangements, policy approaches, and financial allocations that can make progress easier. In addition, there are more experimental initiatives that could be put in place for developing on current activity that looks as if it might have potential.

More specifically, the review of the governance system in Istanbul has highlighted a number of obstacles to be addressed. First there is a scope for clarifying the roles and responsibilities of different levels of government. Although recent legislation has made changes in this respect there seems to be a need for further thought on the division of work between the Ministries, Province, Metropolitan Municipalities and lower level municipalities. This is linked with co-ordination problems between the different levels and agencies of governance. The sector-based approach of central government also works against the co-ordination over a geographical area. The new boundaries of the Metropolitan Municipality, and the overlap with the Province, provide a good basis for co-ordination but improvements are needed as the relationships between the Metropolitan Municipality and the sub-province municipalities move away from a centralist top-down approach towards a more collaborative framework. Meanwhile, the constant evolution of the functional economic area would require developing new collaborative tools with surrounding administrative areas. Istanbul is now endowed with new and elaborated planning tools but the issue of implementation needs to be addressed. A planning system needs to have legitimacy and be enforced so that all development projects and lower level plans conform to the agreed upon metropolitan-wide plan. Finally, the decentralisation process requires co-ordinated policy approaches as well as adequate administrative capacity. This will include ensuring that the financial resources are available to match the devolved responsibilities and that local capacity is upgraded.

This being said, a number of considerations should be made. First, many of the obstacles to well-functioning governance for Istanbul are common to metropolitan regions throughout the OECD. Though the scope and the extent of these challenges are more exacerbated in Istanbul, as it confronts its specific environmental risks and large negative externalities typical to mega-cities. Moreover, both Istanbul and Turkey are "in transition". At the national level, despite important achievements, there is still a wide range of economic, regulatory and institutional reforms to be implemented. At the local level, the emergence of important new actors, especially the rising importance of the Metropolitan Municipality with extended powers and responsibilities is quite recent. Finally, it is important to recall important positive achievements. Major public policies have been developed with positive outcomes in some fields such as water management and international visibility, and more importantly a perceived consciousness of major urban development threats and a will for a pro-active approach to deal with them and to acquire a global status on the international economic scale.

Looking forward, improving governance in Istanbul is both a local and a national matter. At the local level, the Metropolitan Municipality has everything to gain from a comprehensive and deep reform of its management framework. As mentioned above, any decentralisation process should be led cautiously and with strong guarantees of accountability and control. The pre-requisite for any structural change in Istanbul is to enhance local workforce capacity and to improve transparency in decision-making processes. Specific actions include a rationalisation of the administrative framework within the Istanbul Metropolitan Municipality, capacity building programmes for local civil servants, and control and audit procedures on the allocations of resources to various extra-municipal actors including for the attribution of public works contracts. Meanwhile, enhancing the role of civil society in the local decision-making process, through better access to information, and more involvement in municipal decisions-making structures, would contribute to creating a more consensus-oriented approach and overcoming some of the divides in society, and provide a valuable input to policy making. As for the central government, it has perfectly understood the importance of fostering the economic development of its major metropolitan area and dealing with the major urban issues, but these challenges will constantly be a threat so long as the rest of the country is lagging behind. In other words, the implementation of the new regional development policies in Turkey is urgent not only for the development of the country but also for the success and the sustainability of Istanbul.

Notes

1. According to Law No. 5538 (July 2006).
2. In practice they include such competencies as establishing health services, hospitals, and social facilities; dealing with health hazards, planning and controlling for fire risks and natural disasters; planning and co-ordinating public transport; building and maintaining urban roads; parking controls; protecting the environment, water basins, agricultural areas, cultural and historical assets; building and operating district parks, zoos, libraries, museums, sport and entertainment facilities, solid waste management; training in skills and trades; and building facilities for health education and cultural services.
3. The Provinces Bank is a public organisation providing technical services, and distributing the shares of the municipalities and extending loans. Redevelopment plans were prepared free of charge until November 2006 and were charged thereafter.
4. The government of Turkey has announced it will solve this problem in 2007 by application of the so-called "address-based population recording system".
5. In 2005 two mayors were involved in such court cases as a result of political conflicts between central and local governments. One of these two mayors was later reinstated by another court decision.
6. Published in the *Official Gazette* on 08 February 2006.
7. According to OECD/SIGMA (2006), "recruitment procedures in the civil service have long been reputed as being rife with patronage, however some progress has been made in recent years, making it more a historical legacy rather than a recent problem".
8. The Law No. 5234 of 17 September 2004 is an initiative from the central government which attributes all the necessary competences to the Ministry of Public Works, and gathers, according to the same provision, all the available real estate properties under the name of the Turkish State Railways (*Türkiye Cumhuriyeti Devlet Demiryolları*, TCDD). The law also states that some district municipalities must carry out the injunctions of the ministry concerning this particular project. This mechanism is

newly tailored, and meant to be executed in parallel with other ministerial competences. The so-called enforcement is the Ministry of Public Works and Settlement ability 'to act by itself' in cancelling clauses of suspension, publicity and claims for annulment against it, without any prior consultation of the municipalities. Although the Haydarpaşa project has been "put on hold for the moment", this law has been said to have introduced some contradictions within the text of the laws.

9. There are actually six regional committees for Istanbul in the Higher Council for the Protection of Cultural Monuments. According to the law No. 2863 of June 1983, a consensus has to be reached among the various organisations concerned. However, in the absence of a consensus, the ruling of the Supreme Council for the Protection of Cultural and Natural Heritage will be decisive and final.

10. They are the Department of Housing and Urban Development, the Department of Earthquake Risk Management and Urban Development, and the Department of Projects.

11. This shows again that central politicians play a strong role in relation to planning decisions in the city.

12. For a first conceptualisation attempt for the Turkish case, see Göle and Toprak (1996) and Seufert, Vorhoff and Yerasimos (2000).

13. It is chaired by the Istanbul Mayor.

14. OECD/SIGMA (Support for Improvement in Governance and Management), "Turkey: Elements of the Public Integrity System – Assessment June 2005". A joint initiative of the OECD and the European Union, principally financed by the EU.

15. The High Planning Council performs tasks of inter-ministerial co-ordination.

Annex

Regional Disparities in Turkey: A Slow Convergence Process

Throughout the 1990s, Turkey experienced regional convergence. Our analysis took into account β-convergence estimates for three different periods 1987-2000, 1990-2000 and 1995-2000 in order to test possible structural impacts such as the financial liberalisation of the 1990s or the adverse effect of the financial crisis in 1994 (Table A.1).

The results revealed that Turkey has been experiencing a process of convergence characterised by higher growth rates in lagging regions. For all three periods, the results show clear evidence of convergence among the provinces. The deviation coefficient shown by our σ- convergence analysis is decreasing slowly from 0.54 to 0.48 over the 13-year period (Table A.2). Indeed, if we take into account the size of the coefficient in the β-convergence analysis in Table A.1, we can see that regions in Turkey are converging at an average annual rate of 1.4%.

Table A.1. **Summary of β-convergence regressions**

	1987-2000	1990-2000	1995-2000
Coefficient (β)	-0.014523	-0.014566	-0.007045
t-value	-4.810936*	-3.905227*	-1.45171
R^2	0.262580	0.181017	0.027745

* Statistically significant at 1%.

Table A.2. **σ- Convergence**

	1987	1990	1995	2000
Standard Deviation	0.543279	0.521376	0.491148	0.481196

However, convergence is still slow. While β-convergence results for the 1987-2000 and 1990-2000 periods are statistically significant, the shorter period of 1995-2000 yielded no significant results (Table A.1). In fact, the results were weaker the shorter the period evaluated (Figure A.1). If Turkey continues to display convergence at such slow speed, it would take at least 47 years just to cut disparities in half.[1]

Figure A.1. **Average growth rate *versus* initial level of GDP per capita by province**

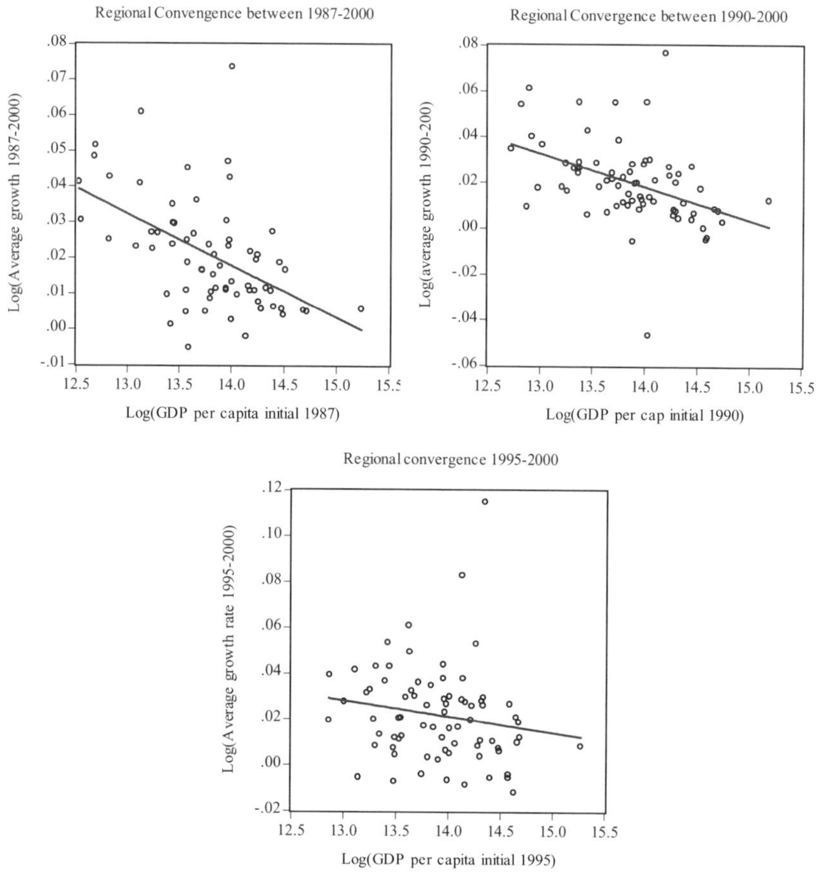

Source: Calculations based on data from Turkish Statistical Institute (TURKSTAT) (*www.turkstat.gov.tr*).

Extending the analysis to include explanations for such convergence trend reveals that regional growth processes in Turkey are complex and not directly attributable to one of the main socio-economic phenomena such as migration, public investment or regional policy. Using two different net migration rates according to the availability of data, as well as linear values of initial public investment (assuming that public investment is an initial investment stock then used throughout the period) and cumulative values for fiscal and other economic incentives for lagging regions, the models presented in this section show that convergence is not fuelled by migration, public investment decisions or even fiscal incentives for lagging regions (Table A.3). The variables included in the conditional model are net migration rates, initial public investment and cumulative investment incentives.

Table A.3. **Conditional convergence regressions for 1987-2000**

	1987-2000					
	Model 1	Model 2	Model 3	Model 4	Model 5	Model 6
Constant	0.2055 (2.8788)**	0.2275 (3.7789)**	0.2208 (2.9483)**	0.2334 (3.8406)**	0.2021 (2.6069)*	0.2014 (2.9228)**
Log of initial GDP per capita	-0.0133 (-2.6227)*	-0.0149 (-3.4498)**	-0.0127 (-2.4593)*	-0.0134 (-2.8496)**	-0.0104 (-1.8003)*	-0.0103 (-1.8244)*
Net migration rate 1985-1990	-0.0279 (-0.5902)	---	-0.0199 (-0.4077)	---	-0.0020 (-0.0384)	---
Net migration rate 1995-2000	---	-0.0167 (-0.2676)	---	-0.0181 (-0.2887)	---	-0.0050 (-0.0789)
Log of initial public investment	---	---	-0.0014 (-0.7037)	-0.0015 (-0.8281)	-0.0008 (-0.3905)	-0.0008 (-0.4022)
Log of cumulative investment incentives for 1995-2000	---	---	---	---	-0.0017 (-0.9387)	-0.0017 (-0.9842)
Adj. R^2	0.2436	0.2404	0.2376	0.2366	0.2362	0.2362

* Statistically significant at 1%.

* * Statistically significant at 10%.

The process of convergence in Turkey is not based on the flow of labour from one place to another (migration). Just as capital flows from one region to the other are motivated by higher returns of investment, migration flows are attracted by the expectation of higher wages. Migrants then represent a drain in the labour force and human capital in the sending region, and a gain for the pooled labour market and for the human capital stock in the destination region. Surprisingly though, strong migration flows in Turkey have been consistent with growth trends and convergence in the country. Despite the fact that migration flows are directed to richer regions (Figure A.2), they are not associated with regional growth dynamics (Figure A.3) nor are they a vehicle of equalisation. However, such results are in line with Barro and Sala-i-Martin's (1995) theory that migration in the United States, the EU and Japan does not determine convergence processes in such regions.

Figure A.2. **Migration and regional income**

Net migration rates and initial regional GDP per capita

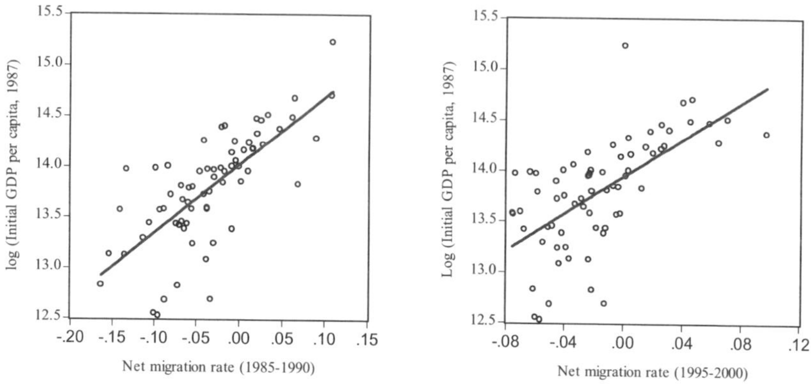

Source: Own calculations based on Turkish Statistical Institute (TURKSTAT), Regional statistics, (*www.turkstat.gov.tr*).

Figure A.3. **Migration and regional growth**

Net migration rates and per capita GDP growth (1897-2000)

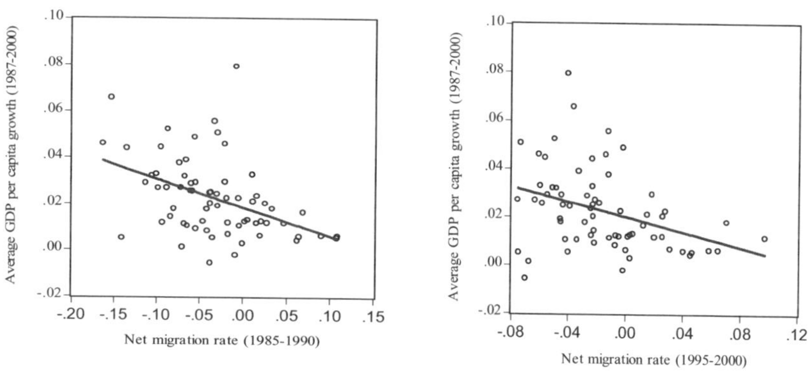

Source: Own calculations based on Turkish Statistical Institute (TURKSTAT), Regional statistics, (*www.turkstat.gov.tr*).

Similarly, the results show that convergence is not related to either public investment or to incentives given by the state for firms settling in lagging regions. Both public investment and value of cumulative incentives display a negative and not statistically significant association to regional growth (Figures A.4 and A.5). One possible explanation is that public investment may be allocated to infrastructure or social development that may improve human development levels, but productive investment (such as industrial estates) may be under-developed. However, further research is needed on the types of investment being allocated to different regions to confirm this hypothesis.

Figure A.4. **Public investment and regional growth**

Initial value of public investment in 1990 and per capita GDP growth (1987-2000)

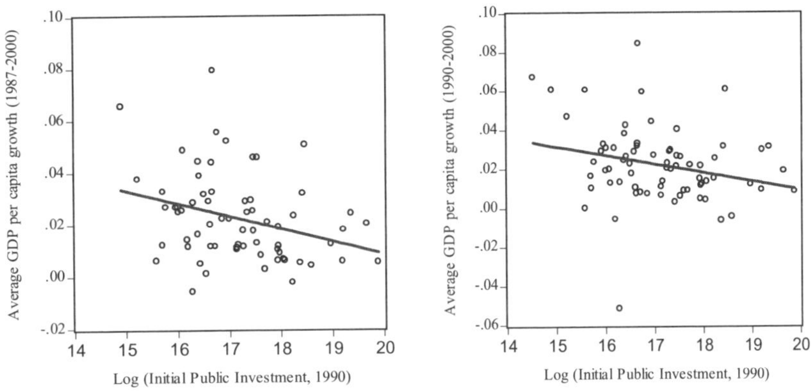

Source: Own calculations based on data from State Planning Organization (SPO), regional statistics (*www.dpt.gov.tr*).

Figure A.5. **Incentives to lagging regions and convergence**

Cumulative value of incentives granted (1995-2000) and per capita GDP growth (1987-2000)

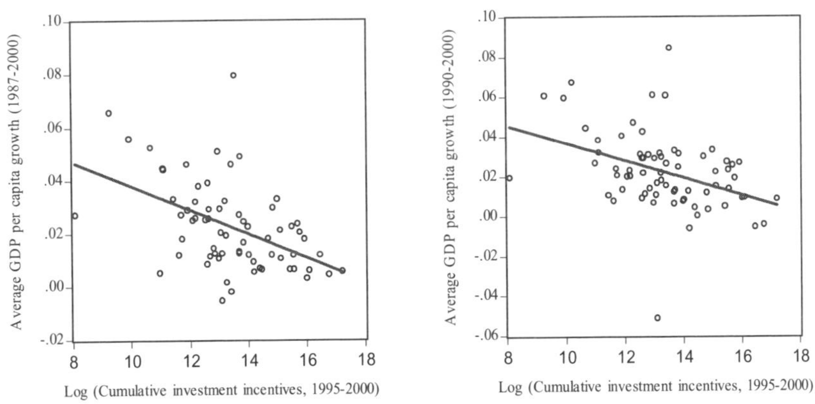

Source: Own calculations based on data from State Planning Organization (SPO), regional statistics (*www.dpt.gov.tr*).

What is surprising in our results is that the cumulative value of incentives granted by the state for industrial location in lagging regions are not behind the positive growth performance in poorer regions. There are two alternative explanations for this phenomenon. Perhaps the process of convergence is more related to private investment decisions based on private investment for business and location solutions such as the "Organised Industrial Zones" or the "Free Zones" that, although geographically selected by the state, are provided by the private sector. On the one hand, it is possible that agricultural policy based on minimum prices for crops or subsidies may have had an impact on the performance of poorer regions. In any case, further research is needed to unveil the determinants of this process of convergence.

Notes

1. The speed of convergence indicates the time that it takes for a region – or a country – to cut inequality in some degree. To cut disparities in half at the current speed of convergence of 1.4523% a year it will take 47 years. Time (t) is calculated to cut the distance between income at the present level log(y(0)) and the desired level log(y*) satisfying the condition $e\text{-}\beta t = ½$ so that $\log(2)/\beta$.

Bibliography

Adams, D. (1994), Urban Planning and the Development Process, UCL Press, London.

Akbulut, Ö (2003), *Yerel Seçim Sistemi Değişmeli (Local Election System should be Changed)*, Cumhuriyet (Newspaper), 19/11/2003, p. 2, Istanbul.

Akçay, E. C. (2005) *The End and the Beginning of Politics: The Case of Istanbul*, Boğaziçi University, Istanbul.

Akçay, Cevdet (2003), "The Turkish Banking Sector Two Years After the Crisis: A Snapshot of the Sector and Current Risks", Barry Rubin and Ziya Öniş (eds.), *Turkey's Economy in Crisis*, Frank Class Publishers.

Akpınar (2004), *Regional Development Dynamics and Institutional Reflections: Development Agencies*, Unpublished Specialization Thesis, State Planning Organization (SPO), Ankara.

Aksoy M. (2002), *Yerel Yönetimlerin Eksiği ve Siyaset (Politics and deficiency of local governments)*, Radikal (Newspaper), 24/02/2002, p. 6, Turkey.

Alada, A (s.d.), Demokratikleşme Sürecinin Dalgalanmaları: Cumhuriyet Döneminde İstanbul'un Yönetimi (Fluctuation in the Process of Democracy: Governance of Istanbul in the Era of Republic), Istanbul Nasıl Yönetilmeli?, Istanbul Dergisi (Istanbul Review), pp.133-138, Istanbul.

Albers, R. (1998), "Learning Democratic Practice, Distributing Government Resources Through Popular Participation in Porto Alegre, Brazil", M. Douglas and J. Friedmann, *Cities for Citizens: Planning and the Rise of Civil Society in a Global_Age*, John Wiley and Sons, pp. 39-66, Chichester.

Allen, K., G Gotz and C. Joseph (2001) *Johannesburg: An African City in Change,* Johannesburg, Zebra Press.

Al Maktoum, B. R (2001), "Dubai: Regional Hub for the New Economy" in *OECD Observer*, January 2001, Issue 224, p 7.

Alpöge, A. (1993), *Halka Dönük Yerel Yönetim (Participatory Governance)*, IULA-EMME & T.C. Başbakanlık Toplu Konut Idaresi Başkanlığı, No. 11, p. 165, Istanbul.

Altınbilek, D. (2006) "Water Management in Istanbul", *Water Resources Development*, Vol. 22, No. 2, pp. 241–253.

Ammour, L. (1994), "Les Élections Municipales du 27 Mars 1994 Dans les Grandes Métropoles et à Istanbul" ("Municipal elections of March 27th, 1994 in the Big Metropolis and in Istanbul"), Lettre d'information, *Observatoire Urbain d'Istanbul*, IFEA, p. 9-13, Istanbul.

Anbarcı, N., A. Filiztekin and H. Kirmanoğlu (2002), "Endogenous Migration: A Theoretical and Empirical Analysis", Discussion Paper Series in Economics, Sabancı University, Istanbul.

Andersen, A. (2000) "Dubai Makes a Bid for E-business", in *International Tax Review*, December 2000/January 2001. Vol. 12, Issue 1, pp. 47-49, London.

Atabek, D.E. *et al.* (1988), "Yerel Yönetimler ve Kent Sorunları" ("Local Governments and Urban Problems"), *Bilim ve Sanat*, No. 93, Istanbul.

Bankacılık Düzenleme ve Denetleme Kurumu (BDDK) (2005), *Road Map for the Implementation of Basel-II*, Banking Regulation and Supervision Agency, Ankara.

Barca F., M. Brezzi, F. Terribile, F. Utili (2004), *Measuring for Decision Making: Soft and Hard Use of Indicators in Regional Development Policies*, Materiali UVAL, Ministry of Economy and Finance, Italy.

Barro and Sala-i-Martin (1991), "Convergence across States and Regions", *Brookings Papers on Economic Activity*, No. 1, pp. 107-182, United States.

Barro and Sala-i-Martin (2003), *Economic Growth*, The MIT Press, United States.

Bayraktaroğlu, M.A (1987), "An Analysis on Istanbul District Municipalities", MA Thesis, Boğaziçi University, p. 57, Istanbul.

Bayramoğlu, A. (s.d.), *Yerel Yönetim ve Ahlak (Local Governments and Ethic)*, IULA-EMME & T.C. Başbakanlık Toplu Konut İdaresi Başkanlığı, No. 10, p. 109, Istanbul.

Bayramoğlu Y.F. (s.d), *Belediyelerde İnsan Kaynağı Yönetimi (Human Resource Management in Municipalities)*, IULA-EMME & T.C. Başbakanlık Toplu Konut İdaresi Başkanlığı, No. 7, p. 93, Istanbul.

Bayramoğlu, Y. F. (s.d), *Çevre ve Yerel Yönetim* (*Environment and Local Governance*), IULA-EMME & T.C. Başbakanlık Toplu Konut İdaresi Başkanlığı, No. 4, p. 108, Istanbul.

Beaverstock, J.V., P.J. Taylor, R.G. Smith (1999), "A Roster of World Cities", *Cities*, Vol. 16, No. 6, pp. 445-458.

Berk, A. (2003), *İller Bankası ve Yerel Yönetimler* (*Provencial Bank and Local Governments*), Sayıştay Dergisi (Review of State Audit Court), Issue 48, Ankara.

Berköz, L. (1998), "Locational Preferences of Producer Service Firms in Istanbul", *European Planning Studies*, Vol. 6, Issue 3, pp. 333-349.

Berköz, L., (2000), "Location of Financial, Insurance, and Real Estate Firms in Istanbul", *Journal of Urban Planning and Development*, 126, (2) pp. 75-88

Berköz, L. (2001), "The Interregional Location of Foreign Investors in Turkey", *European Planning Studies*, Vol. 9, Issue 8, pp. 979-994.

Bilen, G. (2006), *Novel Regional Policy of Turkey in Line With EU Standards*, Development Bank of Turkey, Turkey.

Bilim, S. (2001), "Yerel Yönetimler", Bilim Ve Siyaset, Kis, Yil 1, Sayi 2.

Bölen, F. (1997), *Toplu Konutların Dünü ve Yarını (Today and Tomorrow of the Housing Settlements),* TMMOB ŞPO Publ. (Union Of Chambers Of Turkish Engineers And Architects, Urban Planners Chamber), April, No. 2, pp. 31-36, Istanbul.

Bozkurt, R. (2006), "Küçük ve Orta Ölçekli Aile İşletmelerinde Dönüşüm" ("The Transformation of Family-Owned Small-and-Medium Sized Enterprises"), in Tamer Koçer (ed.), *Aile İşletmeleri ve Girişimcilik Uygulama ve Araştırma Merkezi 2, Kongresi Tutanakları*, Istanbul Kültür Üniversitesi, Istanbul.

Brenner, N. (1998), "Global Cities, Global States: Global City Formation and State Territorial Restructuring in Contemporary Europe", *Review of International Political Economy*, No. 5, pp. 1-37.

Brakarz, J., M. Greene and E. Rojas (2002), *Cidades para Todos: A experiência recente com programas de melhoramentos de bairros* (*Cities For All: Recent Experiences with Neighborhood Improvement*), Washington, DC.

Brito, D. L. (1999), "Congestion of the Turkish Straits: A Market Alternative", *www.ruf.rice.edu/~econ/papers/1999papers/08Brito.pdf.*

Cabinet Office's (The Cabinet Office of the Japanese government) (2002), "Annual Official Report on Disaster Prevention" (Japanese), Japan, *www.bousai.go.jp/index.html.*

Cantz, Hatje (2002), *The Regionmaker: RheinRuhrCity: The Hidden Metropolis*, NRW Forum Kultur und Wirtscahft Düsseldorf, Düsserldorf.

Çetin, U. (2004), *Hayalindeki Istanbul 100 Trilyonluk Start*, Hürriyet (Newspaper), Vol. 4, Issue 1, p. 5.

Chang, Stephanie E. and Nobuoto Nojima (1999), "Measuring Post-Disaster Transportation System Performance: The 1995 Kobe Earthquake in Comparative Perspective", *Transportation Research*, *www.cive.gifu-u.ac.jp/~nojima/pdf/2000_transportation_a.pdf;*

Çiftçi, O. (1989), *Yerel Yönetimlerde Temsil: Belediye Örneği* (*Acting in Local Government: Example of Municipality*), TODAIE, No. 226, Ankara.

Çınar, A., İ. (1997), "Refah Party and the City Administration of Istanbul: Liberal Islam, Localism and Hybridity", *New Perspectives on Turkey*, No. 16, pp. 23-40.

Çınar, A., İ. (1998), "Unsettled Beginnings of the Nation: The Conquest of Istanbul and Turkish National Identity", paper presented at the Middle East Studies Association 32nd Annual Meeting, Panel 054 "Representing the Nation: Negotiations of Turkish National Identity", Chicago.

Centre national de la fonction publique territoriale (CNFPT) (2005) "Les fonctions publiques locales en Europe", Rapport final, *www.cnfpt.fr/.*

Commission of the European Communities (1998), *Sustainable Urban Development in the European Union: A Framework for Action,* Com/98/605 F, CEC, Brussels.

Conway, P., V. Janod and G. Nicoletti (2005), "Product Market Regulation in OECD Countries: 1998 to 2003", *OECD Economics Department Working Paper*, No. 419, Paris.

Cooper, James *et al.* (1994), "The Northridge Earthquake: Progress Made, Lessons Learned in Seismic-Resistant Bridge Design", *www.findarticles.com/p/articles/mi_m3724/is_n1_v58/ai_16112780/pg_2*

Couch, C. and A. Dennemann (2000), "Urban Regeneration and Sustainable Development in Britain: The Example of the Liverpool Ropewalks Partnership", *Cities*, Vol. 17, pp. 137-147.

Cushman and Wakefield (2005), "European Cities Monitor", *www.fco.gov.uk/Files/kfile/European_Cities_Monitor_2005_FINAL.pdf.*

Deveci, A., A. Cerit and O. Tuna (2002), *Determinants of Intermodal Transport and Turkey's Transport Infrastructure*, Dokuz Eylul University, School of Maritime Business and Management.

Dincer, B., M. Özaslan, T. Kavasoğlu (2003), Illerin ve Bölgelerin Sosyo-ekonomik Gelişmişlik Sıralaması Araştırması, Ankara DPT, BGYUGM ISBN: 975-19-3354-4.

Earthquakes and Megacities Initiative (EMI) (2004), *IDMP, Istanbul Earthquake Master Plan*, a report of the International Experts Review Committee.

Eddison T. and C. Tikiz (1993), *Yerel Yönetimde Denetim* (*Audit in Local Government*), IULA-EMME & T.C. Başbakanlık Toplu Konut Idaresi Baskanligi, No. 13, p. 108, Istanbul.

Eder, M., A. Yakovlev, K. Chaudry, A. Çarkoğlu (2002), *Redefining Contagion: Political Economy of the Suitcase Trade Between Turkey and Russia*, final report, The International Research and Exchanges Board (IREX), Washington.

Eder, M. (2003), *From Suitcase Merchants to Organized Informal Trade?: The Case of Laleli District in Istanbul*, European University Institute, Robert Schuman Centre for Advanced Studies, 4th Mediterranean Social and Political Research Meeting, Italy.

Eliçin-Arikan, Y. (1997), "Décentralisation et Urbanisme en Turquie" ("Decentralization and Urbanization in Turkey"), Thèse de Doctorat, Université de Droit, d'Économie et des Sciences d'Aix-Marseille III, Institut d'Aménagement Régional.

Eliçin-Arikan, Y. (1997), "Municipalités Métropolitaines et D'arrondissement En Turquie" ("Metropolitan and District Municipalities in Turkey"), *Cahiers d'Études sur la Méditerranée et le Monde Turco-Iranien*, No. 24, pp. 71-104.

Emrealp, S. (1993), *Belediyelerde Kriz Yönetimi* (*Crisis Management in Municipalities*), IULA-EMME & T.C. Başbakanlık Toplu Konut İdaresi Başkanlığı, No. 5, p. 92, Istanbul.

Emrealp, S. (s.d.), *Belediyelerde Mali Yönetim* (*Fiscal Management in Municipalities*), IULA-EMME & T.C. Başbakanlık Toplu Konut İdaresi Başkanlığı, No. 2, p. 84, Istanbul.

Emrealp, S. (s.d.), *Belediyelerde Proje Yönetimi* (*Project Management in Municipalities*), IULA-EMME & T.C. Başbakanlık Toplu Konut İdaresi Başkanlığı, No. 3, p. 98, Istanbul.

Emrealp, S. (s.d.), *Yerel Yönetim ve Bilgi Teknolojisi* (*Local Government and Information Technology*), IULA-EMME & T.C. Başbakanlık Toplu Konut İdaresi Başkanlığı, No. 12, p. 116, Istanbul.

Emrealp, S. and D. Horgan (1993), *Belediyelerde Alternatif Hizmet Sunma Yönetemleri* (*Alternative Servicing Methods*), IULA-EMME & T.C. Başbakanlık Toplu Konut İdaresi Başkanlığı, No. 6, p. 74, Istanbul.

ENKA-Cleveland Joint Venture (1998), Haydarpasha Taksim, Metro Line, and Haydarpasha, Piyalepasha Motor Way -Preliminary Design-, ENKA Construction Inc. and Cleveland Inc., Istanbul.

Eraydın, Ayda (2001), "New Forms of Governance in the Emergence of Industrial Districts", Taylor and Felsenstein (eds.), *Promoting Local Growth: Process, Practice and Policy*, Aldershot, Ashgate, Blackwell Publishers, pp. 81-104, United States.

Erder, S. (1996), *Istanbul'a Bir Kent Kondu* (*A Squatter Quarter in Istanbul*), Ümraniye, Iletişim Publ., Istanbul.

Erdik, M. (2004), Earthquake Masterplan for Istanbul, *www-megacities.physik.uni-karlsruhe.de/www-mega/downloads/ IstanbulEQMasterPlan.pdf*.

Ergün, N. (2004), "Gentrification in Istanbul", *Cities*, Vol. 21, No. 5, pp. 391-405.

Erkip, F. (2000), "Global Transformations versus Local Dynamics in Istanbul: Planning in a Fragmented Metropolis", *Cities*, Vol. 17, No. 5, pp. 371-377.

Erkut, G., C. Özgen (2005), "European Union Enlargement and Cross-border Cooperation – A Case Study from Aegean Coast on Cooperation versus Needs-Capacities GAP", 45th Congress of ERSA, Amsterdam.

Erman, T. (2001), "The Politics of Squatter (*Gecekondu*) Studies in Turkey: The Changing Representations of Rural Migrants in the Academic Discourse", *Urban Studies*, Vol. 38, No. 7, pp. 983–1002.

Earthquakes and Megacities Initiative and IMM (2004), "Report on Istanbul Earthquake Masterplan", International Experts Review Committee, July 2004, *www-megacities.physik.uni-karlsruhe.de/www-mega/downloads/ IstanbulEQMasterPlan_Review.pdf#search=%22Earthquake%20Master plan%20for%20Istanbul%22*.

Ertugal, E. (2005), "Europeanisation of Regional Policy and Regional Governance: The Case of Turkey", *European Political Economy Review*, Vol. 3, No. 1, pp. 18-53, Brussels.

Ertugal, E. (2005), *Strategies for Regional Development: Challenges Facing Turkey on the Road to EU Membership*, European Stability Initiative (ESI), Brussels.

Eryılmaz, B. (2001), *Yerel Yönetimlerin Yeniden Yapılanması* (*Restructuring in Local Government*), Birleşik Yayıncılık, Istanbul.

European Commission (1996), *Social and Economic Inclusion through Regional Development: The Community Economic Development Priority in European Structural Funds Programmes in Great Britain*, EC, Brussels

European Commission (1999), *European Spatial Development Perspective: Towards Balanced and Sustainable Development of the Territory of the European Union*, prepared by the Committee on Spatial Development, Office for Official Publications of the European Communities, Potsdam.

European Commission (1999), *Sixth Periodic Report on the Social and Economic Situation of the Region in the Community*, EC, Brussels

European Commission. (2001), *Presentation of Trans-European Network, Information–Communication*, Directorate-General for Energy and Transport, Brussels.

European Commission (2002), *2002 Regular Report on Turkey's Progress towards Accession*, EC, Brussels.

European Commission. (2003), *Interreg III B Archimed Programme: Joint Program Document,* EC, Brussels.

European Commission (2004), *3rd Report on Economic and Social Cohesion*, European Commission, Brussels.

European Commission (2004), *Joint Programming Documen: Interreg III A/ Greece-Turkey*, Programming Period 2003-2006, EC, Brussels.

European Commission (2004), *A New Partnership for Cohesion*, Third Report on Economic and Social Cohesion, Official Publications of the European Communities, ISBN 92-894-4911-X.

European Commission (2006), "Commission Staff Working Document", Com (2006) 649 Final., Turkey 2006 Progress Report, November 2006.

Falay, N. (2002), *Yerel Yönetimler Bankacılığı Bağlamında İller Bankası* (*Provincial Bank in Terms of Local Government Banking*), Yerel Yönetimler Sempozyum Bildirileri, TODAİE, Ankara.

Farrell, D., D. Meen and D.D. Baser (2003), *Turkey: Making the Productivity and Growth Breakthrough*, McKinsey Global Institute, Washington, DC.

Ferrari, C., F. Parola and E. Morchio (2006), *Southern European Ports and the Spatial Distribution of EDCs*, Maritime Economics & Logistics, No. 8, pp. 60-81.

Filiztekin, A. (1998), "Convergence across Industries and Provinces in Turkey", Koç University, Discussion Paper, Istanbul

Florida, R. L. and M. Kenney (1986), "Venture Capital, High Technology and Regional Development", *Regional Studies*, Vol. 22.1, pp. 33-48.

Gezici, F. and G.J.D. Hewings (2002), "Spatial Analysis of Regional Inequalities in Turkey", The Real Economics Applications Laboratory, Discussion paper, United States.

Gezici, F. and G.J.D. Hewings (2004), "Regional Convergence and the Economic Performance of Peripheral Areas in Turkey", *Review of Urban and Regional Development Studies*, Vol. 16, No. 2, United States.

Gezici, F. (2004), *New Regional Definition and Spatial Analysis of Regional Inequalities in Turkey Related to the Regional Policies of EU*, 44th Congress of ERSA, Portugal.

Gibson, M. (1994), *Greening Housing Policy: Housing and the Environment*, M. Bhatti, J. Brookes and M. Gibson (eds.), Chartered Institute of Housing, London.

Gibson, M. (1999), *New Labor's Urban Policies and Planning for 21st Century London*, Proceedings of the Second Sharjah Urban Planning Symposium, Sharjah.

Gibson, M. and A. Kocabaş (2000) *Turkish Planning at a Crossroads: False Dawn, or Vision of a New Era?,* Proceedings of the Third Sharjah Urban Planning Symposium, Sharjah.

Gibson, M. and A. Kocabaş (2002), *London: Sustainable Regeneration-Challenge and Response*, Proceedings of the International Urban Design Meeting, International Symposium on Urban Design and Local Specificities in the Process of Globalizations, MSU, Istanbul.

Gibson, M., A. Kocabaş and T. Öztaş (2003), *Istanbul Neighborhood Regeneration Strategy and Investment Program: A Route Towards Earthquake Resistant Neighborhoods*, Istanbul Metropolitan Municipality (IMM), Istanbul.

Giritli, I. (1998), *Türkiye'nin İdari Yapısı* (*Administrative Structure of Turkey*), Der Yayınları Istanbul.

Godard, X. (2004), *Re-exploring some Reasons of the low Capacity Vehicles Success in Public Transport Production in Developing Cities,* WCTRS, the 10th World Conference on Transport, Istanbul.

Göle, N. and B. Toprak (1996), "Authoritarian Secularism and Islamic Politics: The Case of Turkey", in R.N. Agustus (ed.), *Civil Society in the Middle East*, pp. 17-44, Brill, Leiden.

Gomez-Ibanez J., A. and W.B. Tye (1995), *Essay in Transportation Economics and Policy: A Handbook in Honor of John R.Meyer*, C. Winston (ed.), Brooking Institution Press, United States.

Governorship of Istanbul (2004), "European Cities Tourism", Annual Report, *www.tourmis.wu-wien.ac.at/cgi-bin/tmintro.pl.*

Güllüce, I. (2004), *Yerel Yönetimlerin Sorunları ve Çözüm Önerileri* (*The Problems of Local Governments and Suggestions*), Alfa Yayınları, 217, Istanbul.

Güner, Ayse (2003), "Financial Viability of Local Governments in Turkey", Conference paper, September 2003, Istanbul.

Güngör E. and Ç. Nurbanu (2002), *Fundamental Problems of Istanbul Transportation: Administration and its Ramification*, Proceedings of the 13th Mini-EURO Conference, Italy.

Harvard International Review (2005), Eric Lee, "Dynamic Dubai", Vol. 27, Issue 1, pp. 12-13, Cambridge.

Haughton, G. (1997), "Developing Sustainable Urban Development Models", *Cities*, Vol. 14, pp. 189-195.

Healey, P., S.M. Barrett (1990), "Structure and Agency in Land and Property Development Processes", *Urban Studies*, Vol. 37, Issue 1, pp. 89-104.

Heper, M. (1979-80), "Recent Instability in Turkish Policies: End of a Monocentrist Policy?", *International Journal Of Turkish Studies*, Vol. 1, No. 1, pp. 102-113, Madison.

Heper, M. (1987), *Democracy and Local Government: Istanbul in the 1980's*, IFEA, Obs Urb. 265, Eothene Press, p. 62, Walkington.

Heper, M. (1989), *Local Government in Turkey: Governing Greater Istanbul*, Routledge (IFEA), London.

Heper, M. (s.d.), *Dilemmas of Decentralization. Municipal Government in Turkey*, Friedrich Ebert Stiftung (Aus Der Abteilung Entwicklungsländer Forschung), No.123/124, Analysen.

Hyogo Research Center for Quake Restoration (2005), "Lessons from the Great Hanshin Earthquake", translation of selections from *Daishinnsai Hyaku no Kyokun* (*100 Lessons from the Great Hanshin Earthquake*), Creates-Kamogawa Publishers, *www.shinsai.or.jp/hrc-e/publish/lessons_ghe/*.

İnan. E.A. (2004), *Dezenflasyon Süreci ve Düşük Enflasyon Ortamı: Türkiye'de Makroekonomi ve Bankacılık Üzerine Etkileri*, Bankacılar Dergisi, No. 50, pp. 34-56, Turkey.

İnan. E.A. (2005), *Türk Bankacılık Sisteminde Şube, Kredi ve Mevduatın Dağılımı*, Bankacılar Dergisi, No. 54. pp. 21-40, Turkey.

Institute of International Finance (IFF) (2005), *Corporate Governance in Turkey: An Investor Perspective*, IIF, Washington.

International Financial Law Review (2002), "UK Firms Advise on Creation of Dubai Financial Hub", Vol. 21, Iss. 10, Oct 2002, p. 7, London.

International Financial Law Review (2005), "Shanghai and Dubai Top Office Openings Survey", Dec 2005, p. 1, London

International Financial Law Review (2006), "Dubai Exchange Set for Listings Surge", April 2006, p. 1, London.

International Tax Review (2005), "Dubai International Financial Centre Issues New Laws", KPMG, Sep 2005, p. 1, London.

Irmak, H. (1999), "Tarihe Yönelik Çalışmaların Yerel Yönetimlerde Imaja Etkisi (Kağıthane, Fatih)" ("The Effect of Historical Researches on the Image of Local Governments"), MA Thesis, T.C. Marmara University, Istanbul.

Istanbul Chamber of Commerce (ITO) (2001), *Avrupa Birliğine Tam Üyelik Sürecinde ISO Meslek Komiteleri Sektör Stratejileri Geliştirilmesi Projesi: Elektronik ve Telekomünikasyon Sektörü* (*Project of Developing Sectorial Strategies in the Process of Full Membership to European Union*), ITO Sectorial Committees, Istanbul.

Istanbul Chamber of Industry (ISO) (2002), *İmalat Sanayiinin Uluslararası Rekabet Gücü* (*International Competitiveness of the Manufacturing Industry*), Istanbul Chamber of Industry, Istanbul.

Istanbul Chamber of Industry (ISO) (2006), *Türkiye'nin 500 Büyük Sanayi Kuruluşu 2005* (*The Top 500 Industrial Corporations in Turkey in 2005*), ISO, Istanbul.

Istanbul Metropolitan Municipality (IMM) (1998), *1999 Yatırım Programı* (*1999 Investment Plan*), IMM (IFEA), Istanbul.

Istanbul Metropolitan Municipality (IMM) (2002), *Istanbul 1. Kentiçi Ulaşim Şurası* (*First Assembly of Urban Transport in Istanbul*), IMM, Istanbul.

Istanbul Metropolitan Municipality (IMM) and Japanese International Cooperation Agency (JICA) (2002), *Research on Istanbul Earthquake Management Plan*, Vol. 4, final report, Istanbul.

Istanbul Metropolitan Municipality (IMM) and Japanese International Cooperation Agency (JICA) (2002), *The Study on a Disaster Prevention/Mitigation Basic Plan in Istanbul Including Seismic Microzonation in the Republic of Turkey*, IMM, Istanbul.

Istanbul Metropolitan Municipality (IMM) (2003), *Earthquake Master Plan for Istanbu*l, IMM, Istanbul.

Istanbul Metropolitan Municipality (IMM) (2005), Background report delivered to the OECD, IMM, Istanbul.

Istanbul Metropolitan Municipality (IMM), (2007), "Istanbul Functional Area Report", March 2007, Istanbul.

Istanbul Kültür Üniversitesi (2006) Rüştü Bozkurt "Küçük ve Orta Ölçekli Aile İşletmelerinde Dönüşüm" ("The Transformation of Family-Owned Small-and-Medium Sized Enterprises"), in Tamer Koçer (ed.), *Aile İşletmeleri ve Girişimcilik Uygulama ve Araştırma Merkezi 2 Kongresi Tutanakları*.

İsvan, A. (2002), *Başkent Gölgesinde Istanbul* (*Istanbul under the Shadow of the Capital City*), İletişim Press, p. 322, Istanbul.

IULA-EMME and T.C. Başbakanlık Toplu Konut İdaresi Başkanlığı (1993), *Geleceğin İstanbul'u: Demokratik, Etkin ve İnsanca Yaşanabilir Bir Dünya Kenti* (*Future of Istanbul: A Democratic and Effective Word City with High Quality of Life)*, No. 5, Istanbul.

IULA-EMME and T.C. Başbakanlık Toplu Konut İdaresi Başkanlığı (1993), *Konut Politikaları ve Finansmanı* (*Housing Policies and Financing*), No. 3, p. 119, Istanbul.

IULA-EMME and T.C. Başbakanlık Toplu Konut İdaresi Başkanlığı (1993), *Türkiye'de Yerel Yönetim Sisteminin Geliştirilmesi* (*Improving Local Government System in Turkey*), No. 1, p. 163, Istanbul.

IULA-EMME and T.C. Başbakanlık Toplu Konut İdaresi Başkanlığı (1993), *Yerel Yönetim Yapıları* (*Local Government Structure*), No. 4, p. 112, Istanbul.

IULA-EMME and T.C. Başbakanlık Toplu Konut İdaresi Başkanlığı, *Şehircilik ve Konut Bakanlığı* (*Urbanization and Ministry of Housing*), No. 6, p. 113, Istanbul.

IULA-EMME and T.C. Başbakanlık Toplu Konut İdaresi Başkanlığı, *Yerel Yönetim Bankacılığı* (*Banking for Local Government*), No. 2, p. 143, Istanbul.

Japan International Cooperation Agency (JICA) (2002), "The Study on a Disaster Prevention/Mitigation Basic Plan in Istanbul", Final Report.

Japan International Cooperation Agency (JICA) and Istanbul Metropolitan Municipality (IMM) (2002), "The Study on a Disaster Prevention/Earthquake Mitigation Basic Plan in Istanbul", Istanbul.

Japan Bank for International Cooperation (JBIC) (2003) "JBIC Special Assistance for Project Implementation (SAPI) for Emergency Earthquake Recovery Loan", Final Report, SAPI Team for Japan Bank for International Cooperation, Tokyo.

Johnson, Laurie A. (2000), "Kobe and Northridge Reconstruction - A Look at Outcomes of Varying Public and Private Housing Reconstruction Financing Models", presented at the EuroConference on Global Change and Catastrophe. Risk Management:Earthquake Risks in Europe, International Institute for Applied Systems Analysis (IIASA), 8 July 2000, Laxenburg, Austria, *www.iiasa.ac.at/Research/RMS/ july2000/ Papers/johnson_housing0401.pdf.*

Karaman, A., T.B. Levent (2000), *Globalization and Development Strategies for Istanbul*, Globalization and World Cities Study Group and Network, GaWC Research Bulletin No. 53.

Kavasoğlu, T. *et al* (2003), "Indicators Related to the Nomenclature of Territorial Units For Statistics (NUTS)", DPT, BGYUGM, Ankara.

Keleş, R. (1992), *Yerinden Yönetim ve Siyaset (Local Governance and Politics)*, Cem Yayınevi, Istanbul.

Keleş, R. (1996), *Kentleşme Politikası (Politics of Urbanization)*, İmge Kitapevi, Istanbul.

Kerimoglu, *et al.* (2005), *Fiscal Decentralization: A New Approach to Alleviate Poverty and Regional Disparities*, UNDP, Tesev, Istanbul.

Keyder, Ç. (2005), "Globalization and Social Exclusion in Istanbul", *International Journal of Urban and Regional Research*, Vol. 29. pp. 124–134.

Kılınçaslan, İ. (1974), "Büyük İstanbul Şehrinde Hizmetler ve Belediye Giderleri Analizi Üzerine Bir Deneme" ("Essay on Analysis of Municipal Expenditure and Services in Greater Istanbul"), PhD Thesis, ITU Faculty of Architecture, IFEA, Obs, Urb. 190, p. 129, Istanbul.

Kindap, A, SPO (2006), Regional Development and Structural Adjustment Directorate, paper on Development Agencies.

Kıray, M. (1998), *Kentleşme Yazıları* (*Essays on Urbanization in Turkey*), Bağlam Publ., Istanbul.

Kırdar, M. and Ş. Saracoğlu (2006), "Does Internal Migration Lead to Faster Regional Convergence in Turkey? An Empirical Investigation", Middle East Technical University, Discussion paper, Ankara.

Klink J. and A. Cidade-Região (2001), *Regionalismo e Reestruturação no Grande ABC Paulista*, DPA Editores, RJ.

Kocabaş, A. (2000), *Urban Conservation Planning, Mayoral Vision and Development Outcomes in Central Istanbul*, Proceedings of the Third Sharjah International Urban Planning Symposium, Sharjah.

Kocabaş, A. (2000), *Urban Conservation Planning and Development Outcomes in Central Istanbul and Central London: 1969-1989*, South Bank University, London.

Kocabaş, A. and M. Gibson (2003), "Handling Earthquake Threat", *Planning*, p. 16.

Köksal, S. (1990), *Istanbul'daki Sosyal Demokrat Belediye Başkanları ve Gecekondu* (*Social-democrat Mayors of Istanbul and Informal Housing [Gecekondu]*), TÜSES Araştırmalar Vakfı, IFEA: Obs Urb. 260, p. 67, Istanbul.

Köse, E. *et al.* (2003), "Simulation of Marine Traffic in Istanbul Strait", *Simulation Modeling Practice and Theory*, Vol. 11, No. 7, pp. 597-608(12).

Küçük, S. and Ş. Yüzer (1998), *The Growth and Development of Metropolitan Planning Strategies in Istanbul*, 38th Congress of the European Regional Science Association, Vienna.

Kumral, N. and C. Değer, (2006), "The Strategies And Policies for Economic Competitiveness in the Istanbul Metropolitan Region", unpublished OECD expert report, Paris.

Kurtoğlu, A. (1998), "Local Politics and Social Networks in Urban Turkey: The Case Of Keçiören Municipality", PhD Thesis, MTU Department of Sociology, Ankara.

Kurtoğlu, A. (2002), *Hemşehrilik, Patronaj ve Siyaset* (*Hometownship, Patronage and Politics*), Toplum ve Bilim, No. 93, pp. 315-325, Istanbul.

Levent, T.B. (2003), *Globalization and Development Strategies for Istanbul: regional Policies and Great Urban Transformation Projects*, 39th ISoCaRP Congress, Cairo.

Loukaitou-Sideris, Anastasia and M. Kamel Kamel, (2004), "Residential Recovery from the Northridge Earthquake: An Evaluation of Federal Assistance Programs", *www.ucop.edu/cprc/eq%20recovery.pdf.*

Mayor of London (2004), "The London Plan: Highlights from the Mayor's Spatial Development Strategy for Greater London", Greater London Authority, London, *www.london.gov.uk.*

McKinsey (2003), "Turkey: Making the Productivity and Growth Breakthrough", McKinsey Global Institute research report, *www.mckinsey.com/mgi/publications/turkey/index.asp.*

METU, ITU, BU, YTU & IMM (2003), *Istanbul Deprem Master Planı* (*Master Plan of Istanbul Earthquake*), IMM, Istanbul.

Ministry of Science and Technology(2005), Federal Government of Brazil, *The Law on Innovation.*

Nadaroğlu, H. (1989), *Mahalli İdareler (Local Authorities)*, Beta/IULA-EMME, Istanbul.

Newman, P. and A. Thornley, (1996) *Urban Planning in Europe: International Competition, National Systems, and Planning Projects*, Routledge, London.

Newman, P. and A. Thornley, (2005), *Planning World Cities: Globalization and Urban Politics*, Palgrave/ Macmillan, Basingstoke.

Neyaptı, B. (2005), "Equalization via Fiscal Decentralization", Turkish Economic Association, Discussion paper 2005/11.

Nicoletti, G. and S. Scarpetta (2005), "Product Market Reforms and Employment in OECD Countries", *OECD Economics Department Working Paper* No. 472, Paris.

Nishikawa, Satoru (2006) "Progress of Disaster Administration Management in Japan", presentation material, JICA Seminar, June 2006, Istanbul.

Nordas, H.K. (2004), "The Global Textile and Clothing Industry Post the ATC", WTO Discussion Paper.

Ocakçı, M. (2000), "Commuting Patterns of Industrial Labourers in the Istanbul Metropolitan Area", *Cities*, Vol. 17, No. 1, pp. 55-61.

OECD (2000a), *Catastrophic Risks and Insurance*, OECD Publications, Paris.

OECD (2000b), *The OECD Observer*, Paris, October, 2001.

OECD (2001a), *OECD Economic Surveys: Turkey*, OECD Publications, Paris.

OECD (2001b), *The OECD Observer*, Paris, January, 2001.

OECD (2002a), *OECD Economic Surveys: Turkey*, OECD Publications, Paris.

OECD (2002b), *OECD Review of Regulatory Reform: Turkey,* OECD Publications, Paris.

OECD (2003), *Emerging Risks in the 21st Century: An Agenda for Action*, OECD Publications, Paris.

OECD (2004a), *Keeping Schools Safe in Earthquakes,* OECD Publications, Paris.

OECD (2004b), *Large-scale Disasters*, OECD Publications, Paris

OECD (2004c), *OECD Economic Surveys: Turkey*, OECD Publications, Paris

OECD (2005a), *A Framework for the Development and Financing of Dynamic Small and Medium Sized Enterprises in Turkey*, OECD Centre for Private Sector Development, Istanbul.

OECD (2005b) *Catastrophic Risks and Insurance*, OECD Publications, Paris.

OECD (2005c), *Energy Policies of IEA Countries: Turkey*, IEA, OECD Publications, Paris.

OECD (2005d), *OECD Building Competitive Regions*, OECD Publications, Paris.

OECD (2005e) *OECD in Figures*, OECD Publications, Paris

OECD (2005f), *OECD Regions at a Glance,* OECD Publications, Paris.

OECD (2005g), *OECD Territorial Reviews: Busan,* Korea, OECD Publications, Paris.

OECD (2005h), *OECD Territorial Reviews: Seoul*, Korea, OECD Publications, Paris.

OECD (2006a), *Competitive Cities in the Global Economy,* OECD Publications, Paris.

OECD (2006b), *OECD Economic Surveys: Turkey*, OECD Publications, Paris.

OECD (2006c), *OECD Factbook*, OECD Publications, Paris.

OECD (2006d), *OECD Revenue Statistics*, OECD Publications, Paris.

OECD (2006e), *OECD Territorial Reviews: Newcastle in the North East, United Kingdom*, OECD Publications, Paris.

OECD (2007), *OECD Regions at a Glance 2007*, OECD Publications, Paris.

OECD/SIGMA, (2005), Turkey. *Public Service and the Administrative Framework*, Assessment June 2005, assessment report for the European Commission.

Öniş, Z. and B. Rubin (2001), *Turkey and the European Union: Domestic Politics, Economic Integration, and International Dynamic*, Routledge.

Öniş, Z. (2003), *The Turkish Economy in Crisis*, B. Rubin (ed.), Frank Cass and Company Ltd, London.

Örs, H. and S. L. Yilmaz (2003), "Oil Transport in the Turkish Straits System: A Simulation of Contamination in the Istanbul Strait", *Energy Sources*, Vol. 25, pp. 1043-1052.

Özaslan, M., B. Dinçer and H. Özgür (2002), *Regional Disparities and Territorial Indicators in Turkey: Socio-Economic Development Index (SEDI)*, SPO.

Özbay, F. (1999), *Istanbul'da Göç ve İl İçi Nüfus Hareketleri (1985-1990), (Immigration and Movements of Population in Istanbul in the Republican Period in Turkey*), 75 Yılda Köylerden Şehirlere Göç Hareketleri, Tarih Vakfı Publications, Istanbul.

Özcan, Ü. (1988), "Kent Yönetimi, Yöneticiler ve Sehir Plancıları" ("City Administration, Administrators and Urban Planners"), *Planlama*, 1988/2, pp. 3-5, Ankara.

Özer, A. (2000), *Kentleşme ve Yerel Yönetimler* (*Urbanization and Local Government*), Ürün Yayınları, Ankara.

Özkan D. (2000), "Istanbul'un Ulaşım Ana Planı: Haluk Gerçek'le Söyleşi" ("Transportation Master Plan of Istanbul: Interview with Haluk Gerçek"), *Istanbul Dergisi*, No. 35. Pp. 32-33.

Öztürk, A. (1997), *21. Yüzyıl Türkiyesi için Yerel Yönetim Modeli* (*Local Government Model for Turkey of 21st*), Ümraniye Belediyesi Kültür Yayınları, IFEA, p. 228, Istanbul.

Öztürk, A. (2002), "From Oil to Straits: The Caspian Pipeline Politics and Environmental Protection of the Istanbul and the Çanakkale Straits", *Journal of Southern Europe and the Balkans*, Vol. 4, No. 1, pp. 57-74.

Parsa, A., *et al.* (2002), "Emerging Global Cities: Comparison of Singapore and the Cities of the United Arab Emirates", *Journal of Real Estate Portfolio Management*, Vol. 8, Iss. 4, pp. 95-101, Boston.

Parsons, T. (2000), "Influence of the 17 August 1999 Izmit Earthquake on Seismic Hazards in Istanbul", A. Barka (ed.), *The 1999 Izmit and Düzce Earthquakes: Preliminary Results*, US Geological Survey, Washington, DC.

Paskaleva-Shapira, K. (2005), *New Paradigms in City Tourism Management: Reflections on the Legacy of the First World Tourism Forum Istanbul*, ITAS, Turkey.

Petak, William (2000) "The Northridge Earthquake USA and its Economic and Social Impacts", Euro-Conference on Global Change and Catastrophe Risk Management, IIASA, Ladenburg, Austria.

Prud'homme, R. (1991), "Décentralisation à La Turquie (Decentralization in Turkey"), *Revue D'economie Régionale et Urbaine*, No. 2, pp. 253-257.

Reeves, T. (2006), "Turkey's Regional Policy on the Road to the EU", Delegation of the European Commission to Turkey, Discussion Paper, Ankara.

Republic of Turkey (2003), "Preliminary National Development Plan (2004-2006)", SPO, Ankara.

Republic of Turkey (2004), *Pre-Accession Economic Program 2004*, National Report of Turkey, Ankara.

Republic of Turkey (2005), Undersecretariat of Treasury, General Directorate of Economic Research, *Turkish National Economic Outlook*, Ankara.

Riddle, L.A. and K. Gillespie (2003), *Information Sources for New Ventures in the Turkish Clothing Export Industry*, Small Business Economics, Vol. 20, Iss. 1, p. 105.

Rotterdam City Corporation (1993), *Metropolis in the Making,* Rotterdam.

Rydin, Y. (1993), *Urban and Environmental Planning in the UK*, Macmillan (second edition), London.

Safty, A. (2005), *Democracy and Governance: The Global Advance of Democracy*, Bahçeşehir Üniversitesi Yayınları, Istanbul.

Salet, W. and A. Thornley (2003), *Metropolitan Governance and Spatial Planning: Comparative Case Studies of European City-regions*, A. Kreukels (ed.), Spon, London.

Sassen, S. (1991), *The Global City: New York, London, Tokyo,* Princeton University Press, Princeton, NJ.

Scholte, J.A. (2000), *Globalization: A Critical Introduction,* Palgrave/Macmillan, Basingstoke.

Schüler, H. (1999), *Türkiye'de Sosyal Demokrasi: Particilik, Hemşehrilik, Alevilik* (*Social Democracy, Partisanship, Hometownship, Being Alevi*), Iletisim Yayinlari, p. 346, Istanbul.

Seufert, G, K. Vorhoff and S. Yerasimos (2000), *Civil Society in the Grip of Nationalism*, Orient-Insitut/IFEA, Istanbul.

Shrestha, Bijaya (2001), "Disaster Reduction and Response Preparedness in Japan: A Hyogo Approach", The Second Tampere Conference on Disaster Communications, Tampere, Finland 28-30 May 2001, *www.reliefweb.int/telecoms/conference/cdc2001/bks.doc*

Sojo, E. and R. Villarreal (2004), *Public Policies to Promote Productive Occupation and Increase Formality among the Moderate Poor: The Mexican Agenda*, EDGI_WIDER Conference on "Unlocking Human Potential: Linking the Informal and Formal Sectors", Helsinki.

Sönmez, M. (1999), "Istanbul Seçmeninin 50 Yıllık Tercihi" ("The Preference of Istanbul's Voters for Last 50 Years"), *Birikim*, No. 123, pp. 97-103, Istanbul.

State Planning Organization (SPO) (2000), *8th Five Year Development Plan (2001-2005)*, SPO, Ankara.

State Planning Organization (SPO) (2003), *İllerin ve Bölgelerin Sosyo-ekonomik Gelişmişlik Sıralaması Araştırması,* Bölgesel Gelişme ve Yapısal Uyum Genel Müdürlüğü, No. 2671, SPO, Ankara.

State Planning Organization (SPO) (2003), *Ön Ulusal Kalkınma Planı Bölgesel Gelişme Stratejileri*, SPO, Ankara.

State Planning Organization (SPO) and TEPAV (2006), *IX. Bölgesel Kalkınma Özel İhtisas Komisyonu Raporu* (*9th Development Plan Regional Development Policies Experts' Report*), SPO, Ankara.

Tanık, A *et al.* (2000), "A Long-term Management Plan for a Watershed in a World Metropolis- Istanbul", *Environmental Management and Health*, Vol. 11, No. 3, pp. 208–215.

Tansel, A. and N.D. Güngör (1997), "Economic Growth and Convergence: An Application to the Province of Turkey (1975-1995)", Middle East Technical University, Discussion paper, Ankara.

Taylor, D.R.F. and P.J. Walker (2001), "World Cities: A First Multivariate Analysis of their Services Complexes", *Urban Studies*, Vol. 38, No. 1, pp. 23-47.

Taylor, N. (1998), *Urban Planning Theory Since 1945*, Sage Publications, London.

Tekeli I. and T. Okyay (1980), *Dolmuşun Öyküsü* (*History of Shared Taxis [Dolmuş]*), Çevre ve Mimarlık Bilimleri Derneği, pp. 302, Ankara.

Tekeli, I. (1991), *Kent Planlaması Konuşmaları* (*Speeches on Urban Planning*), TMMOB Chamber of Architects Publ., Ankara.

Tekeli, I. (1994), *The Development of the Istanbul Metropolitan Area: Urban Administration of Planning*, Kent Basımevi, Istanbul.

Tekeli, I. (1998), *Türkiye'de İçgöç Sorunsalı Yeniden Tanımlanma Aşamasına Geldi: Türkiye'de Içgöç, Bolu-Gerede*, (*The Problematic of Internal Immigration in Turkey, Bolu-Gerede*), Tarih Vakfı Publ., Istanbul.

Tezer, K. (2004), "Modeling of Land Use-Transportation Interaction in Istanbul", *ITU A/Z Journal*, No. 1, Vol. 2, Istanbul.

Tezcan, S. (1999), *Comparative Study on the 3rd Bosphorus Crossing* (*Submerged Tunnel or suspension Bridge*), Proceedings of the International Seminar on Strait Crossings, Norwegian Public Road Admin., Vol. 1, May 1999, pp. 28-31, Oslo.

Tezcan, S. (2002), *The Marmaray Project – Options of Dr. S. Tezcan-*, Department of Civil Engineering, Boğaziçi University, Istanbul

Toksöz, F. (2000), "Yerel Yönetimler Reform Tasarısı ve Istanbul" ("Draft Local Governments Reform and Istanbul"), *Istanbul Dergisi*, No. 34, pp. 41-43, Istanbul.

Toprak, B. (1996), "Civil Society in Turkey", in R.N. Agustus (ed.), *Civil Society in the Middle East*, Brill, pp. 87-118, Leiden.

Topuz, H. (1998), *Dünyada* ve *Türkiyedeki Kültür Politikaları* (*The Cultural Policies in Turkey and in the World*), Adam Yayınları, Istanbul.

Tümertekin, E. (1997), *Istanbul, Insan ve Mekân,* (*Istanbul, Human and Urban Space*), Tarih Vakfı Publ., Istanbul.

Tuncay, M. (1994), *Kentsel Haklar, Karşılaştırmalı Bir Çerçevede Türkiye* (*Urban Rights, Turkey with Comparative Framework*), Dünya Yerel Yönetim ve Demokrasi Akademisi/World Academy for Local Government and Democracy/WALD Publications, Istanbul.

Turkey National Council (1996), *Turkey National Report and Plan of Action*, United Nations Conference on Human Settlements, Habitat II, Istanbul.

Turkish Industrialists' and Businessmen's Association (TÜSİAD) (1992), *Yerel Yönetimler: Sorunlar ve Çözümler* (*Local Government: Assessments and Recommendations*), T/92-5, TÜSİAD, Istanbul.

TÜSİAD (1999), *Türkiye'nin Fırsat Penceresi, Demografik Dönüşüm ve İzdüşümleri* (*Turkey's Window of Opportunity: Demographic Transformation and Its Consequences*), TÜSİAD, Istanbul.

TÜSİAD and YASED (2004), *FDI Attractiveness of Turkey: A Comparative Analysis*, Istanbul.

TÜSİAD (2005), *Büyüme Stratejileri Dizisi 1-7* (*Growth Studies: 1. Macroeconomic Framework, 2. Sectoral Restructuring, 3. Input-output Patterns, 4. Regional Development, 5. Financing Structure, 6. Capital Formation, 7. Education),* TÜSİAD, Istanbul.

Turkish Institute of Statistics (TUIK), *Regional statistics*, *www.tuik.gov.tr.*

Türkoğlu, H. D. (1997), "Residents' Satisfaction of Housing Environments: The Case of Istanbul, Turkey", *Landscape and Urban Planning*, No. 39, pp. 55-67.

Ulaştırma ve Ulaşım Araçları Uyg-Ar Merkezi (2004), *Ulaştırma Ana Planı Statejisi* (*Strategy of Main Transportation Plan*), TC. Ulaştırma Bakanlığı Ankara.

Ünal, A. (1996), "HABITAT II Etrafında Değerlendirmeler (2)" ("The Assessment of HABTITAT II"), *Zaman* (newspaper), 13/06/1996, Istanbul.

UNCTAD (2005), *World Investment Report 2005: Transnational Corporations and the Internationalization of R&D*, UNCTAD, United States.

UNCTAD (2001), *World Investment Report 2001: Promoting Linkages*, available at *www.unctad.org/en/docs/wir2001_en.pdf.*

Undersecretary of Foreign Trade (2005), *Uluslarlarasi Dogrudan Yatirimlar* (*Foreign Direct Investments*), Ankara.

United Nations Development Programme (UNDP) and State Planning Organization (SPO) (2005), *Millennium Development Goals Report Turkey 2005*, Ankara.

Ünlü, H. (S.D.), *Yönetimler Arası İşbirliği, Yerel Yönetimler* (*Partnership among Local Governments*), IULA-EMME and T.C. Basbakanlik Toplu Konut İdaresi Başkanlığı, No. 8&9, pp. 93&110, Istanbul.

World Bank (2001), *Villes en Mouvement: La Stratégie de la Banque Mondiale* (*Cities in Action: Strategy of World Bank*), World Bank, Washington, DC.

Yayla, M., T.K. Yasemin and I. Ekmen (2005), *Bankacılık Sektörüne Yabancı Girişi: Küresel Gelişmeler ve Türkiye*, ARD Çalışma Raporları 2005/6, BDDK, Ankara.

Yetgin, Ü. (1998), "New Trade Patterns: New Transport Demands in the Black Sea Region Turkish Port", "Infrastructure in International Combined Transport", International Seminar, Antalya.

Yetim, S. and Ozan Gülhan (2005), *Avrupa Birliğine Tam Üyelik Sürecinde Türk Bankacılığı Sektörü*, ARD Çalışma Raporları 2005/7, BDDK, Ankara.

Yıldırım, S. and S. Emrealp (1988), *Metropolitan Government in Istanbul*, Metropolitan Municipality of Greater Istanbul, Istanbul.

Yıldırım, S. (1993), *Local Government and Democracy*, IULA-EMME and T.C. Başbakanlık Toplu Konut İdaresi Başkanlığı, No. 14, p. 200, Istanbul.

Yıldırım, S. and S. Emrealp, (1994), *Yeni Bir Yönetim Organizasyonu: Vilayet Raporu* (*New Governmental Organization: Provincial Report*), *Istanbul Dergisi*, No. 8, pp. 146-148, Istanbul.

Yücel, A. (1994), *Büyükşehir Yönetimi, Istanbul için Model ve İç Göçlerin Yönlendirilmesi* (*Governing a Metropolitan and Managing Internal Migration, a Model for Istanbul*), SPO, Yapısal Uyum Sosyal Politikalar ve Koordinasyon Genel Müd., Planlama Dairesi, Ankara.

Ziyaoğlu, R. (1971), *Istanbul Kadıları, Şehreminleri, Belediye Reisleri ve Partiler Tarihi: 1453-1971-Idari-Siyaset* (*The History of Istanbul Political Life: 1453- 1971Administrative Politics*), Akgün Matbaasi, IFEA, İst16, Istanbul.

Also available in the series of Territorial Reviews on urban and metropolitan regions:

Helsinki, Finland (2003)

Öresund Copenhagen/Malmö, Denmark/Sweden (2003)

Vienna/Bratislava, Austria/Czech Republic (2003)

Melbourne, Australia (2003)

Athens, Greece (2004)

Montreal, Canada (2004)

Mexico City, Mexico (2004)

Busan, Korea (2005)

Seoul, Korea (2005)

Milan, Italy (2006)

Stockholm, Sweden (2006)

Newcastle in the North East, United Kingdom (2006)

Randstad Holland, Netherlands (2007)

Madrid, Spain (2007)

Forthcoming:

Cape Town, South Africa (2008)

Copenhagen, Denmark (2009)

Toronto, Canada (2009)

OECD PUBLICATIONS, 2, rue André-Pascal, 75775 PARIS CEDEX 16
PRINTED IN FRANCE
(04 2008 05 1 P) ISBN-978-92-64-047371-8 – No. 56071 2008